The People's
Historian

JOHN RICHARD GREEN

THE PEOPLE'S HISTORIAN

John Richard Green and the Writing of History in Victorian England

Anthony Brundage

Studies in Historiography, Number 2
John David Smith, *Series Adviser*

GREENWOOD PRESS
Westport, Connecticut • London

Library of Congress Cataloging-in-Publication Data

Brundage, Anthony.
   The people's historian : John Richard Green and the writing of
history in Victorian England / Anthony Brundage.
      p. cm.—(Studies in historiography, ISSN 1046-526X ; no. 2)
   Includes bibliographical references (p.) and index.
   ISBN 0-313-27954-3 (alk. paper)
     1. Green, John Richard, 1837-1883. 2. Historians—Great Britain—
Biography. 3. Historiography—Great Britain—History—19th
century. 4. Great Britain—Historiography. I. Title. II. Series.
DA3.G7B78   1994
941'.007202—dc20
[B]   93-10379

British Library Cataloguing in Publication Data is available.

Library of Congress Catalog Card Number: 93-10379
ISBN: 0-313-27954-3
ISSN: 1046-526X

First published in 1994

Greenwood Press, 88 Post Road West, Westport, CT 06881
An imprint of Greenwood Publishing Group, Inc.

Printed in the United States of America

The paper used in this book complies with the
Permanent Paper Standard issued by the National
Information Standards Organization (Z39.48-1984).

10 9 8 7 6 5 4 3 2 1

Copyright Acknowledgments

The author and publisher gratefully acknowledge permission from the
following to reprint quoted material:

The Principal and Fellows, Jesus College, Oxford, for quoted excerpts
from letters and diaries in the John Richard Green manuscripts.

The Archbishop of Canterbury and the Trustees of Lambeth Palace
Library, for quoted excerpts from letters of John Richard Green in the
Lambeth Palace MS. 1725.

Contents

Acknowledgments

I am deeply indebted for the expert and courteous assistance of the staffs of the various record repositories at which I conducted the archival research for this book. Special thanks go to Dr. D.A. Rees of Jesus College, Oxford, whose kindness and unparalleled knowledge of the Green MSS made my research there particularly enjoyable. I would also like to thank the staffs of the British Library, the Lambeth Palace Library, the Bodleian Library, the John Rylands Library of Manchester University, the National Library of Scotland, and the Edinburgh University Library. Closer to home, the staffs of my own university and the Honnold Library of the Claremont Colleges were very helpful.

I wish to thank the Principal and Fellows of Jesus, College, Oxford, for granting me access to the Green MSS and allowing me to quote from them, as well as for allowing me to reproduce the photograph of Green in the frontispiece. I also would like to express my gratitude to the Archbishop of Canterbury and the Trustees of Lambeth Palace Library for permission to use and quote from the Green Papers in the Lambeth Palace MSS.

Scholars who were kind enough to read portions of the typescript and to offer valuable advice are Professors Philippa Levine, Jonathan Rose, and Albert R. and Martha S. Vogeler. I am greatly in their debt.

Very special thanks go to my wife, Martha, for her encouragement, enthusiasm, critical acumen, and sharp eye.

Abbreviations

HS: *Historical Studies*

LJRG: *Letters of John Richard Green*

shep: *Short History of the English People,* first edition, 1874

SHEP: *Short History of the English People*, revised and illustrated four-volume edition of 1892–94

SS: *Stray Studies*

SSEI: *Stray Studies from England and Italy*

Note on the Text

I have used the revised and posthumously published illustrated edition of the *Short History of the English People* (1892–94) because it is the one most widely available in libraries as well as being a joy to read both for the quality of the paper, binding, and typography, and for the aptness of the illustrative material. Furthermore, it represents not only Green's final statement on his magnum opus, but also his wish to have it illustrated by pictures "which should tell us how men and things appeared to the lookers-on of their own day, and how contemporary observers aimed at representing them." I have indicated in the text and footnotes any changes from the first edition. Quotations from the *Short History* in the text are always from the revised edition, but if there are differences in wording from the first edition, these are indicated in the notes.

The People's
Historian

1. Introduction

Near the end of 1874, Macmillan and Co. published a cheap single-volume history of England by a virtually unknown former Anglican clergyman not yet thirty-four years of age. Designed chiefly as a school textbook, it was expected to sell a few thousand copies. Its author, John Richard Green, had already signed over his copyright to Alexander Macmillan for £350, a sum that both men considered generous. To the astonishment of author, publisher, and everyone else, the *Short History of the English People* sold 32,000 copies in the first year alone and a half-million during the ensuing decades. Among historical works, its sales and popularity were rivaled only by Thomas Babington Macaulay's *History of England from the Accession of James II*, but Macaulay was a respected and well-connected author long before his multi-volume history was published, and its success was not a great surprise.

This great publishing phenomenon was also a major breakthrough in historiography, for Green took seriously the "People" in his title. They, rather than selected kings and statesmen, were the heroes of his history. It was their everyday culture, their works of genius, and above all their persistent quest for freedom that Green celebrated. To be sure, previous historians had sometimes paused in their political, diplomatic, and military narratives to provide a picture of society, Macaulay's well-known Chapter III being a masterful example. In the *Short History*, however, the organizing principle of an entire work was provided by the creative energy and passionate devotion to self-government of the common people.[1] It was a concept clearly in tune with the populist impulses of the period. After the passage of the Second Reform Act in 1867, Britain was a quasi-democratic polity, with considerable radical ferment beneath the relatively calm exterior of parliamentary politics. Serious discussions of formerly taboo topics such as republicanism and atheism moved beyond a fringe of desperate radicals. Demands for freedom from traditional forms of religious, intellectual, and social authority were fueled by the dramatic breakthroughs of modern science. If a new kind of history was necessary for an age of democratic stirrings and waning faith, Green had delivered it.

With the astonishing success of the *Short History of the English People*, it might be thought that writers of history would veer sharply away from their accustomed concern with politics and warfare to undertake social and cultural studies. That this did not happen, at least not until well into the twentieth century, can be attributed to the anomalous position of Green's book, for it ran against the grain of three major developments in nineteenth-century historiography. The first of these was the "great man" theory of history, associated with writers like Thomas Carlyle and James Anthony Froude. True to their Romantic roots, they took the clash of man and destiny as the central dramatic focus of history. In their view, events were shaped by heroic individuals who both transcended and resonated with the spirit of their age. While a biographical approach was by no means absent from Green's book, it was always kept subsidiary to broader social currents.

A second and even more important strain in history writing was a concern with the evolution of the English constitution, particularly a "Whig" version that traced the lineage of modern institutions back to medieval antecedents. Political and constitutional histories of a moderately liberal character continued to attract many readers. The works of Macaulay and Henry Hallam were supplemented by increasingly professional studies based on archival sources. The very year that the *Short History* was published, there appeared the first volume of William Stubbs's magisterial *Constitutional History of England*, a particularly impressive example of an early Germanic or "Teutonist" version of Whig historiography, in which the antecedents of modern English institutions were traced back to Anglo-Saxon communal roots. Such studies may have become more compelling during the unsettling transformations of the Victorian era, for which they provided as an antidote an image of a long, steady process of wholesome change. While constitutional development was certainly an important theme in the *Short History*, Green's presentation of it stressed its connections to broader popular culture, and his analysis was markedly more radical than that of his Whiggish predecessors and contemporaries.

Finally, there was the Positivist strain of historiography, most powerfully represented by Henry Thomas Buckle, which operated on the belief that a dispassionate study of the past would reveal regular patterns analogous to those discerned by the natural sciences. Of the three historical schools, Green was completely at odds only with the last. He rejected the idea that the study of the past could be a science, always insisting that it was the free will of individuals and the aspirations of the people that determined the course of history. The other two did influence his writing, sometimes profoundly. He strove, however, to avoid the bombast and hero-worship of the romantic/biographical school while adopting its vividness and story-telling powers. At the same time, he enlivened the measured phraseology and expanded the limited framework of the Whig constitutional approach. Whatever his debts to these other schools of historical writing, however, the *Short History* belongs in a category by itself—a holistic treatment of English history that was assertively populist and democratic.

There is another major reason that Green, for all the popularity of his book, failed to have an immediate impact on historical writing. The *Short History* appeared at a time when history was undergoing a long transition from being a branch of literature produced by gentlemen amateurs to being a profession. This resulted in part from the labors of antiquaries and others concerned with retrieving and maintaining national and local records. It coincided with the influence of Leopold von Ranke and other European theorists, who insisted that history rest on a massive documentary foundation, necessarily focused on the development of the state. This research ideal took root in Britain in the second half of the nineteenth century, as scholars immersed themselves in archives bulging with increasingly well-catalogued documents.

At the same time, the ancient universities were stirring from their long torpor, responding reluctantly and incompletely to growing demands that they become centers of original research. This occurred just as history was becoming an independent academic discipline. The research-oriented professoriate that emerged in Britain in the final decades of the nineteenth century, while not successful in transforming the intellectual culture of universities, did have a major impact on the kind of history that was published. These scholars tended to disparage "amateur" and "literary" history, as they undertook heavily documented and narrowly focused monographs, laying what they considered to be a firm scientific basis for some eventual attempts at synthesis. This enterprise required that they direct their works to fellow specialists rather than to the general reading public, and that they avoid moralizing judgments and overarching interpretations. Green, with his broad sweep, his literary gifts, his disregard of archives, and above all his popularity, was tried and found wanting by the canons of the new professionalism. He felt the sting of this rejection in the last years of his life, and tried to counter it by writing two narrower, more scholarly books just before his early death in 1883—to no avail.

Green was not alone in being eclipsed by the new professionalism; Victorian historical writing in general was either ignored or denigrated by most professional historians during much of the twentieth century. This process of devaluing necessarily entailed a failure to note significant differences among nineteenth-century historians. Thus Green has been lumped in with the Whig historians or, alternatively, as one of the "Oxford School" along with E. A. Freeman and William Stubbs, even though his work was profoundly different in approach and method.

The only significant published biographical account of Green is in the collected letters and accompanying commentary by Leslie Stephen, published in 1901.[2] Since Green's letters were as delightful, penetrating, and witty as his conversation, the book gives a vivid and on the whole accurate picture of the historian. Stephen did an excellent job editing the correspondence and his commentary is characteristically on the mark. In the relatively brief space he allowed for his analysis, however, Stephen was not able to provide much more than a broad outline of Green as a man and a writer, and he made only the most limited use of Green's manuscript diaries. Moreover, a number of Green's letters, now in the holdings of the Lambeth Palace Library, were unknown to Stephen, including a collection of several dozen from his adolescent years through his time as a curate in London's East End.[3] These throw much interesting new light on Green's relationship with his family and his early intellectual development. Apart from entries in biographical dictionaries and other compendia, a few other studies of Green have been published, most in the decade after the Second World War. W. G. Addison's brief and unimpressive book on Green is concerned chiefly with the development of his religious views and adds little to Stephen.[4] There is a brief and laudatory article on Green by Lionel Angus-Butterworth and a perceptive critique of the *Short History* by R.L. Schuyler.[5] In a 1953 article, Herbert Doherty claims, unpersuasively, that Green's whole point in writing the *Short History* was to trumpet the virtues of the middle class.[6]

If the literature on Green himself tends to be thin and unimpressive, there is much richer fare in the treatment of various facets of Victorian history writing, especially since the late 1970s. Indeed, the quality of the recent scholarship is such that we would be justified in declaring ourselves in the midst of a renaissance of serious interest in the work of nineteenth-century British historians. Among the major themes explored in this recent scholarship are the Victorians' fascination with primitive Germanic antecedents ("Teutonism"), the effects of modern science and religious doubt on history writing, the precise character of Whig historiography, the reasons for and the timing of the reaction against it, the nature and consequences of the new professionalism in history, and the degree of continuity between nineteenth- and twentieth-century practice. On these and other issues, writers like P.B.M. Blaas, J.W. Burrow, T.W. Heyck, Dwight Culler, Rosemary Jann, Philippa Levine, J.P. Kenyon, Peter R.H. Slee, Jeffrey Von Arx, and Christopher Parker have greatly enriched our understanding of Victorian historical scholarship.[7]

The old dismissiveness toward nineteenth-century historians has vanished, and these recent authors have a much better grasp of Green and his contemporaries than did previous commentators. There is still, however, a tendency for Green's distinctiveness to be overlooked. J.W. Burrow, for example, in his otherwise superb study, *A Liberal Descent*, asserts that Green had so much in common with E.A. Freeman "that a separate chapter on him would have involved an unacceptable amount of repetition."[8] Similarly, both Blaas and Heyck are disposed to consider him a junior partner in the Oxford School.[9] To Parker, Green is little more than an example of the "Liberal Anglican" school.[10] Jann, however, considers Green to have been sufficiently important to merit his own chapter, and she explores his distinctive literary qualities as well as his pivotal position as the last great popularizer just as the discipline was becoming professionalized. She also raises the intriguing question of whether such a wide chasm would have opened between professional and popular history had Green not died so young.[11]

The presentation of John Richard Green's life in the following chapters seeks both to build upon and to modify the picture that emerges from the recent scholarship. It is not so much a question of repudiating the analysis of others as pointing out where it is incomplete or misleading. While it will not be denied that Green had some of the characteristics associated with Whiggery, Teutonism, the Oxford School, or Liberal Anglicanism, or that he was a writer of middle-class sympathies, the inadequacy of these categories, each and severally, will be demonstrated. His work was not marked primarily by "picturesqueness," a pious devotion to early folk communities, belief in inevitable progress, or a veneration of modern English institutions, but rather by a vigorous critical voice, by turns harsh, ironic, and humorous, that lashed out at injustices in English society past and present. He was, in a word, considerably more radical than previous analyses have allowed for.

A biographer of a writer should aspire not only to explicate the characteristics of his subject's published work, but also to relate them to the wider social and cultural contexts of the time as well as to family environment and personal experiences. I have attempted to make these connections without becoming overly deterministic about the effects of such things as Green's social marginality or his coming of age just as the Victorian "crisis of faith" got underway. Nonetheless, Green's personal story does reflect many currents of mid-Victorian life: the ambitious strivings of a youth from an obscure family, religious zeal followed by loss of faith, the powerful stimulus of modern science and the advance of democracy, and involvement in the early phases of the social settlement movement and a variety of liberal political causes.

At one level, therefore, an examination of Green's life provides numerous illustrations of the tensions and changes within Victorian middle-class culture. Yet while Green's experiences, beliefs, and aspirations were not atypical of his generation, he alone injected them into the writing of a new kind of history. Thus the major reason for studying Green lies in his crucial role in the history of history writing. He cannot be readily subsumed under any of the major historiographical categories that have been discussed. The *Short History,* with its self-conscious, assertive repudiation of the primacy of politics as a subject of historical writing, must be seen as a unique contribution to its age, one that anticipates twentieth-century concerns and methods more than it reflects nineteenth-century practice.

NOTES

1. Something like this had been attempted ten years earlier by the journalist Charles Knight in his *Popular History of England: An Illustrated History of Society and Government from the Earliest Times to Our Own Times,* 8 vols. (London: Bradbury, Evans, and Co., 1864), but its length and lack of literary quality made it decidedly unpopular.

2. *Letters of John Richard Green,* ed. Leslie Stephen (London: Macmillan, 1901).

3. The only writer to make significant use of the Lambeth Palace letters was W.H. Challen, who used them to construct a rambling, multi-part article on Green's family, chiefly concerned with external and genealogical matters: "John Richard Green, His Mother and Others," *Notes and Queries,* n. s. 12 (1965): 4–9,

56–59, 105–108, 150–54, 185–88, 231–35, 254–58, 294–98, 345–48, 382–83, 425–29, 456–63.

4. W.G. Addison, *J.R. Green* (London: Society for Promoting Christian Knowledge, 1946).

5. Lionel Angus-Butterworth, "John Richard Green," *South Atlantic Quarterly* 46 (1947): 109–18; Robert Livingstone Schuyler, "John Richard Green and his Short History," *Political Science Quarterly* 64 (1949): 321–54.

6. Herbert J. Doherty, Jr., "John Richard Green: Historian of the Middle Class," *London Quarterly and Holborn Review* 178 (1953): 69–73.

7. See the Bibliography for the works of these authors, some of which are discussed in subsequent chapters.

8. J.W. Burrow, *A Liberal Descent: Victorian Historians and the English Past* (Cambridge: Cambridge University Press, 1981), 7.

9. P.B.M. Blaas, *Continuity and Anachronism: Parliamentary and Constitutional Development in Whig Historiography and in the Anti-Whig Reaction between 1890 and 1930* (The Hague: Nijhoff, 1978), 186–95; T.W. Heyck, *The Tranformation of Intellectual Life in Victorian Britain* (London: Croom Helm, 1982), 141–45.

10. Christopher Parker, *The English Historical Tradition Since 1850* (Edinburgh: John Donald, 1990), 38–39. The concept of Liberal Anglicanism was introduced by Duncan Forbes, *The Liberal Anglican Idea of History* (Cambridge: Cambridge University Press, 1952).

11. Rosemary Jann, *The Art and Science of Victorian History* (Columbus, Ohio: Ohio University Press, 1985), 141–69.

2. An Oxford Boyhood: Outside Looking In

John Richard Green was born in Oxford on 12 December 1837, shortly after eighteen-year-old Victoria began her long and momentous reign. His birthplace was both the seat of England's premier university and a thriving market town with a proud history. Its population of nearly 25,000[1] included a multitude of trades, some of which catered chiefly or exclusively to the university. The historian's father, Richard Green (1799–1852) was a maker of silk gowns for Fellows. In addition to becoming a father for the second time in 1837, he was also made registrar of births, deaths, and marriages under the Civil Registration Act of that year. While this appointment attests to some useful connections among the city's political leadership, Richard Green was a hard-working tailor in often straitened financial circumstances. His social status was probably little different from that of his father, John Green (1763–1834), who had also been a tailor as well as serving as parish clerk of St. Martin, Oxford.

There was, however, a tradition of academic eminence in the family represented by Richard's uncle William West Green (1759–1820), a vice principal of Magdalen Hall.[2] It was this worthy who was constantly held up for emulation to John Green and his younger brother Richard. As the historian's wife, Alice, put it many years later, the boys were "brought up in the idea that they were to take him as an example, and to restore the family to a better position." An economic dimension to this family decline was represented by a great-grandfather who, according to Alice Green, left money that was "found not to exist. He is supposed to have come down in the world."[3] John's mother could neither boast an eminent forebear nor lament a vanished family fortune. Rachel Hurdis Green (1801–81) was of obscure origins, there being apparently no foundation to stories of her belonging to the family of an eighteenth-century professor of poetry.[4]

John Green was born at 5 St. John Street, but the 1841 census found the four-year-old lodging with his parents, his older sister Adelaide, younger brother Richard, and his mother's cousin, Christopher Graham, at a house in Pembroke Street owned by Sarah Dell, a laundress.[5] A fourth child, Ann Mary Castle Green (Annie) was born in 1846. John was a frail, sickly child who surprised his family by surviving infancy. Writing about his childhood in an 1873 letter, he noted that it was "not a happy one," and that he recalled little of it beyond "a morbid shyness, a love of books, a habit of singing about the house, a sense of being smaller and weaker than other boys." Yet he harbored affectionate memories of his father, who "encouraged me in my love of books, or shielded me from the harsh rebukes of people who could not understand my absent, shy, unboyish ways."[6]

Considerable ingenuity must have been required to gratify Green's passion for books since there were few in the house beyond *Pilgrim's Progress, Don Quixote,* and a ponderous life of Christ.[7] The Milton appears to have been a loan from his uncle John, whose suspected atheistic tendencies led to a family rupture, with the result that the boy lost all contact with his namesake.[8] This meager reading fare was supplemented by a stray volume of David Hume's *History of England,* then the standard work used in the schools. Although Green would later reject Hume's essentially conservative political premises, the volume that fell to his lot, particularly its account of Elizabeth's reign, stimulated his interest.[9] Even more exciting was his first encounter with a book he later remembered as *Merchant and Friar,* almost certainly *Truths and Fictions of the Middle Ages: The Merchant and the Friar* by Sir Francis Palgrave (1788–1861), Deputy Keeper of the Queen's Records and a major figure in the promotion of medieval studies.[10] Years later he described Palgrave's colorful evocation of medieval town life as "the first book which gave me . . . a notion of what history was."[11] Beyond this, most of his early knowledge was acquired by reading the *Penny Journal.*[12]

The boy was raised in a High Church and Tory atmosphere in which reverence for established institutions was strongly marked. Even an otherwise exciting expedition to London for the Great Exhibition in 1851 was the occasion for a sermon by his father on the wickedness of the mob, prompted by observing the iron shutters on Apsley House, the duke of Wellington's residence. The shabbiness of the public house in which the family lodged during the visit and the long walk occasioned by a lack of money for the omnibus fare were a further trial. Still, thirteen-year-old John was thrilled to see the Iron Duke's back and delighted by the machinery at the Crystal Palace.[13]

A succession of events in 1852 altered the fourteen-year-old's life drastically. He had to bear the loss of both his father and his sister Adelaide, who died about the same time. A year and a half older than John, Adelaide had doted on him, making her loss a particularly bitter blow. As Alice Green later remarked, "John [was] passionately attached to her, and felt her death terribly."[14] The sudden removal of the close, maternal attachment of his sister left an emotional void, for his mother was far more aloof. This deprivation stimulated a lifelong yearning for close feminine companionship, which he was to find in a few notable friendships and finally, in the last six years of his life, in marriage. His father's death, in addition to removing a steady, caring force in Green's life, necessitated the breakup of the family. Rachel took five-year-old Annie off to live in a small cottage in Hertfordshire, while John and his twelve-year-old brother Richard were taken in by their paternal aunt Mary and her husband, Nathaniel Castle, a hatter in Oxford. Life in the ultra-conservative Castle household, where strict obedience and constant gratitude were demanded, was to prove a severe trial to the adolescent boys.

Another defining event of 1852 was Green's expulsion from Magdalen College School. He had been admitted there as a scholarship boy, possibly on the strength of his connection to the former vice principal of Magdalen Hall. Entering school at the age of eight, undersized and of delicate health, made him feel at first "dazed among so many strange faces and rough boy-ways," yet he recalled years later that "I was soon happy enough, and the new fun of games, small and weak though I was, carried all shyness away." At that time the grammar school was housed in the college, and suddenly to belong to a place of such beauty and antiquity was a powerful spur to Green's imagination:

> All that innerness of life, that utter blindness to outer things which leaves my childhood such a blank to me, disappeared at Magdalen. The college was a poem in itself; its dim cloisters, its noble chapel, its smooth lawns, its park with deer browsing beneath venerable elms, its "walks" with "Addison's walk" in the midst of them, but we boys thought less of Addison than wasps' nest and craw-fishing. Of all the Oxford colleges it was the stateliest and most secluded from the outer world, and though I can laugh now at the indolence and uselessness of the collegiate life of my boy-days, my boyish imagination was overpowered by the solemn services, the white-robed choir, the

long train of divines and fellows, and the president, moving like some myste-
rious dream of the past among the punier creatures of the present.[15]

Green was fascinated that the president of Magdalen College, Dr. Martin
Routh (1755–1854), who was over ninety years old and the last man in
Oxford to wear a wig, could recall seeing Samuel Johnson striding down
the High. The venerable Dr. Routh once presented Green with a prize,
shook his hand, and told him he was a clever boy. A quarter of a century
later, the historian was still deeply impressed that he "ever shook hands
with a man who had seen Dr. Johnson."[16]

Green's quickness was soon perceived by his teachers and by the
headmaster, Dr. James Ellison Millard, who appointed him librarian of a
small collection of books above the porch. Such marks of favor did not,
however, exempt the boy from his share of floggings, especially for his
difficulties with arithmetic. While this brutal pedagogy was the common
lot of all English schoolboys, it was especially hateful to Green, whose
father had never struck him.[17] Moreover, the masters soon discovered the
boy's mocking, iconoclastic streak. When Millard showed him a picture
of Noah in the Ark, Green responded with unbecoming levity that the pa-
triarch looked like a "Jack-in-the-Box."[18]

Although such behavior was exasperating to the Headmaster, the prize
essay incident proved to be intolerable. A medal had been offered for an
essay on Charles I, and Green had read Hume's *History of England* and
other works in preparation for it. In spite of Hume's sympathetic treatment
of the Royalist cause, Green concluded that the king had been in the
wrong and that Parliament was the true defender of English liberties. The
examiner, Canon Mozley, was fair-minded enough to give the prize to
Green over the head of older boys, even though he disagreed strongly with
his conclusion. Such impugning of the "royal martyr" by an impertinent
schoolboy proved too much for Dr. Millard, however. He insisted to
Green's uncle that John be removed from Magdalen and sent to study with
a private tutor. Millard wrote that "my experience of John Green's peculiar character and disposition during the past term has convinced me that it
would be disadvantageous to him to remain any longer in his present position."[19] The sting of this rejection, and a galling sense of unfairness, remained with Green for many years and helped shape the rebellious, anti-
establishment thrust of his later writings. An intense anti-royalism was to
be a marked feature of his treatment of the Civil War in the *Short History
of the English People*, which specialists like S. R. Gardiner and James
Gairdner would never be able to convince him was one-sided.[20]

Although Millard could not abide Green's continuing at Magdalen, he was concerned enough to recommend to Nathaniel Castle that James Ridgway of Kirkham, Lancashire, would be a good choice to tutor the boy. Millard contacted Ridgway directly, telling him that his instructing the lad offered a "possible chance of reclamation for him."[21] Ridgway agreed to take the boy and assured Castle that nothing about the goings-on at Magdalen need be revealed in Kirkham. He warned sternly, however, that if young Green "exercises a bad influence over my other pupils I must return him to you at once."[22]

The fear of liberal contagion of the other boys proved unfounded, for Green spent a good deal of time by himself and "wandered about the fields thinking."[23] Castle was pleased to hear of his nephew's improved behavior and even more, to receive from John a deferential reaction to his account of British exploits in the Crimean War. Green, who in the 1870s was to take an active part as a "pro-Russian" agitator against Turkish atrocities and British power politics, replied to his uncle with schoolboy bravado: "I read out to the delight of everyone your account of the Nemeses and Hecla. I am sure it was only our scanty numbers prevented our giving a good cheer. I hope our Admiral will do something better than that half-finished job, the bombardment of Odessa."[24]

While such patriotic effusion no doubt pleased his uncle, Green parted company with him over a controversial proposal to open the reading room of the Oxford Library on Sundays. Castle, a strict Sabbatarian, must have been unhappy to receive the following letter, in spite of the qualifications his nephew placed on his liberal opinions:

> I see by Ann's letter that you and the Conservative party (for so it really is) have been floored by the Rads on the question of the reading Room. [T]here is a great deal of (excuse the word) Puritanism in the people of England, and many a workman who shy up his cap and shout "Hooray Charley" would be awfully scandalized at what they would deem a profanation of the Sabbath. For my part however I am rather in favour of the motion, that is of its principle. If the proposition were, as I hope it is, to open the reading Room in the afternoon, or at some time out of service hours, I think that a certain degree of Recreation on a Sunday is perfectly proper, though of course I would not approve of the abuse of this principle.[25]

Beyond showing Green's continuing streak of independence, this letter is also of interest in the somewhat negative attitude toward Puritanism it expresses. Green came to harbor a deep ambivalence on this topic: In the *Short History*, he would praise the Puritans for their stalwart defense of liberty against Charles I, while regretting (as he did in this adolescent letter) the narrowness of Puritan life and culture.

Castle had begun to entertain doubts about Ridgway's suitability, for he had ambitions for his nephew to prepare himself for a career in the Indian Civil Service. Ridgway himself, with the Northcote-Trevelyan report of 1854 clearly in mind, had already written that it was imperative for the boy to go to university in order to do well on the new competitive exams.[26] One scholar whom Castle consulted wrote that while Ridgway was "certainly of abundantly sufficient powers and attainments to teach young boys," he would "never do as a trainer for Candidates for Scholarships for Academical honors."[27]

A possible lack of academic rigor in Green's tutor was not the only thing for his uncle to worry about, for the boy had fallen in with a priest in Lancashire and announced his intention of converting to Roman Catholicism. It is difficult not to conclude that, whatever the attractions Green felt for the ancient faith, it was a most excellent means of infuriating his guardian. Several years earlier he had managed to provoke his uncle's wrath by ridiculing Lord John Russell's Durham Letter of November 1850 on "Papal Aggression." Green denounced the absurdity of the anti-Catholic agitation and legislation with such vigor that his uncle had refused to admit him to his house for some time.[28]

Considering this background, Castle showed remarkable restraint in calmly securing from his nephew a promise that he would delay the conversion until he came of age. As he had hoped, John's enthusiasm for Rome quickly waned.[29] But now that it seemed prudent to remove the boy from Lancashire on religious as well as academic grounds, the services of a new tutor were quickly secured. The choice was an excellent one. Charles Duke Yonge (1812–91), the author of a number of educational manuals, would later become professor of modern history and English literature at Queen's College, Belfast. He charged £100 a year to tutor John Green, a sum that Castle tried without success to negotiate downward.[30]

Studying with Yonge involved a move to Leamington Spa, which was as much to Green's liking as it was his uncle's. On the academic side, Yonge had to tell Castle that while his young charge was a good student, "he has been very badly taught."[31] A week later, Yonge wrote: "I make him work very hard, and he is not at all afraid of work."[32] Among the works Green was introduced to under Yonge's tutelage was *The Decline and Fall of the Roman Empire*. He instantly became a devotee of Gibbon: "What a new world that was!"[33]

A judicious amount of leisure was also part of the regimen at Leamington. A holiday was granted to the boy by his tutor, who "thought I had well earned it by my industry." Green chose nearby Stratford-on-Avon, to "pay my respects to the relics of the immortal Shakespear." Having ridden to Stratford on top of a coach in a driving rain, he presented himself at the house claiming to be the Bard's birthplace, where he was met by a "very ladylike widow" who escorted him upstairs. Green's characteristic irreverence is evident in his reaction to the experience: "Here he was born, and here I ought to have fallen into a rhapsody. But how could one with a wet jacket? (and with a loquacious guide)." Finishing his sightseeing four hours before the return coach, he walked the ten miles back to Leamington in order to save the fare.[34]

Castle, pleased at his nephew's academic progress, was eager for him to go on to university, a desire that he expressed to Yonge. Green himself saw a notice in the *Oxford Herald* of a scholarship competition for Jesus College, Oxford, "open . . . to all English counties." Jesus, with an almost exclusively Welsh student body and staff, was perhaps the least distinguished of the Oxford colleges of the 1850s, and his tutor offered guarded encouragement, "as he supposes it is one which would not be much sought after." Green asked his uncle to make inquiries, noting that it would be "well to know its worth etc. and whether it leads to a fellowship."[35] Yonge expressed to Castle some misgivings about the scholarship attempt: "I shall be exceedingly glad to hear of his success at Jesus, but do not feel sanguine about it, as I hardly contemplated his going up for an Examination so soon."[36] On another occasion he told Castle that he was against boys going up early, noting that it would be "as easy to get a first class [degree] at 22 as a second at 21." He recommended waiting until the following year, when two scholarships at the more prestigious Trinity College would be available.[37]

In the event, the uncle's impatience and desire to save money prevailed. Green, who was as eager as his uncle to get on with his education, secured the Jesus College scholarship, and Yonge responded with warm congratulations. Green's own interest in an academic career had by now been thoroughly roused, and he received an encouraging response from his tutor: "I spoke of the Fellowships of Jesus and any chance of getting one. He said it did not matter much, for he thought if I continued steadily working as I was doing now there seemed nothing to prevent me getting a First, and then it would not be difficult to get any fellowship."[38]

While excited at the opportunities that were opening to him, he was apprehensive and not a little sad to leave Yonge, declaring that he had "never been so happy before, as I have been here, and it is a great chance whether I should be ever so happy again."[39]

NOTES

1. 23,834 in the 1841 census.

2. W. H. Challen, "John Richard Green, His Mother and Others," *Notes and Queries,* n.s. 210 (1965): 106.

3. Notes by Alice Stopford Green on John Richard Green's family, Jesus College MS. 242, J 49/3.

4. This claim is made by Leslie Stephen in the introduction to *The Letters of John Richard Green* (London: Macmillan, 1901), 1, but has been rejected by W. H. Challen.

5. Ibid., 7.

6. Ibid., 3.

7. Ibid., 7–8.

8. Ibid., 2.

9. Ibid., 4.

10. For Palgrave's importance, see P. B. M. Blaas, *Continuity and Anachronism: Parliamentary and Constitutional Development in Whig Historiography and in the Anti–Whig Reaction between 1890 and 1930* (The Hague: Nijhoff, 1978), 77–83 *et passim.*

11. Ibid., 170. By the time he had graduated from Oxford and begun his own scholarly labors, Green had become much more critical: "Sir Francis writes like a man who had lived in the times he was writing about, but he moves with the crowd and never climbs a step to get a *general* effect. His philosophical part seems great twaddle." Green to E. A. Freeman, n.d. [1864–65], LJRG, 153.

12. LJRG, 8.

13. LJRG, 10.

14. Notes by Alice Stopford Green on John Richard Green's family, Jesus College MS. 242, J 49/3.

15. LJRG, 5.

16. Ibid., 6.

17. Ibid., 7.

18. Ibid., 11–12.

19. Millard to Nathaniel Castle, 17 April 1854, Lambeth Palace MS. 1725, fo. 147.

20. Blaas, *Continuity and Anachronism,* 191.

21. James Ridgway to Castle, 19 Apr.il1854, Lambeth Palace MS. 1725, fo. 148.

22. Ibid., fo. 149.

23. LJRG, 12. Leslie Stephen assigned the Lancashire experience to 1853, but the Lambeth Palace MSS. show that Green's expulsion and his interlude with Ridgway were in 1854. Stephen was consistently off by a year in dating all the events of Green's life between leaving Magdalen and entering Jesus College.

24. Green to Castle, 8 June 1854, Lambeth Palace MS. 1725, fo. 1.

25. Ibid., n.d. [1854], fos. 35–36.

26. Ridgway to Castle, 27 Jan. 1855, Lambeth Palace MS. 1725, fos. 152–53.

27. Thomas E. Espin to Castle, 7 Oct. 1854, Lambeth Palace MS. 1725, fo. 139.

28. LJRG, 9.

29. LJRG, 13.

30. Yonge to Castle, 11 May 1855, Lambeth Palace MS. 1725, fos. 156–57.

31. Ibid., 30 April 1855, fo. 166.

32. Ibid., 7 May 1855, fo. 168.

33. LJRG, 13. It is intriguing to compare Green's near conversion to Catholicism with Gibbon's brief embrace of the ancient faith—both events in the early adolescence of two historians born almost exactly a century apart—but there is no evidence that Green was aware of this episode in Gibbon's life.

34. Green to Castle, 24 June 1855, Lambeth Palace MS. 1725, fos. 11–12.

35. Ibid., n.d. [1855], fo. 23.

36. Yonge to Castle, n.d. [1855], Lambeth Palace MS. 1725, fo 158.

37. Ibid., 7 May 1855, fos. 168–69.

38. Green to Castle, 17 Mar. 1856, Lambeth Palace MS. 1725, fos. 15–16.

39. Ibid., fo. 15.

3. An Ambivalent Undergraduate: The Jesus College Years

Green was granted the scholarship to Jesus College in November 1855. Since it would be nearly a year before he could enter the college, he remained through the winter in Leamington studying with Yonge, returning to Oxford in March 1856. During this time he tried his best to maintain cordial relations with his querulous uncle, congratulating him on becoming a magistrate and chiding him good-naturedly on his reluctance to use "Esq." after his name. In the same letter, Green managed to craft a quite restrained reply to one of Castle's many demands that he express some sense of the many advantages that were being accorded him. He assured his uncle that his "kind expressions" were appreciated and that he was indebted to him for "giving me that start in the world which makes the after course so comparatively easy." As for Castle's concern that his nephew might not be making the best use of his opportunities, Green promised that he would do his very best to succeed, and would endeavor "in years to come to show to others the same generosity which you have shown to me."[1] Few of his other replies to his uncle on this touchy subject would be as diplomatic as this one.

The ambitious young man, dreaming of prizes, honors, and fellowships, who entered Jesus College in 1856 was soon to become disillusioned by the general low standards and laxness of the place. Even the best of the colleges in the 1850s were in a relatively unreformed condition. Jesus College was no citadel of learning. Green came to refer to it as "that vile place" where the Fellows had "nibbled down to nothing the reforms proposed by the Commissioners."[2] The reference here was to the foot-dragging by his own and other colleges, which delayed for a generation the reforms of the Oxford University Commission of 1852.[3] That Royal Commission sought a major overhaul of the way colleges allocated their financial resources, and urged giving more attention to research conducted by an expanded corps of professors.

The commission also recommended reform of the curriculum, stressing more modern and professionally oriented programs. It would be a generation before some of these changes were being implemented, and even then the tutors would manage to maintain their control of undergraduate education and prevent the emergence of a German-style professoriate. In Green's day both Oxford and Cambridge were very much Church institutions, and most tutors thought of themselves as in a comfortable holding pattern, awaiting well-paid livings in country parsonages. The terms of their fellowships entailed celibacy, an additional reason that most of them chose to abandon academic life at the first favorable opportunity.

Green quickly came to despise the dons for their narrow, illiberal learning, pettiness, and indolence. Being far more widely read than most undergraduates, he found but few to stimulate his intellect. He was ambitious and a good conversationalist, however, with a desire to achieve high honors and put himself in line for a fellowship. Such a combination of attributes has often been translated into brilliant academic and social success. In Green's case it did not. After some initial attempts to distinguish himself, he tended to adopt a bemused, sarcastic attitude. He began to ignore the syllabus and took to reading widely and intensely in subjects that interested him, principally literature and history. Eventually, he gave up all thought of sitting for an honors examination, contenting himself with a pass degree instead.

The intellectual torpor of his college does not alone account for Green's determination to slip through his university years in as undistinguished a fashion as possible. It is likely that the ongoing struggle with his uncle was at least as much to blame. Castle's ambition for his nephew had by this time progressed from Indian civil servant to barrister, but Green expressed a marked distaste for the law. Although modern history was now a degree field (thanks to the Oxford University Commission), he would have nothing to do with it because its study was combined with jurisprudence. His uncle's insistence on a legal career for him almost certainly stimulated Green's repugnance for the subject.

Compounding the struggle over a field of study and choice of career was the older man's hectoring manner over Green's alleged moral failings and ingratitude. At one point Castle urged his charge to embrace religion in order to avoid "falling into the Pit of Destruction ere you know where you are." Green replied hotly: "Such a reproof might well form a fitting rebuke to a life of Sin and Vice. A course of utterly abandoned conduct, a character entirely cool and ruined could scarcely have been more strongly denounced or more energetically condemned." He went on to defend his life as one "which though blotted with a few errors has never been tainted with a single vice, a character which though faulty and imperfect though it may be has never cast away the restraints of Morality and Religion, though it may have lightly treated their outward profession."[4]

On another occasion, Castle stressed the need for his nephew to be dutiful and submissive to the college authorities because of his "humble" station. Green's response was, first, to assert that even were he "reduced to a mechanic's station this moment I should not feel a whit degraded." Furthermore, he continued: "In Jesus there are many in no better, some in a worse station than myself, yet you speak as though a wide difference of station existed between me and the rest of the College. I would have this childish exaggeration cease."[5]

Even more galling was to be reminded of the "disgrace" of his expulsion from school. This rebuke touched a raw nerve, generating a spirited response: "I look back on my expulsion with no regret, for moral fault I see none in my conduct, but rather with a triumphant satisfaction." He went on to claim that "a Divine Providence did convert that injustice, ruinous as it was meant to be to all my future prospects, into the very means of opening still wider prospects and more decidedly furthering my Fortune."[6] But the emotion roused by this issue was surpassed by what Green felt when again being chided for his ingratitude:

> However an occasional outburst from Aunt has made us feel deeply the sting of dependency, yet our treatment on the whole is such as to demand our most thoughtful acknowledgment. It demands in short our gratitude. But if gratitude consists in a tame subserviency, I had almost said slavery to Benefactors, as we see in some; or if as we see in others it consists in profuse and sickening expressions of affection and fawning and flattery, in false and fulsome adulation, I will say at once that gratitude such as this I cannot stoop to, even if I would.[7]

By no means was the relationship between Green and his guardian always as strained as these quotations suggest. A tone of cordiality pervades much of their correspondence, and it is clear that there was a fair measure of affection on both sides. It is also clear, however, that the tone of wounded pride, a kind of persistent adolescent truculence, that runs through many of these letters, was quite authentic. The loss of his father at the age of fourteen and the need to rely on the charity of relatives who demanded constant expressions of gratitude reinforced Green's natural spirit of independence. His ardent love of liberty, thus stimulated by the troubled relationship with his guardian, would find full expression in his writings, most notably in the *Short History*. At the same time, there was a profound ambivalence: A genuine affection and attachment wrestled with his resentment. A similar ambivalence characterized his attitude toward the university and the church, institutions that he came to criticize bitterly yet continued to love deeply.

Within his first year, Green joined the Oxford Union. He also participated actively in two important organizations in his college: the Literary and Debating Society and the College Junior Common Room and Debating Society. While these involvements were a promising beginning, a scathing satire published about this time was attributed to Green, with unfortunate but hardly unexpected results. Titled the "Gentiad," it was based on Alexander Pope's "Dunciad" and began by invoking his muse:

Mute is the lyre that moved of old the rage
And scourged the rampant follies of the age;
Hushed is the voice whose one satiric word
Pierced ten times deeper than the keenest sword;
And, see! e'er yet its echoes faint are hushed
Start into life the vices it had crushed.
Oh wake once more, satiric harp; too long
Have ninnies gloried in thy silenced song![8]

The poem proceeded to skewer the members of the college so effectively that Green was excluded from much of college society.[9] While it is by no means certain that he was the author, the poem reflects his interest in and knowledge of the biting satirical literature of the eighteenth century. Furthermore, that he was so widely believed to have written it testifies to perceptions of him as an acerbic critic of collegiate life.

His partial exclusion from the social life of Jesus College intensified his disdain for the place and its practices. Nonetheless, he did establish several close and lasting friendships there. By far the most important was with William Boyd Dawkins (1837–1929), a science student who became an archaeologist and the first professor of geology at Owens College, Manchester. It was Dawkins, or "Dax," as Green called him, who stimulated his interest in science and who would influence his career and writing in important ways. And even though Green's college years led him to develop a jaundiced eye regarding Wales and Welshmen, he could count among his friends a Jones, a Griffiths, and a Morgan.[10] One younger Welshman Green formed an especially strong liking for was Henry Llewellyn Browne, who had just come up from Llanrwst School. The traits that he professed to admire in Browne were in fact strikingly like those of Green himself:

> This Browne—a freshman and a Scholar—with his clear-cut brow, quiet eyes and stern ascetic life—his brusque sentences and heady manner—is a Triton whose advent seems likely to make a stir among the minnows. They cry out against his bumptiousness. . . . I like him because in a college of liars I find in him a Truth Teller. He has no bump of reverence—he is a restless sceptic, rather let me say destructive, and a rash theorist but in his wildest speculations he is struggling for light and striving towards the Truth. . . . His brain teams with high quixotic notions. He loves Scholarship.[11]

Llewellyn Browne's recollection of Green's relationship with his fellow undergraduates was still vivid twenty-five years later. He described Green's "terrible gift of sarcasm," which he claimed was used "sometimes for the pleasure of using it." Llewellyn Browne recalled Green's decisive power in debate, yet noted that his "repartee was instantaneous and decisive, never spiteful nor malicious." As a result of these qualities, he concluded, Green was not popular with his contemporaries: "Such persons seldom are; the fault was more often theirs than his."[12]

In spite of his friendship with Llewellyn Browne and other Welshmen, Green still nurtured some typical English attitudes:

> To the Welch [sic] mind in especial any choice is unintelligible. They have no notion of individuality—of eccentricity—they cannot live in themselves they must have fame—and the coarser must have gold. This is the reason why their manuscript authorities for their national histories lie dust covered in their libraries while those who should disentomb them are spouting trash about Llewellyn and independence.[13]

Yet even this stereotyping embraced the notion that the stimulation of Welsh pride through a study of the principality's culture and history was a worthy undertaking. He blamed his own college, which had been established in the sixteenth century to meet such needs, for abdicating its responsibility. In 1862 Green helped launch a new magazine, *The Druid*, under Henry Llewellyn Browne's editorship. Green asked rhetorically, in a letter which appeared in the first issue: "What in past times has the College done—what does it now for Wales? . . . What does it do for Welsh literature, Welsh history, Welsh archaeology, Welsh philology, Welsh patriotism in its higher and nobler sense?"[14] To help supply the deficiency of scholarship on Welsh studies, Green contributed to a subsequent issue of *The Druid* an article on the Welsh poet and Jesus College alumnus William Vaughan (1577–1641).[15]

Green's undergraduate years were by no means consumed with railing against the shortcomings of the dons and students. Walking with his friends through the town, the other colleges, and the countryside, attending the theatre, visiting coffee houses and taverns, fishing, even on one occasion pitching into the annual town-gown affray—these and other student diversions brought him considerable pleasure. Neither was he immune to the charms of Oxford's young ladies. Like many other undergraduates, Green was frequently falling in and out of love. His attachments to women at this point in his life were characterized, not unsurprisingly, by an adolescent romanticism. His attraction to a "Miss J.," notable for "the inexpressible purity and delicacy of her expression," was typical. This young beauty, who reminded Green of Gretchen in *Faust*, had "a dove-like, guileless repose about her." But Miss J. was no means the only girl to catch his eye. Green was quite enchanted by his discovery of the joys of dancing. After telling "a young damsel of twenty summers" that he did not know how to dance: "A dozen instructors are instantly at hand, and in another minute I am in the thick of quadrilles and waltzes. . . . I owned to myself that I had not spent so happy or so unphilosophical an evening for years."[16]

By the end of his undergraduate career, Green's thoughts had begun to turn to marriage, though it was clear that his concept of a wife did not yet include real intellectual companionship. He wrote to Dawkins in 1859:

I believe I shall end in marriage,—and with whom? I have not settled on the individual, but I can tell you the species. Not the beautiful—your Junos, Minervas, or Venus's—but some quiet, demure little party whose beauty at best will be that of expression; who won't mind pets, humours, and eccentricities; who will never invade my study or pop in on my musings with some vapid suggestion to visit the Blinks's or some bothering inquiry about papering and painting. Some one who won't talk of her love, or expect demonstrations in return, but whose love will be like sunshine, cheering and warming and comforting, and lighting up all the dark corners of one's morbid temperament. Some one who can decipher my horrible scrawl and copy my manuscripts for the printer.[17]

Considering this near-parody of the ideal Victorian wife, it is fortunate that Green did not marry for another eighteen years, by which time he had come to appreciate a partnership of minds.

His intellectual development during these years was mostly the result of self-study. History and literature continued to be his principal interests, though he also found time to delve into works of philosophy, including J. S. Mill's *A System of Logic*.[18] What he called his "sunny memories" of his rooms at Jesus College were linked to his reading—memories of

> hours of poring over musty old chronicles while the clocks chimed the hours after midnight; of lounges all the long summer afternoons on the old sofa over *Ariosto* or *Rape of the Lock;* of pacings round and round the room, Pope's *Homer* in hand, chanting out the lines which, criticise them as you will, have got a ring of old Homer in them.[19]

Science also came to absorb his interest, thanks in part to the influence of his friend Dawkins. Indeed, science would ultimately prove the most important intellectual stimulus he acquired as an undergraduate, profoundly affecting the course of his religious and historical thinking.

Green declined to read for the newly established degree field of modern history, protesting that its linkage to jurisprudence in the curriculum made it unpalatable. He further objected to the tendency of his tutors to purvey history in the form of snippets from various authors, rather than using works in their entirety. This time-honored method of study was closely linked to the system of honors examinations, in which those seeking "class" degrees (as distinct from a mere "pass") sought to "get up" their subject in the most expeditious manner possible. Students seeking maximum results with minimum efforts had only to consult a useful volume titled *Pass and Class*, by Montagu Burrows, who was to become Chichele Professor of Modern History in 1862. While Burrows cautioned against superficiality, clearly his cram manual encouraged precisely that.[20] Green, seeing the full, grand flow of Gibbon's narrative carved into fragments for the purpose of cramming, was repulsed. He read classics instead, but only in a fitful manner. At the last moment, one of his tutors tried to put his name down for modern history, but Green withdrew it. Instead, he suddenly opted for physical science, a subject that included little of the exciting and controversial new work that was just coming to a head with the publication of Charles Darwin's *Origin of Species*. He "got up" just enough of his degree field to squeak through with a pass.[21]

Green's poor showing can be viewed both as an attempt to register his dissatisfaction with the system and as a method of further aggravating his uncle. There is certainly an air of defiance in a letter to Dawkins a month before taking his degree:

> You may have guessed—what is for the present a secret—that I do not intend to go up for a class. This will fall like a bombshell among the Dons, and I will have to endure a few skirmishes . . . and not a few black looks from quarters which I care more about. But people are beginning to comprehend that what I will to do, I do; and if they are philosophers the Dons will soon give over in which they cannot but be beaten.[22]

"Bombshell" was an exaggeration. Green's decision may have proved disappointing to some of the dons, but most had probably written him off as an eccentric and malcontent. Undoubtedly his tutor, Robert Owen, was disappointed. Owen coached Green in ethics and Livy during his last year, and praised him for his rapid progress. Green professed himself gratified at Owen's favorable opinion of him, but qualified it by noting that it was "in spite of my own adage that a fool's flattery may please because it may happen he believes it—a clever man's flattery must be odious because it implies an underlying sarcasm."[23] His influence on Green must have been slight, for in spite of being the modern history tutor, Owen was unable to convince his pupil to take a degree in that subject.[24]

A crucially important encounter with Arthur Penrhyn Stanley during Green's last year bolstered his decision to renounce academic honors. It also helped to propel him into a career in the church, and restored his dedication to the study of history. Stanley (1815–81), one of the leading Oxford liberals, was Professor of Ecclesiastical History and a Canon of Christ Church. A critic of Oxford education, he had served as secretary of the Oxford University Commission. One day Green, in a disconsolate mood, wandered into Stanley's lecture on the Wesleys. Several years later he described to Stanley the impact of that experience. Two years of residence, Green wrote, had left him "idle and irreligious" and he "rebelled doggedly" against the Oxford system, turning his back on history and standing apart wearily from the various religious factions:

> I was utterly miserable when I wandered into your lecture-room, and my recollection of what followed is not so much of any definite words as of a great unburthening. Then and after I heard you speak of work, not as a thing of classes and fellowships, but as something worthy for its own sake, worthy because it made us like the great worker. . . . I took up my old boy-dreams,—

history—I think I have been a steady worker ever since. And so in religion, it was not so much a creed that you taught me, as fairness.[25]

Green was excited to hear Stanley conclude his lecture with the phrase, *Magna est veritas et praevalebit* (Great is truth, and will prevail). Springing to his feet, he shouted: "*Magna est veritas et praevalebit* is the motto of the town!" Delighted at this show of knowledge and enthusiasm, Stanley asked the young man to walk him home and invited him for dinner. The date appointed, in early November, turned out to be the occasion of a town-gown row, with passage through the streets a dangerous affair. When Stanley asked how he had managed to come at all, Green replied, echoing Samuel Johnson: "Sir, it is a great thing to dine with a Canon of Christ Church."[26] A friendship between the two men developed quickly. The attraction of Stanley's Broad Church views for someone of Green's temperament is readily apparent. Impatient with authority and resistant to the narrow ambitions and social snobbery of Oxford life, Green found meaning in a liberal doctrine of work and service. Furthermore, this doctrine allowed him to pursue a career in the church while at the same time developing the kind of scholarly life that did not seem possible within the university.

Another area of interest that opened to Green during his final year at Oxford, largely through his friendship with Dawkins, was archaeology. Dawkins took Green with him to Somerset to explore Wookey Hole and other caves, both for scientific and archaeological research. These expeditions led to a plan for a jointly authored history of Somerset, in which chapters on the geology, flora, and fauna of the region would lead into the later historical sections—a scheme not unlike the later *Victoria County History* series.[27] Although the book on Somerset was never written, the two men would continue to discuss it and similar collaborative projects for many years.

The Somerset connection through Dawkins also proved important in that it led to Green's introduction to Edward Augustus Freeman. In truth, it was a reintroduction; while still at school, he had first encountered Freeman in Oxford through a shared interest in architecture. Green had developed his close knowledge of ecclesiastical building styles by dint of long hours in the churches of the town and surrounding countryside, saving up his sixpences to pay sextons for admission and the right to take brass rubbings. It was at Magdalen College School that thirteen-year-old Green met Freeman, who would carry "little Johnny" on his shoulder around Dr. Millard's library because the boy was "so well up in mould-ings."[28]

The year 1859 brought Green his first opportunity to publish something historical. Immediately after his finishing his studies at Jesus College, he was commissioned by the proprietors of the *Oxford Chronicle* to write a series of articles on Oxford life in the eighteenth century. An earlier series by another writer had proved unsatisfactory, and a fresh approach was needed. The choice could not have been better. Green was a native-born citizen of Oxford, proud of the town's history and traditions. Furthermore, he had already developed an impatience with the traditional manner of presenting history as a chronicle of major political events.

In the preface to the edition that combined both series, the change of author was explained as growing partly out of the unexpected refusal by the city authorities to grant access to the archives:

> It [thus] became impossible to persevere in the original project without rendering the papers a mere dull summary of petty and uninteresting events. It was determined, therefore, on the change of authorship . . . to adapt them, as far as possible, to our existing sources of information; and since we could not present a chronological history, to depict in as lively a manner as possible the Life of the Times which were so fast passing away from us.[29]

There is something odd about this explanation. As Leslie Stephen aptly remarked, "It does not seem to be obvious that the dulness [of the first series]—which is undeniable—would have been remedied by the use of city archives."[30] It was probably a face-saving expedient for the original author. Whatever the reason, it offered a perfect opportunity to write the kind of history that would foreshadow the social and cultural framework of the *Short History of the English People*.

Green was excited to be working at what he loved while also earning money. He was ensconced in a spare room in his uncle Nathaniel Castle's house, which was just across the High Street (at number 13) from Jesus College. From there he wrote to Dawkins in July 1859, describing the makeshift study in which he was happily surrounded by "a very sea of books, papers, notes, extracts, memorandums, pens in all stages of crushableness, paper in all degrees of rumble-fication." For each paper (consisting of four handwritten pages) he received a guinea, and as he planned to write ten papers that week, he looked forward to receiving that many "fresh new sovereigns with a golden chink." He professed to be indifferent to having his work published anonymously, proclaiming that, "as to fame I begin to despise that with the class list. No—a fig for fame—a cosy vicarage, a heap of books, a good pen and a deluge of paper, and I could be as happy as a king."[31] It is well to treat with skepticism Green's protestations of love of anonymity and of joy in scholarly labors for their own sake. He was eager for public acclaim.

In the articles on Oxford during the previous century, Green ranged widely over social, economic, and cultural history, in some cases reaching back to the Middle Ages and beyond the confines of the town. The writing was colorful, displaying what came to be one of Green's principal strengths: the ability to sketch striking verbal portraits with considerable economy. Whether the resulting picture was accurate or fair is, in some cases, open to doubt. An example is Green's treatment of the history of the Jews:

> The picture which Scott has given us in *Ivanhoe* of Isaac of York, timid, silent, crouching under oppression, accurately as it represents our modern notions of the position of the race during the Middle Ages, is by no means borne out by historical fact. In England at least the attitude of the Jew is almost to the end an attitude of proud and even insolent defiance. His extortion was sheltered from the common law. His bonds were kept under the royal seal. A royal commission visited with heavy penalties any outbreak of violence against the "chattels" of the king. The thunders of the Church broke vainly on the yellow gabardine of the Jew.[32]

This image might be seen as a modest echo of his friend Freeman's almost pathological anti-Semitism. But Green followed up this rather negative sketch with the observation that the Jews brought learning with them, especially in science and medicine, and that Jewish capital led to economic development and improvement in urban architecture, such as stone houses.[33]

Several points are worth observing about Green's initial foray into writing history. First, it was written in a vivid style for a popular readership. Second, he was self-consciously writing a social and cultural history, and consequently slighted many political or institutional matters that other authors would have emphasized. Third, Green did not hesitate to range considerably beyond the chronological and geographic confines of his subject. Altogether, it was an impressive beginning and clearly prefigures his later work. He regretted that the series was discontinued, thus denying him the opportunity to turn his attention to eighteenth-century religion and education. He also conceded that "the social part is over-coloured. It is the almost necessary consequence of using memoirs or pamphlets, etc. as authorities before one has learnt the use of a little wholesome criticism."[34] Such self-criticism was both accurate and characteristic, and Green turned it to good account. His later scholarship does indeed demonstrate tighter control and more skepticism regarding sources, though without sacrificing the strengths of his early work.

After completing this writing project, Green still had to wait for some months before going ahead with his plan of becoming a clergyman in the Church of England. In September 1859 he visited Ireland. In Dublin, he was regaled with stories about Jonathan Swift by a verger at St. Patrick's. Outside the city, he employed his keen observational powers and sensitivity to landscape while being driven "by a civil, dare-devil, gambling scamp into some of the most delicious scenery in the world." He went on to describe a country "of bogs and rocks, where the turf piles lay like brown dots around, and the stone walls cut up every field into infinitesimal portions." Ruminating on these experiences, Green displayed that acute sensitivity to geography that would be such a marked feature of his historical publications The Irish landscape, he noted, was of a type that he had "never observed elsewhere; there are none of those reaches of field upon field, those long sweeps of crops or meadow, without sign of man or man's dwelling-place that often gives me a sense of almost painful loneliness in the midst of an English landscape."[35]

A "prosy sermon" he was forced to endure caused him to reflect on the oppressive features of British rule in Ireland. When a prayer was offered for the Lord Lieutenant "that he may wield the sword committed to his hand by Her Most Gracious Majesty," Green noted that this was "a raw-head and bloody-bones way of teaching loyalty."[36] Opposition to high-handed measures of government, in Ireland or other parts of the British Empire, was an enduring feature of Green's thinking, and found its way into his later historical writing. In a brief visit to Belfast, he was relieved to find "no screaming or shrieking" at a chapel, in spite of the fact that Ulster was then in the grip of a fervent Protestant revival. After seeing that natural wonder of the northern Irish coast, the Giant's Causeway, he was back in Oxford in late September.[37] He could not resist writing immediately to his geologist friend Dawkins, crowing over the basaltic formations he had seen in northern Ireland. Also included was a bit of doggerel verse he had composed about the trip, each stanza of which ended with effusive praise for Irish whiskey.[38]

Much of the time between taking his degree and receiving Holy Orders Green devoted to the study of science. He spent part of the winter and spring of 1860 in the Somerset village of Theale, as a kind of apprentice to the local clergyman. Although he found ample time for "geologising, archaeologising, physiologising, studying bone-caves, old ruins, and stomachs," he also had to involve himself in the frustrating duty of training the local rustics to sing in the choir.[39] Back in Oxford, he read *The Elements of Geology* by Charles Lyell; he became so enthralled that his thoughts were on the book all during a sermon, and he heard not a word of it. He wrote to Dawkins, in an unselfconscious assertion of the "presentism" that he and other Victorian historians were to engage in (and ultimately to be convicted of): "The great value of the whole book consists, to my unscientific mind, in its scrupulous adherence to the rule of reading the Past by the Present."[40]

The impact on Green made by reading Lyell was powerfully reinforced by another experience in the summer of 1860: his presence at the famous debate between T. H. Huxley and Bishop Wilberforce of Oxford. Green, by paying a small subscription, had recently become an associate of the British Association for the Advancement of Science, with the right to attend meetings. On his way to this momentous conference, he fell in with one Jenkins, who announced excitedly that he was going "to hear the Bishop of Oxford smash Darwin." "Smash Darwin! Smash the Pyramids," declared Green. Jenkins's retort, that Wilberforce's first class degree in mathematics gave him the authority "to treat on scientific matters," did not impress Green, who entered the hall eager for the fray. Afterward, he reported with delight to Dawkins that Huxley, "young, cool, quiet, sarcastic, scientific in fact and in treatment, . . . gave his lordship such a smashing that he may meditate on with profit over his port at Cuddesdon."[41] No doubt the spectacle of one of the representatives of Oxford "learning" suffering such a humiliating public defeat was as gratifying to Green as the triumph of the new science.

One of Green's final activities before quitting Oxford was to engage enthusiastically in "beating the city boundaries." He cherished this historic and somewhat riotous public ceremony (held once every eight years) partly because of its color and antiquity. More importantly, it reflected deep civic pride and the spirit of local autonomy, elements that Green held to be at the core of the true patriotism of the English people. He was overjoyed that the mayor invited him to participate, possibly on the strength of the articles he had written for the *Oxford Chronicle*. A love of every geographic and social detail is evident in his description to Dawkins of marching with the mayor and aldermen, in full civic regalia and accompanied by the rifle band, down the High Street and across the countryside.

The mud-spattered but magnificent assemblage made its way to the various boundary markers, their progress enlivened by encounters with groups like the Sclavonians, a club of firemen arrayed in aldermanic costume. The King of the Sclavonians was presented with a bottle of gin, "whose head he graciously condescended to knock off, and then to swallow its contents." Pressing onward, the procession was disconcerted to find that the traditional tribute offered by the tenant at Hincksey to the mayor, a barrel of beer, had been stolen. Still, there was bread, cheese, pipes, and ale at Godstow, along with a raucous but good-natured exchange of taunts with the locals. "The Mayor," Green concluded, "did wonders, and reflected credit on the city. The mace made oft acquaintance with the mud."[42]

It was well that Green took such delight in this high-spirited civic pageant, as there would be little opportunity for such exuberance during the coming decade of clerical service.

NOTES

1. Green to Castle, 20 Feb. 1856, Lambeth Palace MS. 1725, fo. 13.

2. Green to Freeman, 19 Oct. 1866, LJRG, 166.

3. Arthur Engel, "The Emerging Concept of the Academic Profession at Oxford, 1800–1854," in *The University in Society*, ed. Lawrence Stone (Princeton: Princeton University Press, 1974), 1: 305–52.

4. Green to Castle, n.d. Lambeth Palace MS. 1725, fos. 33–34.

5. Ibid., fos. 25–26.

6. Ibid., fo. 26.

7. Ibid., fo. 27.

8. LJRG, 15.

9. J. N. L. Baker, *Jesus College, Oxford, 1571–1971* (Oxford: Oxonian Press, 1971), 49–50.

10. Ibid., 50.

11. Ibid., 51.

12. H. Llewellyn Browne, "Some Personal Reminiscences," *The Academy* 23 (1883): 187.

13. Ibid., 53.

14. *The Druid* 1 (1862): 80.

15. Reprinted in HS, 301–16.

16. Green to M. M. [?], n.d. [1858], LJRG, 26–27.

17. Green to Dawkins, 25 July 1859, LJRG, 31.

18. Green to George[?], 26 March 1857, Lambeth Palace MS. 1725, fos. 131–32.

19. Green to B[?], n.d. [1859], LJRG, 29.

20. Peter R.H. Slee, *Learning and Liberal Education. The Study of Modern History in the Universities of Oxford, Cambridge, and Manchester, 1800–1914* (Manchester: Manchester University Press, 1986), 45–49.

21. LJRG, 14–15.

22. Green to Dawkins, September 1859, LJRG, 38–39.

23. Quoted in J. N. L. Baker, *Jesus College, Oxford, 1571–1971*, 52.

24. Green commented to Freeman in 1868: "There was somebody I know got a modern history first or a modern history second or something [at Jesus]; I know it cured me of any wish to distinguish myself in *that* school." LJRG, 198.

25. Green to Stanley, Dec. 1863, LJRG, 17–18.

26. Green's MS. Diary for 1859–62, Jesus College, fos. 71–72. Leslie Stephen misquotes this diary passage as "the Canons" instead of "a Canon" in LJRG, 16.

27. Report of a lecture given by Professor William Boyd Dawkins at Owens College, *Manchester Guardian*, 27 Jan. 1885.

28. LJRG, 10.

29. *Oxford During the Last Century, Being Two Series of Papers Published in the Oxford Chronicle and Berks and Bucks Gazette During the Year 1859* (Oxford: Slatter and Rose, 1859), iii.

30. LJRG, 19.

31. Green to Dawkins, 25 July 1859, LJRG, 29–30.

32. John Richard Green, *Oxford Studies* (London: Macmillan, 1901), 7–8. This volume is a reprint of Green's 1859 articles on Oxford, with an introduction by Alice Stopford Green.

33. Ibid., 9–10.

34. Ibid., xxiii. This extract from a letter of Green's in 1859 was inserted by Alice Green, along with some of his diary entries of the period, into the introduction to the 1901 edition of the Oxford articles.

35. LJRG, 34–35.

36. Ibid., 35.

37. Ibid., 35–36.

38. Ibid., 37.

39. Green to M. T. [?], LJRG, 39.

40. Green to Dawkins, 26 June 1860, LJRG, 41.

41. Green to Dawkins, 3 July 1860, LJRG, 44–45.

42. Green to Dawkins, 2 Oct. 1860, LJRG, 47–48.

4. The Church, the World, and the Self: A Clergyman's Struggles

Studying for the required examination by a bishop was a prudent course for aspirants to the Church of England clergy. A standard list of authorities, including William Paley's *Evidences*, formed the basis of the examination. Yet Green, ever disposed to resist the conventional approach and the orthodox authorities, wrote to Dawkins in October 1860, a few weeks before his interview with Bishop Tait: "I have been naughty as to work lately—reading Goethe and Schiller instead of Paley and Pearson—I know from which one learns the *truest* theology."[1] It was fortunate that he was to be examined before the Bishop of London, A.C. Tait, who had already taken a liking to the intense young graduate. He was also fortunate to have A.P. Stanley intervene for him. Since Green flatly refused to read Paley, on the grounds that the arguments were out of date, Stanley convinced Tait that it could be dispensed with. The same indulgence was granted for John Pearson's *Exposition of the Creed*, another required work to which Green objected.[2]

Green stayed with Bishop Tait at Fulham Palace during part of this time, remarking in his diary that his host was "hospitality itself—unpretentious, full of honest fun, but always open and sincere. His charge at our conclusion today embodied all my feelings on charity towards others in the Church and without it. They were noble words—not soon, by God's grace, to be forgotten"[3]

Green was ordained as a deacon by Tait on Christmas Day 1860 and as a priest exactly a year later. The bishop was to have a major influence on Green's clerical career, and few young clergymen can have had such a sympathetic episcopal patron. Not that this opened the door to a comfortable country parsonage or any other tangible evidence of preferment, as most Victorian clergy (and readers of Trollope) would have understood it.

On the contrary, Green, still under the spell of Stanley's gospel of ennobling toil, insisted on the most difficult assignments in the East End of London.

His first ecclesiastical posting was as a curate to the Rev. Henry Ward, incumbent of St. Barnabas, King's Square, Goswell Road. Green chose this challenging working-class parish in preference to a much easier West End curacy that was proffered, ironically, by Stanley. If Stanley's nostrums of work and service helped Green make this decision, so did the Christian Socialist doctrines of F. D. Maurice. Like many of his contemporaries in the upper and middle classes, Green responded to Maurice's call to undertake missionary-type labors among the lower orders.[4] Attacking the country's massive social problems with zeal, sympathy, and intimate involvement in the lives of the poor appealed to those who, like Green, had grown weary of theological disputes or had begun to feel their faith waning. As much as he was inspired by Maurice's sense of mission, however, Green was described by a friend and fellow clergyman, H.R. Haweis, as "entirely unaffected by the Maurician method, and entirely unable to stop at the Maurician half-way house, in which the Bible, although admitted to be human, was almost too sacred to be treated as history, and the Prayer-Book was regarded as an almost inspired document."[5]

One of the most attractive features of life at St. Barnabas was being an integral part of a large and cultivated household. Henry Ward and his wife Jane made Green feel like a member of the family, permitting him a degree of domestic happiness denied him as a child. His love of children found ample scope in playing with and tutoring the numerous Ward offspring. With one of the children, Humphry, Green formed a lifelong friendship, one later broadened to include his wife, Mrs. Humphry Ward (née Mary Arnold), the best-selling novelist of the late nineteenth and early twentieth centuries.[6] Humphry Ward later recalled how Green had guided and enlivened his studies while he was a student at Merchant Taylor's School, noting that "under his touch things that had been mere names became full of meaning. Thucydides took his place in universal history; the life of the Roman forum took the colours of reality, and in proportion as he shook down the edifice of Bibliolatry on which I had been brought up, the Bible became interesting."[7]

Green developed an even closer attachment to Jane Ward. Humphry Ward wrote that his mother, "ever genial, sunny, and cheerful, and supported by a happy and extremely simple religious faith against the difficulties of a large family, a huge parish, and narrow means," was like "an elder sister" to Green. This comparison was apt. There was something of Green's fierce attachment to his elder sister Adelaide in his devotion to Jane Ward. There was, in addition, the displaced sexual drive of a young man with a persistent need for close feminine companionship. While the friendship was one of complete rectitude, it was also, on Green's part, a deeply romantic one. He wrote to Dawkins that it was important "to have one who loves me for my own sake, not as some do, for my head, and who gives me, what I have never known—a *home.*" The simple, unqualified affection he received from Jane Ward was a soothing balm, and may have kept him attached to his clerical career longer than if he had been left to his own devices. For Green, she became "an Ideal of Christian Womanhood—which hushes and awes my own sceptical brain into a silent reverence and love."[8]

Another comparison with his sister Adelaide, a tragic one, is to be found in Jane Ward's early death—attributable in large part to her having borne seventeen children, five of whom failed to survive childhood. When she died at the age of forty-two in July 1862, Green was shattered. To his uncle Richard Castle he bitterly lamented the loss of "my friend, my sister, my more than mother."[9] He delivered the sermon at her funeral, and it was one of his most impassioned.[10] Even nine years later, the intensity of his feelings and his sense of loss are evident:

Ah, when I think of that freshness, that nobleness, wrought out in a life so hampered and bound down to the commonplace, I turn angrily from all my moans, and other people's moans at their life rendering real greatness impossible. I see people straining after power, longing to be able to influence and what not. I long to tell them, "There has been in my whole life among the thousands I have met one person, and one only, who has influenced *me*, before whom my whole soul bent in reverence and adoring love. And she was the quiet wife of an East End parson, in a dingy London square, who would have laughed at the thought of 'influencing' anybody."[11]

There was scant opportunity for grieving in the endless labor and bustle of ministering to the East End poor. It would have been a punishing schedule for anyone. Green's health had always been delicate, but now his lungs were rapidly deteriorating in the foul air of London's worst quarters. Still, he drove himself remorselessly. Striving to improve the lot of the district's children was a high priority, and one of the principal means of achieving this was organizing daytrips to nearby Epping Forest or to the seaside. This involved an unending round of fund-raising, usually of very trifling sums, among his hard-pressed parishioners. It also meant hitting up friends like Dawkins, who was asked for half a crown "to give five poor white-cheeked little wretches a day of great enjoyment—I am sure you will not refuse."[12] In a similar begging letter to his uncle Richard Castle, Green declared: "Fresh air and green fields and trees are such every day friends of ours that we sometimes forget that to our East End London children they are *luxuries*, to be tasted perhaps for one day in a year."[13]

Another group of Green's unfortunates was the district's many prostitutes. There was a particularly pressing need for such a ministry in Hoxton, a derelict parish to which Green was transferred, at Tait's urging, in 1863. The description he gave to Dawkins of his first meeting with the women of the streets indicates his clear-headed powers of social analysis, even in the presence of so many "sinners":

> I was at an odd meeting the other day,—a midnight meeting of girls from the *pave*. It began at eleven with tea, and ended at half-past two. Some 150 were present, and few other friends save myself and the City Missionary. No scene could have been more interesting, principally because it stripped away all romance from the matter. (1) All I have investigated looked on it as a matter of £ s. d. Some had been driven by sheer want, others by gaiety and the attractions of high wages, others by the "independence" of the life. I did not find one case of *seduction*,—save by similar girls of their own stamp. (2) Most were willing to return if the £ s. d. question were settled. There were few cases of violent disgust or great remorse. That the step upward seemed so little to them, showed that the step downwards had not been great. We must not transfer the gulf which in *our* lives parts virtue from vice to the lives of the London poor. (3) All knew the hymns, "Rock of Ages," etc. Nearly all had been to Sunday School. Religious teaching has reached them, the "fundus" of our population, and the result proves that means "so successful" are fallible after all. A face at once encouraging and disheartening.[14]

Such Mayhew-like powers of observation refined Green's understanding of human nature and social relations, maturing him for his subsequent historical labors.

The success he enjoyed with the various segments of Hoxton working-class life made it difficult for him to leave there in 1864, but the state of his health mandated a move. Tait, concerned lest the dedicated young priest should expire from overwork and bad air, had him transferred at the end of 1863 to the West End, as a curate to the Rev. Philip Gell at Notting Hill. Green described his transfer as "a terrible blow. The people like me and I like them, and that makes it hard to leave."[15] But it was hoped that the salubrious environment and far less crushing burden of work would restore his health. Another benefit would be that he might be able to turn his serious attention to writing history. Indeed, even in the midst of the trials of his East End ministry, he had found some time to continue his studies.

His connection with Somerset, first established through Dawkins, provided an opportunity for him to present a paper, which led in turn to his reintroduction to E. A. Freeman. The occasion for the meeting of the two men was a conference sponsored by the Somerset Archaeological Society in 1862, at which Green spoke on "Dunstan at Glastonbury," deeply impressing Freeman with his literary flair and command of the sources. During Green's talk, Freeman recognized him as the schoolboy he used to carry around on his shoulder. From the time of the renewal of their acquaintance, Green and Freeman developed a close friendship, which was to exercise a profound influence on Green's scholarly and literary career. Freeman developed a proprietary interest in his protégé's career, taking every opportunity, as he said, "to blow Green's trumpet."[16]

Yet in spite of this propitious meeting, and the publication of the Dunstan paper in the Somerset Archaeological Society's *Proceedings*,[17] Freeman was not given an opportunity to trumpet Green's abilities for several more years. Initially, Green expressed his satisfaction with Notting Hill, enjoying "walks in a country stillness beneath Kensington elms."[18] Soon, however, he was restive and unhappy, eager to be back in the East End maelstrom. He was ill at ease with his middle class congregation, delivering sermons to comfortable and preoccupied parishioners. As he explained to Dawkins:

A crowded church full of upturned faces is a mere solitude to me. A little group of people I know rouses all my energy and fire. What I did in Hoxton, I did because I *knew* my people—why I failed here is because I did not know them. If I succeed again in the East it will be because dock labourers and costermongers are not mere "faces in pews" to me. . . . A "respectable congregation" has its formula of faith; if yours doesn't square with it you are practically unintelligible. Costermongers at least have no formulae.[19]

Seeing his unhappiness, Tait allowed him to return to a "real" congregation, as a mission curate at St. Peter's, Stepney.

In part, Green's restiveness at Notting Hill reflected his anguish over his own growing religious doubts. In the East End, the palpable need for his ministrations and the sheer time and labor he had to devote to them allowed the troubled inner voices to be stilled. If he could not accept the orthodox prescriptions of the Church of England, at least he was performing useful service. Not that he ignored the intense theological debates of the time. One would have needed to be a singularly dull-minded careerist to have done so in the early 1860s. To begin with, there was the intense furor over Darwin's *Origin of Species* (1859), as Evangelicals, Tractarians, Catholics, and Nonconformists halted their attacks on each other to turn on the common enemy of infidelity masquerading as science.

Another challenge to orthodoxy attended the publication in 1860 of *Essays and Reviews*, which created a brouhaha that continued unabated for the next few years. The ecclesiastical liberals who wrote the essays in this contentious volume insisted on a flexible, historical, framework for interpreting the Scriptures. The essayists, inspired by the critical studies of the life of Jesus by such scholars as David Friedrich Strauss and Ernest Renan, included some eminent churchmen. Perhaps the best-known was Benjamin Jowett of Balliol College, Oxford, who horrified the pious by his statement that the Bible should be read "like any other book." Convocation condemned two of the essayists in the Court of Arches (one for "denying the doctrine of Eternal Punishment"), though this was reversed on appeal to the Judicial Committee of the Privy Council in 1864. Nearly half the clergy in the Church of England signed a declaration affirming, against *Essays and Reviews*, the doctrine of the divine inspiration of Scripture.

A further shock came with the publication of John William Colenso's *Critical Examination of the Pentateuch* in 1862. Colenso, bishop of Natal, concluded that the first five books of the Old Testament were written many centuries after the events they described. Deposed and excommunicated by the bishop of Capetown in 1863 for these heretical views, he was reinstated by the law courts three years later. While the Colenso case, like that of the essayists, shows that the government and judiciary were disposed to moderate the severity of the ecclesiastical authorities, this was small comfort to liberal clergy. An embattled minority, they felt themselves forced to defend their broad, tolerant views, and could feel little hope of remaking the church in their image.

In spite of his worsening health and arduous labors, Green followed these various controversies closely, taking an active part in defending the liberal critics against censure. Even in 1861, before the full flood of reaction had broken, Green expressed to Dawkins his "anxieties about the future of my opinions—church theories and the like. Where am I drifting to?"[20] The following year he told Dawkins he wished to remove from

Christianity "the theological dogmas encrusted upon it." He set himself the task of performing radical surgery on Anglican doctrine in order to bring it into conformity with scientific truth:

> To make Science in its discovery and advance the Revealer of Christianity— to show how, as it has progressed step by step, it has removed one after another the false interpretations which men have placed on the True Revelation,—to point out how providential in its course the disembarrassing of Christianity is—how it must go on—and how it would be better to welcome than to distrust it—to make it the rule of our exposition of Christianity—and our aid to understanding its real nature—would be the great plan of my undertaking.[21]

He would feel less and less sanguine about effecting such a reconciliation of science and religion. After his first meeting with him in 1865, Stopford Brooke, a fellow clerical liberal who was to become a close friend and experience a similar erosion of faith (and ultimate "secession" from the church), described Green as "a very gifted man, but in a state of theological 'yeast' which is curious and somewhat painful to see."[22]

Green's markedly secular brand of religious belief is evident in a lecture series he developed in 1862, possibly for delivery to his parishioners or perhaps to the Curates' Clerical Club. He recorded in his diary an outline for lectures on the Galilean Ministry of Christ. Heavily influenced by the "historical Jesus" school, he saw Jesus' ministry as being shaped by the geography and local culture of each of the discrete parts of Palestine. The coast was the "Graecized, Herodianized" seat of government for which Jesus displayed "deep scorn" and "ardent Galilean opposition." Jesus is depicted as a product of the "wild hill country" who yet rejects its disorder and extremism:

> Amid its lawlessness and frenzied enthusiasm he grows up in silence—to leave them—to be misapprehended by them—to be rejected. He passes thence to choose as the seat of His labours the third division, the Lake-country. Here he found the enthusiastic patriotism of the Hills in the deep enthusiastic generous hearts of the fishermen of the sea, but without narrowness: broadened by great lines of commerce and the busy traffic of the district and the daily contact of strangers for the spread of His Religion, the intense earnestness of the Jew and the social freedom, the mobility, and propagandism of Galilee.[23]

This passage is of interest both because of its autobiographical component (hostility to authority, being "misapprehended" and "rejected" by those among whom one grows up, finding a life of "social freedom" without "narrowness") and because we can see elements of historical theory and method that become evident in his later published works: the crucial influence of geography, the freer, more cosmopolitan nature of commercial societies.

In 1863, Green took a leading role in the attempt to launch a Church Liberal Association, one of whose aims was "to promote unity of action amongst those clergy and laity who desire freedom of thought and teaching in the Church of England." Another purpose was to bring to the notice of Anglican clergy and encourage discussion of "such works of foreign theology as appear to be exercising a prominent influence on the progress of religious thought on the Continent."[24] Although stymied in this project, Green set about organizing a clerical college, confiding to Dawkins that he was "amused to see how quietly it is taking the shape of the old Liberal Association, which every one put down as too extreme when I first proposed it."[25] Two weeks later, he was able to exult over the Privy Council's reversal of the heresy conviction of two of the essayists.[26] By the following year, he was heavily involved in raising money for the Colenso defense fund, writing to Dawkins only half in jest: "You MUST stump up 5 shillings old boy—or never hope to dine here again."[27]

During these years Green was also in the midst of considerable family turmoil. The most pressing concern was his younger sister, Annie. At the time of his father's death in 1852, she had gone with her mother to live in a small cottage in the countryside, while Green and his brother Richard were taken in by the Castles. Since Rachel Green's income was meager, Annie grew up with no advantages, in the lower strata of rural society. After a visit there, John Green described her as "a magnificent girl—but rather skittish and hard-mouthed."[28]

Worse was to come. Still a girl herself, Annie gave birth to a daughter. Green certainly shared in the general sense of horror regarding illegitimacy that was so marked a feature of Victorian middle-class life, but there was also a measure of guilt, as he contrasted the favorable opportunities that had come his way with his sister's hard lot. Annie's plight perhaps reminded him of his own social marginality—how easily he too might have been swallowed up in rustic ignorance and squalor. His sister's sexual activities did not cease with the birth of her child. As Green wrote despairingly to his uncle Richard Castle:

It makes my heart bleed every time I go up there, that there has been some fresh outbreak of the old sin—but so it is, tho' since Christmas she has been comparatively better. . . . Poor soul, God help her! It is just one of those pitiful cases which we are forced to leave to him, and to his "Mercy which Endureth Forever"—and that mercy which knows and weighs what we can never know or weigh, the pressure, the temptation, the care, the suffering, the want of society, the degradation social and moral, which produced and perhaps still continues it.[29]

Green's avoidance of harsh judgments and attempts to comprehend the social basis of his sister's behavior were similar to his attitude towards the prostitutes of Hoxton. In her case, however, there was an additional complication, which went to the root of his role as a clergyman: Annie refused, for a considerable time, to have her daughter christened.[30] Something practical had to be done, which would certainly entail bringing Annie and her child to live with him. This was impossible as long as he was a member of the Ward household. His appointment to the derelict parish of Hoxton in 1863 provided him with his own house, though this would require several months to build. There was a problem, however, in getting Annie to agree to the arrangement. She harbored considerable resentment against her older brother, and Green had to report to Richard Castle that he had "again invited Annie to come and stop with me, but all I get is reprisals."[31]

Before the Hoxton parsonage was completed, Green's health had broken down and he was transferred to Notting Hill. The rooms he occupied there ruled out anything more than short-term stays by his sister and niece, but again Annie was unwilling.[32] She was staying with Richard Castle and his family in Oxford, receiving tutoring for which Green was paying the fees. This was an expense he could ill afford, considering his own meager stipend and the needs of his parish. Eking out financial assistance from one's own modest resources to help an ungrateful relative is apt to produce resentment, and Green was no exception. It was compounded by the fact that he was also involved in trying to help his brother Richard. At one point, John Green was moved to comment bitterly that Annie "shares with Richard the peculiar sort of affection which forgets one till a bill is to be paid or some difficulty to be met."[33]

Richard's difficulties began with his rakish behavior as an Oxford undergraduate. He fell in with a dissolute crowd and showed little interest in his studies, which made his announced intention of pursuing a legal career seem impossible to attain. John Green respected his brother's intellectual

44

abilities but doubted his character. He suggested a year away from Oxford, an absence that "will have thinned away most of his associates and broken his ties to the rest."[34] Either the furlough did not occur or it was ineffective, for the next year John Green had to go to Oxford on the "painful errand" of removing his brother's name from the books at Pembroke College. The transgression that led to Richard's expulsion was spending "Sunday afternoon in the house of Grainge the pawnbroker with the servant, Grainge himself being from home." Such blatant sexual dereliction was not tolerated in Victorian Oxford, and John Green did "not think the punishment unjust."[35]

In the aftermath of this disgrace, a plan was hatched to have Richard live with some country clergyman for a year and then enter Cambridge. The miscreant balked at the prospect of rural exile, however, and other arrangements had to be worked out. Richard still wished to enter Cambridge, but John Green, beset by doubts, weighed various alternatives:

> Cambridge would of course expose him to the same risk as those which have just caused his shipwreck. As to entering an office, he would have to change his whole nature and pick up business habits—a thing not so easily done as he supposes. And from what I have seen of the clerks in City houses they are rather a gay, wild lot. If one only knew of some steady fellow to whom he might go out in the Colonies.[36]

In the interval before starting Cambridge, Richard managed to land a position as Undermaster at Tower Hamlets School. The proximity of the school to Hoxton led Richard to urge on his brother a plan that the two of them share a house and bring Annie and her child to live with them. This scheme was rejected by John Green on the grounds that Richard's "habits and mine are so utterly incompatible that there would always be squalls."[37]

In the midst of these painful dealings with his siblings, Green also had to contend with a bitter and protracted struggle over the will of his uncle, Nathaniel Castle. Castle died in November 1860, after being thrown from his horse while fox hunting, and left £250 to John Green.[38] The difficulties arose concerning the testamentary disposition of Castle's widow, Green's Aunt Mary, who died in 1862. Richard Castle (probably Nathaniel's brother) was made executor of the estate, which amounted to over £3,000. Green advised his aunt before her death about making provision for his own brother and sister in her will, but other family members intervened to undercut these efforts. Learning of this, Green wrote hotly to Richard Castle "to repudiate any responsibility for a will made contrary to my advice and, as I am bound to add, contrary to justice."[39] He did manage to convince Mary Castle to add a codicil making Annie, Richard, and himself residuary legatees for at least a small portion of the estate.

With a host of greedy cousins descending upon the legacy, however, and complications arising out of prior loans within the family and charges of misuse of portions of the estate, the wrangling over the will went on for years. At one point, suit was brought in the Court of Common Pleas, though ultimately the matter was arbitrated within the family. It would take another five years for matters finally to be wound up, with John, Richard, and Annie getting several hundred pounds apiece.[40]

Green probably did not receive much, if anything, when the affair was settled, for he had already borrowed substantial sums from Richard Castle against his expectations. In his letters to Castle, Green tended to adopt the airs of a rising young professional whose borrowings were simply investments in a successful future. This was not entirely an affectation: he *was* ambitious to advance himself in the Church. In 1862 he was offered the post of Vice-principal of a training college at £300 annually (twice his stipend as a curate) by his old tutor Ridgway, the recently appointed principal. Explaining his refusal of the post to Castle, he wrote that "it leads to nothing" and that to move "save on some certain and positive prospect of promotion, would be ridiculous."[41] He did not mention his reluctance to give up his missionary labors among the London poor, though this was certainly a powerful factor.

To Dawkins, he gave as an explanation for refusing the training college position "that it would be a sore trial to leave London, both in a literary sense and as parting me from my dear little ones here."[42] As this indicates, he had by no means renounced the thought of making his mark (and perhaps a good income) as a writer. In fact, he went on to declare in the same letter that failure to secure a good clerical incumbency would entail "*relinquishing all hope or outlook for clerical preferment*, and throwing my future wholly on literature."[43] But his very real commitment to his social work and educational functions, plus his hope of finally landing an incumbency, led him to defer that step indefinitely. When he returned to the East End from Notting Hill to take up a "mission curacy" at St. Peter's Stepney, his expectations continued to rise and fall. He wrote to Dawkins in September 1865: "Did you see the *Times* calculation that a curate's chance of a curate's getting a living are 19 to 1?—Yours faithfully, 1/19th of an Incumbent."[44] It was also during this difficult curacy that he described himself as "sick—ill—suicidal—blank—ignorant" and signed himself "Gone to Pot."[45]

Just two months later came the long-hoped-for appointment to an incumbency, at nearby St. Philip's, Stepney. He exclaimed to Dawkins:

> In plain English, I am Incumbent of St. Philip's, Stepney, ... There is a good church, a fine choir, a capital parsonage, and good schools—16,000 people, of whom 6000 are cut off to form a mission district. Two curates work with me at the church, two more are in charge of the Mission. There is an Institute, Church Association, and what not. The nominal stipend is £300, but various deductions reduce it to two-thirds of that amount; but I hope to get part of my burthens borne by other shoulders.[46]

To Richard Castle he described it as "a glorious place for one who is as young as I am and has his spurs to win, and such as a Bishop seldom gives to a man only five years in orders." He asked to borrow £500 to furnish a suitable clerical establishment since he was obviously now "on the road to high preferment" and the money was "a mere investment of capital."[47]

The initial excitement Green felt over the appointment quickly gave way to depression, compounded by ill health. The day after Christmas he wrote Dawkins that he had settled into his own parsonage and sent for his sister, both long-term ambitions. Yet they failed to produce satisfaction: "Now that the home I longed for has come it is like the Sodom apple— ashes in the mouth."[48] Partly this despair was a reaction to the desperate financial state of his new parish. The claims on his meager funds seemed endless, and even the large loan from Richard Castle would soon be exhausted. He lamented to Freeman that he had been "signing cheques . . . ever since I came here, and it is only now when my solitary £500 is exhausted, my bank account closed, my cheque book a vanity, and myself a beggar that I let the bills pour in and 'lie on the table.'"[49]

Having Annie and her child with him did bring satisfaction, but this was eclipsed by the old feelings of resentment on his sister's part. She still felt he was censorious, despite his efforts to appear loving and forgiving. She also sensed that he was uneasy around her, Richard, and indeed the whole family, including the Castles. Annie was not the only member of the family to feel this. On a visit to his mother, Green wrote Annie to answer her charges that he had shown considerable discomfort during a family gathering in Oxford at Easter 1866. He denied, somewhat unconvincingly, that he had been restless and uneasy during a family gathering in Oxford, concluding that people simply did not understand him: "It is easy to ford the shallows of one's character, it is harder to sound its depths."[50]

Yet the family difficulties were on the verge of reaching a resolution. The final settling of the tangled disputes over legacies in 1867 tended to soothe the troubled relations within the Green and Castle clans. As for Richard and Annie, a marked improvement in both their situations paved the way for John Green to have a far less troubled relationship with them. Richard Green graduated from Corpus Christi College, Cambridge, in 1865 and became a clergyman, first as an East End curate and then as a vicar in rural Cambridgeshire.[51] Annie was married at St. Peter's, Stepney, on 30 March 1869, to John Cooper Pearse, a Cambridge graduate and friend of Richard's from Sherborne School in Dorset. John Richard Green performed the ceremony.[52]

While Green had less and less cause at Stepney to worry about his siblings, the needs of his district gave ample reason for concern. A resident incumbent had increased responsibilities, and finances remained precarious. He gave a good description of his multifarious duties to Dawkins:

> The fall of the year has brought its usual sick-list—the Institute is starting anew, and its classes have to be arranged; our District Visiting Society to be set again on foot; the Sunday School has lost its three most useful teachers; the Church Decoration Society on the other hand is *too* energetic and requires holding in; we are setting up two night schools; and I have the whole parish, Sunday and week-day, on my hands without aid. This for a lazy beggar is rather a grind.[53]

The cholera outbreak of 1866 found him in the thick of the desperate efforts to help the victims and their families, working, according to one observer, "day and night amidst the panic-stricken people, as officer of health, inspector of nuisances, ambulance superintendent, as well as spiritual consoler and burier of the dead."[54] He was assisted in these fearful labors by some of the district's prostitutes, with whom he had established a rapport through the midnight missions. As his friend and clerical colleague H. R. Haweis later recalled, "It was no uncommon thing to see Mr. Green going down the lowest back streets in Stepney, on his way to some infected house, between two women of the town, who had volunteered with him on sad and perilous service to the dead and dying, as was daily to be done, and was daily being left undone, in those dismal times."[55]

Despite the crushing burdens of such labors, Green agreed to take part on the local Board of Guardians as an ex-officio guardian. The Poor Law

Board enlisted his services, along with those of many of the East End clergy, because of the paucity of "gentlemen" to take the lead on the local boards. The distress of the East End was very severe, and numerous overlapping charities attempted to grapple with it, alongside Anglican and other clergy and, of course, the Poor Law authorities. Green quickly perceived the enormous waste and inefficiency of so many uncoordinated efforts and tried to impose some order, thus anticipating the system-building efforts of the later Charity Organization Society (COS).

He also anticipated the COS in his opposition to overly profuse relief, especially the indiscriminate charitable-giving stimulated through mass advertising. He denounced what he called "this newspaper appeal dodge" because it was "sapping all independence." The clergy, he exclaimed, "should throw up the relief business altogether."[56] He also turned his guns on lax Poor Law administrators. Having become a *Saturday Review* writer during 1867, he made the Poor Law and charity mess the subject of a number of articles, denouncing the pettiness and short-sightedness of his shopkeeping colleagues on the board.[57] On one occasion he delivered a sermon on the topic, not knowing that G.J. Goschen, the recently appointed President of the Poor Law Board in Gladstone's first cabinet, was in attendance.[58] Goschen was soon to make rigorous administration by boards of guardians a central feature of his Poor Law policy. It would, however, be long after Green gave up his clerical office and poor relief functions that significant reforms of this type were put into practice in both the public and private relief sectors.

Green's attacks on undiscriminating giving, lax administrators, and cunning beggars were no Scrooge-like mutterings. He continued to give his time and energy without stint, going deeply into his own pockets to help the poor of the district. In 1868, Green, with Edward Denison, John Ruskin, and the Rev. Brooke Lambert, hatched the idea of helping the poor by living among them, sharing in their lives and worries, and shaping character through example.[59] This was a far cry from the periodic materializations of West End charity types, dispensing coal tickets and returning to their comfortable homes puffed up with a sense of their own benevolence.[60] The settlement house movement thus inaugurated would not come to fruition for many years, partly because of Denison's early death in 1871 and the necessity for Green to abandon his labors. The incessant financial pressures undermined Green's body and spirit as much as did the foul air and overwork. Having, on one occasion, to pay £43 of his own to balance the school books, he complained to Denison that "these incessant money-worries simply kill all vigour of life and thought in me."[61]

Worn out, downcast, and not a little disillusioned, Green yearned to escape the grinding pressures of the East End and devote himself to writing. He was already contributing to the *Saturday Review*, but the reviews and essays he had to churn out, partly from financial pressure, did not constitute a satisfying literary career. Ephemeral and unsigned pieces written under pressure in the scant few hours each week he could steal from his parochial labors would do little for his reputation. In February 1869, he told Dawkins: "I have made up my mind to quit these eastern climes, and for a while to withdraw quietly from any conspicuous *clerical* position." In the same letter, he mentioned two possibilities: a position as Censor of King's College, London or Senior Librarian at Lambeth Palace (the Archbishop of Canterbury's London residence). The latter became a distinct possibility with Bishop Tait's elevation to the primacy in 1869.

The King's College position paid £120 a year plus room and board. Since the duties were light and the British Museum nearby, it would have been an ideal base for writing his long-deferred history. It would also allow him to continue as a clergyman: "I have a great wish not to part cable altogether,—the hold the Church has over one, however slight, is a really healthy hold to a mind like mine."[62] But his outspoken liberalism was a decided liability: F.D. Maurice had been forced out of his position at King's College in 1854 for his liberal views.[63] Green was found unacceptable, and he reported to Freeman that the appointment "vanished before my 'notorious broad-churchism.'" He did, however, get the unpaid position at Lambeth, joking to Freeman: "I get no pay nor rooms nor muttonchops, but I get the librarianship which gives me a 'steak' in the Church still."[64] Even though the position was honorary, Tait sent him "a handsome cheque" in recognition of his acceptance.[65] To Dawkins, Green remarked that with the Lambeth Palace job, "that terrible question, 'Who is he?' receives an archepiscopal reply."[66]

His predecessor in the librarianship was the celebrated medievalist William Stubbs (1825–1901). He and Green had met in 1863 on a train on their way to stay with Freeman for a meeting of the Somerset Archaeological Society.[67] A long friendship ensued and Stubbs, appointed Regius Professor of Modern History at Oxford in 1866, was a guest of Green's at Stepney on at least one occasion. Green was amused by Stubbs's punctilious behavior, and could not resist telling Freeman of the older historian's discomfiture at an evening gathering:

I hurried him away at last, for every lady fell in love with him, and I felt that the last and deepest foundation of my faith would be shaken if Stubbs—if Stubbs! But the pertinacious and utterly inaccurate way in which he *would* moan for a bed-candle (there being nothing but gas in the house)—and his steady and conservative refusal to believe himself awake at eleven, though he was flirting at that very moment with at least three lovely women—these things proved that in spite of all mental and affectional perturbations Stubbs was Stubbs.[68]

Green also noted the humor in a scholarly dilemma faced by Stubbs: "The Purfessor is in a hole about his Dictionary of Christian Antiquities—he is sub-editor of all Canon Law matters and his contributors have taken most of the articles off his hands. But there are two which no one will take, and he will have to do himself, and those are 'Abortion' and 'Adultery.' Conceive the position of the learned Professor."[69]

When Green received a congratulatory letter from Stubbs on the Lambeth librarianship, he could not avoid the conclusion that Stubbs had "half-expected" to be reappointed to the position himself.[70] And Stubbs told Green, at the end of his letter: "I was afraid that your peccadillo de Colenso [Green's fundraising efforts for the heretical bishop] would have stood in the way. But no doubt you have repented; if you have not, don't tell me."[71] Green had most certainly not repented, but Stubbs, who was theologically conservative but tolerant, harbored no grudges over this or over the Lambeth appointment. Indeed, Stubbs had strongly endorsed Green's candidacy.[72] For his part, Green could not contain his joy over being liberated from the daily grind of parish labors: "Oh Freeman, my good fellow, how I wish you were here. I am in such tearing spirits at the prospect of Freedom. William Tell, ora pro nobis—Oh Leonidas, Garibaldi, all illustrious bards of Freedom, hoorah-te pro nobis."[73]

The freedom Green so ardently celebrated in 1869 was almost certainly freedom from something more than overwork and bad air. In a portion of a letter of 13 January 1869, not used by Leslie Stephen in the collected letters, Green wrote to Freeman from St. Philip's: "There is a past which clings about this place which I would fain get rid of, but which I can only get rid of by running away—never to see the East End or recall its memories again." He concluded by characterizing his years of clerical ministry as "so much real earnestness and work mingled with so much sin and worthlessness."[74] Green was clearly referring to himself, and his use of the word "sin" is important. It is almost surely a sexual reference, for one of the few times he used the word previously was to describe his sister Annie's sexual transgressions.

This interpretation of the remorse expressed in the letter is reinforced by considering the bitter correspondence between Alice Stopford Green and John Richard Green's friends following his death, a conflict that will be taken up more fully in the final chapter. It concerned Mrs. Green's attempts to gather in all her late husband's letters so they could be edited and published. Alice Green came across something in one of Freeman's letters to Green that was obviously a response to some very confidential revelation Green had made. Naturally wishing to see this particular letter from her husband, besides needing to have all the letters for the planned collection, she pressed Freeman to send her all of Green's side of the correspondence.

Freeman refused to turn over certain letters to Mrs. Green, as did Dawkins. Samuel Rawson Gardiner, whom she prevailed upon to act as go-between, had to report that his mission was unsuccessful:

> Freeman spoke of the great love which both he and Dawkins had for your husband, and how that love was based on his not being perfect. If he had been perfect, he said, we would not have loved him so. Then I fancy that they are afraid lest a correspondence in which all the temptations and trials of early life were revealed, and perhaps falls before temptations, would come as a shock to you, and also that this fear was one if not the principal motive which made them hold back letters from you.[75]

The most that Dawkins was willing to provide was verbatim transcripts of Green's letters, "with the exception of certain blanks, which had better remain blank."[76] As anyone familiar with Victorian culture is well aware, "temptation," "fall," and "sin" almost invariably refer to illicit sex. Whether it was with one of the many prostitutes Green ministered to, or indeed if it was heterosexual at all, is not known, but his guilt over it generated a powerful impulse for abandoning active clerical life.

NOTES

1. Green to Dawkins, 22 Sept. 1860, LJRG, 46.
2. LJRG, 22–23.
3. Green's MS. Diary, 1859–62, Jesus College, fo. 77.
4. LJRG, 52.

5. H.R. Haweis, "John Richard Green: In Memoriam," *Contemporary Review* 43 (1883): 739.

6. For a discussion of John Richard Green's influence on her, see John Sutherland, *Mrs Humphry Ward: Eminent Victorian, Pre-Eminent Edwardian* (Oxford: Clarendon Press, 1990).

7. LJRG, 53.

8. Green to Dawkins, 16 Sept. 1861, LJRG, 87.

9. Green to Richard Castle, n.d. [1862], Lambeth Palace MS. 1725, fo. 61.

10. The full text of Green's sermon is printed as an appendix to LJRG, 485–95.

11. Green to Louise von Glehn, 11 Feb. 1871, LJRG, 284–85.

12. Green to Dawkins, 23 Aug. 1861, LJRG, 85.

13. Green to Richard Castle, n.d. [1861], Lambeth Palace MS. 1725, fo. 52.

14. Green to Dawkins, 5 Aug. 1863, LJRG, 132.

15. Green to Richard Castle, 3 March 1863, Lambeth Palace MS. 1725, fo. 90.

16. LJRG, 62–63.

17. Reprinted in HS, 29–53.

18. Green to Dawkins, 14 Dec. 1863. LJRG, 135.

19. Green to Dawkins, 15 March 1864, LJRG, 141–42.

20. Green to Dawkins, April 1861, LJRG, 80.

21. Green to Dawkins, 23 April 1862, Jesus College MS. 198, J 49/2.

22. L.P. Jacks, *Life and Letters of Stopford Brooke* (London: John Murray, 1917), 1: 183.

23. Green's MS. Diary, 26 April 1862, Jesus College, fos. 5–6.

24. Green to Dawkins, 14 Aug. 1863, LJRG, 132–33.

25. Green to Dawkins, 1 Feb. 1864, Jesus College MS. 199, J 49/3.

26. Green to Dawkins, 14 Feb. 1864, LJRG, 140.

27. Green to Dawkins, July 1865, Jesus College MS. 204, J 49/8.

28. Green to Richard Castle, n.d. [1861], Lambeth Palace MS. 1725, fo. 84.

29. Green to Richard Castle, n.d., Lambeth Palace MS. 1725, fo. 82.

30. Ibid.

31. Green to Richard Castle, n.d. [1863], Lambeth Palace MS. 1725, fo. 92.

32. Green to Richard Castle, n.d. [1864], Lambeth Palace MS. 1725, fo. 105.

33. Green to Richard Castle, 10 Jan. 1863, Lambeth Palace MS. 1725, fos. 76–77.

34. Green to Richard Castle, 18 March 1861, Lambeth Palace MS. 1725, fos. 42–43.

35. Green to Richard Castle, n.d. [1862], Lambeth Palace MS. 1725, fo. 80.

36. Ibid., fo. 81.

37. Green to Richard Castle, n.d., Lambeth Palace MS. 1725, fo. 92.

38. W. H. Challen, "John Richard Green, His Mother and Others," *Notes and Queries* 210 (1965): 234.

39. Green to Richard Castle, 19 July 1861, Lambeth Palace MS. 1725, fo. 64.

40. The correspondence relating to these tangled proceedings is scattered throughout Lambeth Palace MS. 1725, culminating in a letter of 10 Oct. 1867 from John Green to Richard Castle (fos. 115–16).

41. Green to Richard Castle, n.d., Lambeth Palace MS. 1725, fos. 72–73.

42. Green to Dawkins, 20 Nov. 1862, LJRG, 111.

43. Ibid., 112.

44. Green to Dawkins, 10 Sept. 1865, LJRG, 156.

45. Green to Dawkins, n.d., LJRG, 156.

46. Green to Dawkins, 17 Nov. 1865, LJRG, 159. There is a misprint in the published letter, so that the year is given, incorrectly, as 1869.

47. Green to Castle, n.d. [1865], Lambeth Palace MS. 1725, fos. 109–10. Castle made the requested loan, against the security of Green's expected legacy, in December (fos. 37–38).

48. Green to Dawkins, 26 Dec. 1865, Jesus College MS. 199, J 49/3.

49. Green to Freeman, n.d., Jesus College MS. 199, J 49/3.

50. John Richard Green to Anne Green, n.d. [1866], Lambeth Palace MS. 1725, fo. 125.

51. J. A. Venn, *Alumni Cantabrigiensis* (Cambridge: Cambridge University Press, 1900), Part 2, Vol. 3, 130.

52. W. H. Challen, 461. Richard died in 1911, Annie in 1934.

53. Green to Dawkins, 19 Oct. 1866, LJRG, 166.

54. LJRG, 55.

55. Haweis, "John Richard Green: In Memoriam," 737–38.

56. Green to the Rev. Isaac Taylor, n.d. [1867], LJRG, 188.

57. See, for example, *Saturday Review*, 28 Dec. 1867.

58. Green to Freeman, 13 Jan. 1869, LJRG, 220.

59. Sutherland, *Mrs Humphry Ward*, 215–16.

60. George Kitson Clark, *Churchmen and the Condition of England 1832–1885* (London: Methuen, 1973), 282.

61. Green to Denison, 18 Oct. 1868, LJRG, 203.

62. Green to Denison, 8 Jan. 1869, LJRG, 206.

63. Kitson Clark, *Churchmen*, 308.

64. Green to Freeman, n.d. [Feb. 1869], LJRG, 228.

65. H. R. Haweis, "John Richard Green: In Memoriam," 742.

66. Green to Dawkins, 2 Feb. 1869, LJRG, 227.

67. William Stubbs, *Seventeen Lectures on Medieval and Modern History* (Oxford: Clarendon Press, 1887), 431.

68. Green to Freeman, n.d., Jesus College MS. 199, J 49/3. Original emphasis.

69. Green to Freeman, n.d. [May 1868], Jesus College MS. 199, J 49/3. Leslie Stephen omitted this passage when he printed the rest of the letter in LJRG, 193.

70. Green to Freeman, n.d. [Feb. 1869], LJRG, 228.

71. Stubbs to Green, 20 Feb. 1869, Jesus College MS. 204, J 49/8.

72. Stubbs to Archbishop Tait, 24 Dec. 1868, Lambeth Palace, Tait Papers 163, fos. 190–91.

73. Green to Freeman, n.d. [1869], LJRG, 232.

74. Green to Freeman, 13 Jan. 1869, Jesus College MS. 199, J 49/3.

75. Samuel Rawson Gardiner to Alice Stopford Green, 30 Nov. 1884, Jesus College MS. 223, J 49/16.

76. Dawkins to Alice Stopford Green, 8 Oct. 1892, Jesus College MS. 223, J 49/16.

5. Writing for the *Saturday Review:* Self-Revelation and Historical Apprenticeship

One of the ways E.A. Freeman had in mind to help "blow Green's trumpet" was to bring the young cleric into the stable of writers for the *Saturday Review*. Freeman had been asked by the editor to look out for "promising young men," and approached Green during the latter's visit to Somerset in 1862. Green confided to his diary that he was "thunderstruck but promised to try." He then added: "I don't suppose I shall do."[1] Although he would not begin writing for the *Saturday Review* for nearly five years, it was certainly not because of lack of talent or confidence. His clerical labors, the state of his health, Annie's and Richard's troubles, and his intense involvement with various liberal Anglican causes required him to defer his career as a reviewer and essayist.

In many respects he was an almost ideal writer for a weekly that had a reputation for iconoclasm and a certain breeziness of style. The *Saturday Review* was founded in 1855 by Alexander James Beresford Hope (1820–77), a Conservative MP who sought to promote High Church principles. He had also acquired the *Morning Chronicle* for similar purposes, and brought many of the staff, including its editor, John Douglas Cook, over to the *Saturday Review*. Under Cook's editorship, which lasted until his death in 1868, a number of the leading mid-Victorian intellectuals were brought aboard. These included Goldwin Smith, who resigned in 1858 to become Regius Professor of Modern History at Oxford, John Morley, Leslie Stephen, and E.A. Freeman. With a staff such as this, it was not possible to hold to the journal's original conservative principles. The *Saturday Review* became rather unpredictable politically, with liberal and conservative views jostling each other in the same issue. But lively writing and a tone of irreverent, often caustic criticism (it was dubbed the "Saturday Reviler") raised its circulation to 10,000 by 1868.[2]

When Green did start writing for the *Saturday Review*, at the beginning of 1867, it had as much to do with his financial needs as with his desire to launch a literary career. The stipend from his perpetual curacy at St. Peter's Stepney was never sufficient to keep his parish afloat, and the money he earned by his pen provided a necessary supplement. Even with this, he was often financially strapped. Almost a year and a half after starting to contribute to the review, he was forced to asked Richard Castle for £50 to tide him over till he got his next £100 payment from the *Saturday Review*. Teachers and nurses had to be paid for the next two months, and other heavy bills had been incurred to keep the parish going. "I dare say," Green continued, "my bank would let me overdraw the amount, but in districts like these a clergyman's credit must not be suspected if he is to retain his position and influence, and a whisper of debt would ruin both."[3]

Thus while the income from his essays mitigated the desperate financial conditions somewhat, it certainly did not create any abundance. And of course the relentless pressure of writing against deadlines further taxed his limited physical resources. The sheer volume of his contributions would have been impressive even for someone whose time and energy were not so fully committed. In all, 164 of Green's essays were published in the *Saturday Review* between 2 March 1867 and 10 January 1874.[4] Four more appeared in *Macmillan's Magazine* and one in the *Contemporary Review*.[5] While his arduous clerical labors came to an abrupt halt with the resignation of his living at St. Philip's in February 1869, he was heavily engaged thereafter in researching and writing the *Short History of the English People*.

Green's contributions to the *Saturday Review* can be classified into book reviews, historical sketches, essays on contemporary political and religious controversies, and "middles"—light-hearted pieces of social description and humor inserted between the lengthier, more weighty fare at the beginning and end of each issue. These categories, however, are less clearly demarcated than they might seem. Like many Victorian (or, indeed, present-day) reviewers, Green frequently used book reviews as a take-off point for his own extended historical essays. His critiques of contemporary policies were often framed in a historical perspective, and his middles, even when humorous, frequently addressed significant problems.

Broadly speaking, most of Green's contributions to the review were historical, and therefore represented a further apprenticeship. His Oxford history series, published in 1859, had been an important beginning, and he had by no means abandoned historical scholarship during the early part of his clerical career. In addition to his paper on Dunstan before the Somerset Archaeological Society in 1862, he had presented one on "Earl Harold and Bishop Giso" to the same group the next year. In 1864, his paper on the Ban of Kenilworth was presented to the Historical Section of the Archaeological Institute of Great Britain and Ireland. One titled "London and the Election of Stephen" was read at the London Congress of the Archaeological Institute. All were published in the proceedings of the various societies.[6] He was also involved in research for a book on England under the Angevin kings. This project was seen by Freeman as a gratifying continuation by a protégé of his own work on the period of the Norman Conquest. While Green never completed this work, the materials he was gathering for it were used in some of his *Saturday Review* pieces as well as in the *Short History*.

His first contribution to the *Saturday Review* was a review of Stubbs's Inaugural Lecture as Regius Professor at Oxford. The Regius Chairs of Modern History, established in George I's reign at the two English universities, were designed to provide a practical grounding in history for those entering government service. "Modern" was defined as anything post-classical, and thus there was nothing anomalous about Stubbs, an eminent medievalist, holding a chair of modern history. In his inaugural address, Stubbs emphasized the fundamental differences between ancient and modern. The fall of Rome and the rise of Christianity provided the great watershed in history.[7]

This classification found favor both with sincere Christians and ardent Teutonists; Stubbs was both. So, for that matter, was Green, but he made his disagreement on the ancient-modern divide the centerpiece of his review. While praising Stubbs's abilities, he faulted him for "the elaborate contrast he draws between the world of classical and medieval history."[8] In a letter to Freeman reporting Stubbs's lecture, he expanded on this theme: "I am not likely to be prejudiced in favour of the age of Pericles; but is it true that Age is dead to us, and the Age of Dunstan living? . . . [The ancient world's] thoughts on philosophic, artistic, literary, scientific subjects are our thoughts—Dunstan's are utterly alien to us."[9] In the review Green deprecated Stubbs's over-emphasis on the importance of Christianity, arguing that its principal importance was as a vehicle for preserving the culture of antiquity, which still formed a vital part of western institutions and thought. Universities, he wrote, are places where the two worlds mingle, "and we cannot but regret that the Regius Professor should have missed the special opportunity which the place suggests of vindicating the true unity of the history of man."[10]

Shortly after this came his two-part review of the first volume of Freeman's *History of the Norman Conquest*. As with his assessment of Stubbs's lecture, Green adopted a critical stance in spite of close friendship. He began by describing the great transformation in social thinking since the French Revolution, which had turned men's eyes "from the mere appreciation of the outer aspects of national or political life to a perception of the spiritual forces from which these mere outer phenomena proceed. History shared the change that passed over poetry, over music; in the startling advance from Pope to Wordsworth, from Gainsborough to Turner, from Haydn to Beethoven."[11] Having firmly established his romantic credentials, Green lamented the incomplete advance of an authentic but unsentimental romantic approach to the writing of history. Regarding Macaulay's search for "accuracy and justice" as well as the "poetic insight" of Froude, "one cannot but feel how the real life of the people has escaped the constitutional and political research of the one, and how the deeper principles on which all hope of human progress rests are caricatured by the sentimentalism of the other."[12]

After a lengthy exposition of his own view of history, Green finally offered an assessment of Freeman's work. He praised his friend's literary gifts, and on the whole gave the book a favorable review. But he kept up a running critique on the basis of the philosophy he had already spelled out:

> There is evidently a powerful attraction for Mr. Freeman in the outer aspects of war and policy which throughout tends to lead him away from an examination of those deeper questions which lie beneath them. . . . [T]here is too much of wars and witangemots, and too little of the life, the tendencies, the sentiments of the people.[13]

As subsequent volumes of *The Norman Conquest* were published over the next several years, Green reviewed them in the *Saturday Review*.[14] Although the assessments were, on balance, positive, he continued to maintain a critical stance. When Freeman was hurt by one review, Green replied that if it had been too complimentary, "people would say 'there is the S. R. buttering Freeman.'"[15] He was determined not to be drawn completely into the Stubbs-Freeman axis lest his name be added to Thorold Rogers's delicious couplet on the two men's habit of heaping praise on each other's work:

See! ladling butter from alternate tubs,
Stubbs butters Freeman, Freeman butters Stubbs.[16]

A third friend and mentor, who came in for an even more severe treatment at Green's hands, was A.P. Stanley, who had become Dean of Westminster in 1864. When Stanley published his *Historical Memorials of Westminster Abbey* in 1868, Green reviewed it and was unsparing in his criticism: "The book is hardly a book at all; it strikes one, as one reads, as a series of lectures, essays, papers, loosely strung together, with little artistic unity and less historic purpose."[17] This blunt appraisal produced a severe rupture in his relationship with Stanley. Almost nine years later, informing his future wife Alice that he had been invited to the Stanleys' for dinner, Green commented: "I used to dine there often, but after my review of his *Westminster Abbey* in the *S.R.* Lady Augusta avenged herself by not dining me, and this is a sort of reconciliation dinner, I suppose—though as a matter of fact Stanley and I have always been on very good terms."[18]

He did, of course, continue to inject his views on the philosophy and scope of history, especially the need for presenting the "inner life" of the people. In a review of James Thompson's *An Essay on English Municipal History*, for example, he called for a vigorous effort to find and publish town records. The calendaring and publication of central government documents, which antiquarians, historians, and public officials had so far concentrated on, usually permitted only a dry institutional story to be told: "No history of medieval England has as yet attempted to reveal the actual life and thoughts of its people; in a word the real history of our country rests buried in the dusty archives of its towns."[19]

He further expanded on the significance of archival materials in an essay on "Historic Study in France."[20] This time, however, the emphasis was on the pitfalls of the sudden availability of a mass of published records. In the tendency to worship at the altar of primary-source research, Green saw the danger of historians becoming narrowly focused, dry-as-dust antiquarians. While his criticisms were directed at the state of historical scholarship in France, they had obvious application to Britain:

So prodigious has been the store of original documents, charters, rolls, dispatches, memoirs which have of late been disinterred from the archives of the past, that history has retrograded into annals. It is not everyone who can deal with enormous masses of uninteresting facts as de Tocqueville dealt with them in *L'Ancien Régime*, extracting all that was really living and essential from the forms in which it lay buried. It is easier to transfer the whole mass of facts to the pages of so-called histories, and to let the distracted reader do the sifting. Histories grow longer in extent, shorter and shorter in the time they cover, simply because historians read more and think less than their predecessors.[21]

He did credit the French with having good history books for schools, noting that "it is a disgrace to English literature . . . that we have no short history of our country which is not at once blundering and dull."[22]

In another article on French history, which appeared in the *Contemporary Review* in 1868, he elaborated further on the importance and proper use of provincial, as distinct from central, archives. Titled "The Revolution in a French Country Town," it was the only one of Green's articles that was signed.[23] In it he praised Michelet and Tocqueville, the one for penetrating the life of the people, the other for basing his account of the French Revolution on provincial research. Breaking free of the distorted images reflected in central records, Green claimed, was the key to achieving a truer and more fully rounded picture of the past. "A right appreciation of the social conditions, the economic changes, the intellectual phases of an age," he asserted, could be based only on "a mass of incidents to be found, for the most part, in the common and domestic life of men, and to discover and record which . . . is the legitimate business of local research."[24] He showed how very different the Revolution appeared from the perspective of a small community, where historic associations, customs, and hierarchies managed to weather the storm. In an obvious swipe at Carlyle's *French Revolution*, Green suggested that accounts like Tocqueville's offered a Revolution "stripped of its heroisms as of its butcheries, of its Charlotte Cordays as of its Marats, in the streets of a Norman country town."[25]

A historical sketch in *Macmillan's Magazine* on "Abbot and Town"[26] afforded Green a vehicle for extolling the liberty-loving ways of medieval burghers and decrying the malign influence of the church in those towns where an ecclesiastical magnate held sway. It also provided the opportunity for another indirect attack on Carlyle, for Green offered a decidedly revisionist interpretation of Abbot Samson, the hero of Carlyle's *Past and Present*. Instead of a wise and even heroic ad-ministrator guiding his great establishment through troubled times, Samson in Green's hands comes off as one of a long line of haughty abbots whose saving grace was his willingness to renew the municipal liberties of Bury St. Edmund.

Green also held that the baronage had been of secondary importance in opposing royal tyranny. It was England's townsmen who took pride of place, and he saw himself as challenging the established historical orthodoxy in insisting on this point. His ardent belief in the central importance of towns as hatcheries of liberty is evident in the following passage:

> Unnoticed and despised, even by the historian of today, they had alone preserved the full tradition of Teutonic liberty. The right of self-government, the right of free speech in free parliament, the right of equal justice by one's peers,—it was these that the towns had brought safely across the ages of Norman rule, these that by the mouth of traders and shopkeepers asked recognition from the Angevin kings. No liberty was claimed in the Great Charter for the realm at large which had not in borough after borough been claimed and won beforehand by plain burgesses whom the "mailed barons" who wrested it from their king would have despised.[27]

As for the "inner life" of the inhabitants of English medieval towns, this he claimed was best revealed by "reading" the town itself. James Bryce later described Green's genius for quickly grasping the lineaments of a town's history through its lanes and buildings, "darting hither and thither through the streets like a dog trying to find a scent."[28] An illustration of this ability is found in the depiction of Bury St. Edmunds in "Abbot and Town," in which his powerful sense of place was deployed to reveal the essence of past lives: "In the quiet, quaintly-named streets, in the town-mead and in the market-place, in the lord's mill beside the stream, in the ruffed and furred brasses of its burghers in the church, lies the real life of England and Englishmen, the life of their home and their trade, their ceaseless, sober struggle with oppression, their steady, unwearied battle for self-government."[29]

Green was by no means naive in his understanding of the relationship between towns and liberty. He was fully aware of the tendency for oligarchies and social tensions to develop in urban communities. Indeed, this was to be an important theme in the *Short History*. He also realized the powerful inhibiting role of the church—a major element in "Abbot and Town." In a review of the late Dean Milman's *Annals of St. Paul's*, he explained how Londoners had the good fortune of being able to expand their liberties in the very shadow of St. Paul's itself.[30] Elsewhere, he noted, authoritarian ecclesiastics worked to stifle freedom, especially in cathedral cities. This was especially true in the case of Oxford, as he explained in an 1871 article in *Macmillan's Magazine* on "The Early History of Oxford."[31] Green wrote to Freeman that Stubbs would certainly disapprove when he read it, for "the thesis is twofold, (1) that the University killed the city, and (2) that the Church pretty well killed the University."[32]

A baneful ecclesiastical influence, Green complained, continued to be exercised in the scholarly societies of his own day, especially in archaeology. In an essay on "St. Edmundsbury and the Archaeological Institute" he attacked the dominant influence of those interested in church architecture. The field had been "abandoned to country parsons and old maids simply because men take it at its own evaluation, and look on it, not as any broad and general investigation of the past, but simply as a study of ecclesiastical architecture slightly tempered by an enthusiasm for Roman camps and old helmets."[33] Furthermore, a spirit of junketing pervaded the archaeological meetings, so that "the only papers which receive much attention are those which are read in the sunshine, to the genial accompaniment of the clatter of forks and the fizz of champagne." He also found galling the invariable practice of inviting some local lord or baronet to chair the meetings.[34] Although often depicted as an "amateur" historian, Green clearly comes across, in his strictures on Victorian archaeology, as strongly committed to greater rigor and professionalism.

Some of Green's most overt expressions of his political views were inserted into historical reviews. His review of a book by Goldwin Smith is a notable example. Smith, who had resigned as Regius Professor of Modern History in 1866 partly out of disgust at Oxford conservatism, was about to emigrate to America to become a professor of history at Cornell before finally settling in Toronto. His book, *Three English Statesmen: Pym, Cromwell, and Pitt*, was published as part of a fund-raising effort by the Jamaica Committee, those spirited liberals who attacked Governor Eyre for his brutal response to the insurrection of exploited former slaves. This was one of the most contentious political issues of the decade and, considering the origin of Smith's book, Green felt no hesitation in using it as a point of departure for expressing his own opinions on contemporary politics as well as on history.

In his review, Green once again deployed Froude and Macaulay as the Scylla and Charybdis of historical methodology, but while Froude was still (as in the Freeman essay) guilty of sentimentality, Macaulay was now said to exemplify "middle class Philistinism." The likeliest source for this characterization was Matthew Arnold, whose essay on Heinrich Heine (1863) had injected the term into cultural discourse in England. Philistinism would of course be a central critical concept of Arnold's *Culture and*

Anarchy (1869). So would the idea of a "saving remnant" of the middle class by whom higher cultural values might be sustained. While Green had a less elitist concept of culture, there was much in Arnold's formulation to attract someone seeking a unifying theme for a history of the English people. In the *Short History*, the middle class, or at least a substantial portion of it, was to be implicitly portrayed as the "saving remnant" of English history.[35]

Of the three subjects of Goldwin Smith's book, Green praised Pym for his attachment to traditional liberties. Such "manly Liberalism," he asserted, was sorely needed in the present, since the Second Reform Act was about to bring into the House of Commons men who would at last tackle a host of pressing constitutional problems. There is a remarkably republican cast to Green's enumeration of these, "namely the best means of dispensing with party government, the abolition of a State Church and an hereditary Peerage, the compatibility of an hereditary Sovereign with free institutions."[36] This review made it clear that Green's political opinions were far in advance of those of scholarly friends like Freeman and Stubbs. Other *Saturday Review* essays underscore his radicalism.

In 1867, Green reviewed *Essays on Reform*, an important collection of essays by Leslie Stephen and others. While agreeing with many aspects of the contributors' essays, he took them to task for failing to consider the complexity of the voteless class, especially since both parties' reform bills at that point aimed to pull the "respectable" artisans into the electorate. With his close knowledge of the social gradations of the "lower orders" gained in years of face-to-face dealings, he called his readers' attention to "the rift on either side of the artisan class, which is deeper below than it is above," and noted that "the artisan is really more connected in feeling and interest with the small shopkeeper than he is with the unskilled workman." The latter's "sullen grudge and dull sense of injury," Green feared, "would become a far keener feeling when the class whose monopoly practically shuts him out from the chance of rising in the world had sheered right away into the mass of the governing class."[37]

While the Second Reform Act managed to avoid the worst of these pitfalls, thanks to Benjamin Disraeli's audacity, Green found policy making in the new democratic age wanting. An advanced Liberal in politics, he viewed the party leaders as lacking a clear vision of the nation's real problems. His discontent was focused, quite naturally, on Gladstone, and was expressed in a February 1868 article on "Mr. Gladstone and the Session." He took the premier to task for emphasizing non-essential policies

such as Irish church disestablishment when pressing needs were so palpable. He went on to outline the philosophy that should guide Liberalism:

> A large and generous way of viewing social problems, a reasonable reliance
> on the good sense which underlies half the rant of the working-class, a hearty
> acceptance of their new position and resolve to fit them for it, a wide and far-
> reaching sympathy with the progress and variance of thought which shall en-
> able its possessor to understand before he pretends to deal with the complex
> religious and ecclesiastical questions of the day, a determination to substitute
> some more rational and intelligible system of foreign policy for the meddling
> non-Intervention of the Foreign Office, while avoiding the enthusiastic non-
> sense of alliances based on anything but our national interest in the peace of
> the world—these we take to be the great lines along which the policy of any
> real Liberal leader in the future must run.[38]

At about the same time, in reviewing Gladstone's *Ecce Homo*, Green
suggested that the Liberal leader, judging by the evidence of his book, had
missed his calling: "All that portentous solemnity, that insensibility to
humour, that tendency to monologue which bore us in politics, are the attributes of a great preacher."[39] This sarcastic tone, characteristic of the
"Saturday Reviler," did not fully reflect Green's attitude towards Gladstone, which was a good deal more ambivalent. And his feelings were to
warm considerably during the next decade, as the "People's William" began to champion the cause of oppressed nationalities during the Bulgarian
atrocities agitation.

At any rate, it was not only Gladstone and the Liberal leaders that
Green criticized, but the party rank-and-file as well. While most Liberals
exulted in the electoral victory of 1868, Green complained to Edward
Denison, whose return as MP for Newark he considered one of the few
bright spots, that the new Parliament "out-Palmerstons Palmerston. 'No
philosophers, no artizans,' seems to have been the winning cry." He continued: "The fact is the governance of England is still in the same shopkeeping hands, and their sympathies are just where they were, with a quiet
Liberalism which changes as little as possible."[40]

If the Philistinism of shopkeeping Liberals was one of Liberalism's
shortcomings, another was the growing influence of narrow, militant
Nonconformity. In an 1870 article on "Morleyism,"[41] he decried the
growing influence of Samuel Morley, proprietor of the *Daily News* and
munificent builder of chapels, who as MP worked tirelessly for the removal of all the Dissenters' grievances. Green agreed that many of the
grievances were genuine, especially those concerning the Church of Eng-

land's attempts to control education. He had already expressed himself unequivocally on the issue to Freeman: "What hinders Reform? The want of education among the people. And what hinders education but the present attempt at a sectarian and not a national system? And what hinders a national system but the Church?" The clergy, he continued, "know that a thoroughly educated people and that people without any uneducated class would be the ruin of their Establishment."[42]

Green expressed support for the interdenominational National Education League, founded by Joseph Chamberlain and others in Birmingham in 1869, which insisted on non-sectarian education: "On this platform Churchmen and Unitarians united with the general mass of the Nonconformists, and, with only parsons and squires before it, the League counted on an easy victory." The rabid Nonconformists under Morley's direction, however, would have no part of such secularization: "Morleyism has no more notion of 'a godless education' than the parson or the squire. Of culture in itself, of free human development, of intellectual liberty, Little Bethel knows and desires to know nothing."[43] The similarity in his attitude toward the Nonconformists of his own day and the Puritans of the sixteenth and seventeenth centuries, as the latter would be portrayed in the pages of the *Short History,* is striking. While the dissenting sects were often in the vanguard of resistance to oppression, the intellectual and spiritual environment they created tended to be a crabbed, narrow one.

As this article makes clear, Green was an ardent libertarian, impatient of any attempts to check thought or action, from whatever quarter and however nobly motivated. An instructive example is provided by his posture toward the Princeites, a sect in Somerset that flourished during the mid-Victorian period. In 1867 William Boyd Dawkins published a not unsympathetic account of the group in *Macmillan's,* in which he described a well-ordered, agrarian commune whose inhabitants appeared prosperous and happy. Dawkins pointed out that the recent adoption by the leader (a former clergyman) of the principle of free love had split the community, but criticized the magistrates and gentry of the area for their unremitting hostility to the sect.[44] Green congratulated his friend on the article with the observation: "To me the chief question it suggests is the one which Mill treats in his book on Liberty—have we . . . yet reached any clear conception of the right of every man to think and express his thoughts as he will consistently with the safety of the state. The persecution of the Princeites doesn't look like it."[45]

On the vexed issue of religious freedom itself, Green had little to say in the pages of the *Saturday Review.* This was perhaps due to the editor's reluctance. Cook had asked Green to do more political pieces following the *Essays on Reform* review,[46] but apparently no similar offer was made for articles on religious topics. When Green did address himself seriously to religious issues in the *Saturday Review*, they tended to be institutional ones like the Ecclesiastical Commissioners' policy of establishing perpetual curacies. In an 1867 article on "The Cry of the Curates," he denounced the formation of a Curate's Augmentation Fund, which was designed to increase the number of curates in poorer districts by providing annual stipends of £100 each. Green argued that remuneration in the clerical profession should be left to market forces, noting that there was "no other profession in which, without any special exertion, a dunce is sure of a hundred pounds a year."[47] Green was clearly aware of the financial needs of curates, having toiled as one for years in straitened circumstances. His concern was that the artificial multiplication of curates would tend to attract men of low abilities.

There was a further, disturbing aspect to the fund, as Green observed in an article a few weeks later: the alternative uses to which the money could be put. By concentrating on the curates' fund, the commissioners were draining resources from an array of services that enriched national culture. Among the instances he cited was the need to pay a decent stipend to the Librarian of Lambeth Palace. It is possible that his ambitions had already begun to turn to that post, but the argument was based on a deeply felt sense of the church's broad cultural mission. By depriving the church of the resources to maintain its vital role in shaping national culture, he claimed, the Ecclesiastical Commissioners were showing their "Philistinism."[48]

Another way of dealing with religious questions in the *Saturday Review* was through the "middles," which Green was rather fond of writing. When Freeman criticized his spending time on such light fare, Green defended himself by noting that one should have loyalty to the journal, "and it absolutely needs 'trivial middles' to keep it up and induce people to read our weightier musings."[49] This was not the whole truth: Many of the middles, while done in a humorous or ironic vein, addressed important matters. This is especially true of the pieces on clergymen, most of which are, not surprisingly, autobiographical. One of his early articles, "The Curate's Progress," reveals his inner struggle. Contrasting an older clergyman with a youthful one, he wrote that the former "has quietly grown into the world of thoughts and ideas which his younger brother is so earnestly plunging into, and if he makes less fuss about them it is because they are natural to him." The church and the world, he asserted, "are still wrestling for mastery in the breast of the latter, and this doubleness makes him the more interesting of the two." He went on to note the social disadvantages of a young cleric: "Nothing is quite denied him, but everything is given with a difference. He may ride, but not hunt; if he dances, it must be very cautiously; and his laugh must be a little softer than other men's."[50]

A tone of bitterness crept into some of Green's writings. Shortly after resigning his living, he wrote a piece on "The Parson's Vigil" in which his disaffection from his parishioners is evident:

> Little by little he discovers that he is inaudible in the galleries and unintelligible to the "free seats." He becomes brief, bitter, sarcastic. At last he preaches his farewell sermon on "Let the dead bury their dead." "You have never understood me, and I have never cared to understand you, my brethren; but never mind, I am going and we shall see each other no more—let the dead bury their dead." So preached a young Levite once in our hearing to an unsympathetic congregation, and disappeared.[51]

A similar despair over the moral condition of his flock was expressed in a transparently autobiographical article on "The Curate's Wife": "The ideal poor, grateful and resigned, proved cross and greedy old harridans. The world of peace, of nobleness, of serenity, died into a parish of bustle and scandal and worry."[52]

Green had the same recourse to a feminine front in a slashing attack on the church hierarchy in an 1868 article titled "The Priesthood of Women." Convocation, he lamented, was downright "feminine" in its methods:

> There is the same interminable flow of mellifluous talk, the same utter inability to devise or to understand an argument, the same bitterness and hard words, the same skill in little tricks and diplomacies, the same practical incompetence, which have been denounced as characteristics of woman. . . . The caution, the finesse, the sly decorum, the inability to take a large view of any question, the patience, the masterly inaction, the vicious outbursts of temper which now and then break the inaction of a Bishop may sometimes lead us to ask whether the Episcopal office is not one admirably suited for the genius of woman.[53]

This attack, sharp as it was, was blunted by being encased in a "humorous" middle, and even it did not directly address the question of the Church of England's muzzling of dissidents. This was as burning an issue at the end of the 1860s as it had been at the beginning, and Green was if anything even more vexed by ecclesiastical tyranny. The great issue of the day was the Voysey judgment. Charles Voysey (1828–1912) was neither an intellectual nor a leading figure in the Broad Church movement. Like Green, he had been an underpaid, overworked curate who had served in several East End parishes before securing, with A. P. Stanley's help, a perpetual curacy in a Yorkshire village. He had come to doubt the doctrine of eternal punishment and began preaching this heretical view. He then published some of his sermons, hoping to goad the ecclesiastical authorities into prosecuting him.

Though initially reluctant, the Archbishop of York finally decided to take action in 1869. Voysey, defended by James Fitzjames Stephens, argued that the Privy Council's overturning of the condemnation of the two essayists in 1864 meant that clergy were free from doctrinal controls. The church court in York decided otherwise, and Voysey was deprived of his living. He was confident, however, of being vindicated on appeal, and clearly relished the role of martyr of conscience. A defense fund appeal was launched, headed by A.P. Stanley and including leading liberal churchmen like Benjamin Jowett, even though Voysey's opinions (by now including a denial of Christ's divinity) went well beyond their own. It was a major blow to Anglican liberals when the Judicial Committee of the Privy Council delivered a unanimous judgment against Voysey in February 1871.[54]

Green followed the case with the deepest interest, hoping that another victory before the Privy Council would cement the rights of clergy to shape and promulgate their own theological views. He was especially hopeful in that Archbishop Tait was the only clerical member of the Judicial Committee for this case. When the verdict was announced, he was stunned and deeply disappointed by what he saw as his mentor's capitulation to the forces of reaction. He wrote to Olga von Glehn of his "sad tumble back after the wild excitement into which I had managed to work myself over the Voysey judgment." Viewing the case in the light of the vital issues raised in Darwin's just-published *Descent of Man*, he exclaimed: "How in the presence of vast problems such as these all these Theological controversies sink into littleness, into absolute unreality." He still clung to hope of fostering a truly rational religion, "but we can only reach it by flinging to the owls and the bats these old and effete 'Theologies' of the world's childhood."[55] His outspokenness on the case irritated his more conservative friends. Stubbs wrote to him testily: "How the Voysey [judgment] affects you I do not see. If I thought you believed what you pretend to me to do, I should not be writing to you."[56] Freeman, who refused to support Voysey, was censured for his "Toryism in ecclesiastical matters" by Green, who went on to declare that if he did remain a clergyman, it would be with the purpose "to force the Church of England into open accordance with, or into open opposition to, the conclusions of reason, of science, and of historical criticism."[57]

That few of Green's tumultuous feelings on these issues found their way into print cannot be necessarily ascribed to editorial timidity at the *Saturday Review*. Green may have found the short article format unsatisfactory for presenting opinions on matters that were so complex and so important to him. At any rate, he had a more powerful and magisterial vehicle for projecting his views—the *Short History of the English People*, on which he had started work well before the Voysey judgment.

NOTES

1. Green's MS. Diary, 1859–62, Jesus College, fo. 96.

2. See Merle Mowbray Bevington, *The Saturday Review, 1855–1868: Representative Educated Opinion in Victorian England* (New York: Columbia University Press, 1941).

3. Green to Richard Castle, 9 Aug. 1868, Lambeth Palace MS. 1725, fos. 119–20.

4. The complete list is given in LJRG, 500–02.

5. Leslie Stephen listed the *Macmillan Magazine* pieces in LJRG, 500 (all four essays are reprinted in SSEI), but he seems to have been unaware of Green's essay on "The Revolution in a French Country Town" in the *Contemporary Review* 7 (March 1868): 416–28. This omission is the more surprising since it is the only one of Green's articles that was signed.

6. Ibid., 503. These four essays are reprinted in HS.

7. For the full text of his inaugural address, which was delivered on 7 February 1867, see William Stubbs, *Seventeen Lectures on the Study of Medieval and Modern History* (Oxford: Clarendon Press, 1887), 1–28.

8. *Saturday Review*, 2 March 1867. Reprinted in SS, 192–202.

9. Green to Freeman, 12 Feb. 1867, LJRG, 176.

10. *Saturday Review*, 2 March 1867.

11. *Saturday Review*, 13 April 1867.

12. Ibid.

13. Ibid.

14. All nine reviews of Freeman's *Norman Conquest* are reprinted in HS, 54–147.

15. Green to Freeman, n.d [1869], LJRG, 230.

16. W.G. Addison, *J.R. Green* (London: Society for Promoting Christian Knowledge, 1946), 46.

17. *Saturday Review*, 18 Jan. 1868.

18. Green to Alice Stopford, 22 Feb. 1877, LJRG, 446. Freeman was originally suspected of having written the caustic review. Although Green promptly told Lady Augusta that Freeman was not the culprit, he failed to confess his own authorship for some time. Green to Freeman, Jan. 1868, LJRG, 190–91.

19. *Saturday Review*, 13 July 1867.

20. *Saturday Review*, 17 Oct. 1868. Reprinted in SS, 175–82.

21. SS, 180–81.

22. Ibid., 182.

23. *Contemporary Review* 7 (1868): 416–28.

24. Ibid., 417–18.

25. Ibid., 418.

26. *Macmillan's Magazine*, October 1869. Reprinted in SSEI, 183–205.

27. SSEI, 186–87.

28. James Bryce, *Studies in Contemporary Biography* (London: Macmillan, 1903), 153.

29. Ibid., 189.

30. *Saturday Review*, 2 Jan. 1869. Reprinted in SS, 63–72.

31. *Macmillan's Magazine*, Oct.– Nov. 1871. Reprinted in SSEI, 283–307.

32. Green to Freeman, 6 Feb. 1871, LJRG, 283.

33. *Saturday Review*, 31 July 1869. SS, 86.

34. SS, 93.

35. It is noteworthy that Green and Arnold were to become friends in later years. LJRG, 395.

36. *Saturday Review*, 10 Aug. 1867.

37. *Saturday Review*, 6 April 1867.

38. *Saturday Review*, 15 Feb. 1868.

39. *Saturday Review*, 8 Feb. 1868.

40. Green to Edward Denison, 19 Nov. 1868, LJRG, 205

41. *Saturday Review*, 8 Jan. 1870.

42. Green to Freeman, 23 Jan. 1867, LJRG, 171–72.

43. *Saturday Review*, 8 Jan. 1870.

44. "Brother Prince," *Macmillan's Magazine* (16 Oct. 1867): 464–73.

45. Green to Dawkins, 7 Oct. 1867, Jesus College MS. 199, J 49/3. For some reason, Leslie Stephen chose to omit this passage when he printed the rest of the letter in LJRG, 189.

46. Green to Freeman, 11 April 1867, LJRG, 184–85.

47. *Saturday Review*, 24 Aug. 1867.

48. *Saturday Review*, 14 Sept. 1867.

49. Green to Freeman, 23 Jan. 1868, LJRG, 192.

50. *Saturday Review*, 6 July 1867. This may have been the article that Green described as "autobiographical" when forwarding it to Freeman. Green to Freeman, n.d., Jesus College MS. 199, J 49/3.

51. *Saturday Review*, 23 July 1870. How different from this bleak self-appraisal was that of James Bryce, who recalled later his reaction on first hearing Green preach in 1866: "I shall never forget the impression made on me by the impassioned sentences that rang through the church from the fiery little figure in the pulpit with its thin face and bright black eyes." *Macmillan's Magazine* 48 (May 1883): 73.

52. *Saturday Review*, 18 Jan. 1868.

53. *Saturday Review*, 7 March 1868.

54. M. A. Crowther devotes a chapter to the Voysey judgment in her *Church Embattled: Religious Controversy in Mid-Victorian England* (Hamden, Conn.: Archon, 1970).

55. Green to Olga von Glehn, 20 March 1871, LJRG, 292.

56. Stubbs to Green, 15 March 1871, quoted in W.H. Hutton, *William Stubbs, Bishop of Oxford* (London: Archibald, Constable, and Co., 1906), 101–02.

57. Green to Freeman, 20 March 1871, LJRG, 295.

6. The *Short History of the English People*

While Green's deteriorating pulmonary condition was certainly a factor in his abandonment of clerical work and resolve to dedicate himself to writing history, the choice of a general history of the English people is by no means as clear as Leslie Stephen suggested. In his commentary in Green's published letters, Stephen presented it as simply a question of Green's wanting to leave something worthy behind if his physician's warnings that it might not be possible to arrest the desperate condition of his lungs proved true.[1] The evidence Stephen relied on was a letter to Freeman in 1869 in which Green reported that he had just signed a contract with Macmillan for a £350 advance to write *A Short History of the English People*. The book was to be 600 pages and, as he commented somewhat off-handedly, "might serve as an introduction to better things if I lived, and might stand for some work done if I didn't."[2]

There is no question that Green feared an early death and with it, the failure to attach an enduring intellectual legacy to his name. But this explanation still fails to consider why he chose not to pursue his history of England under the Angevins. This was, after all, a project that his mentor Freeman was most eager to see him pursue, as it would pick up where he had left off with his studies of the earlier periods. In the preface to his book on the Norman Conquest, Freeman warmly acknowledged the help of "Rev. J.R. Green of Jesus College, a rising scholar to whom I look for the continuation of my own work."[3] And indeed, in a letter to Freeman written sometime in the late 1860s, Green evinced his determination to write a History of the Great Charter, "the *magnum opus* I mean for my life's work."[4] When Green ultimately decided against pursuing this book or a somewhat broader work on England under the Angevins, Freeman was deeply disappointed.[5]

In part, the writing of the *Short History* had to do with Green's determination to be his own man and not fall into the orbit of Freeman or Stubbs, a determination evident in his criticism of their works. More important, however, the *Short History* was an expansion of his concept of a history of the Archbishops of Canterbury. From his first East End curacy, in 1862, Green wrote to Dawkins explaining the evolution of his thinking. He had resolved at Oxford to become the historian of the Church of England, but the more he considered it, the more difficult it was to discover any unity in the theme, especially after the Reformation:

> The prospect widened as I read and thought. On the one hand, I could not fetter down the word "Church" to any particular branch of the Christian communion in England; . . . . On the other hand I could not describe the Church from the purely external and formal point of view taken by the general class of ecclesiastical historian; its history was, with me, the narrative of Christian civilisation. And to arrive at a knowledge of this, it was necessary to know thoroughly the civil history of the periods which I had passed through; to investigate the progress of thought, of religion, of liberty, even the material progress of England.[6]

The next day he recorded in his diary his intention of becoming the "historian of England," adding, somewhat grandiloquently:

> With full consciousness of many great deficiencies, I devote myself to the task. The greatest of them is, perhaps, a dislike for abstract thought, which would ever tempt me to subordinate general tendencies to particular events and principles to individuals. But two great helps I can—and by God's help, purpose to bring to its execution,—unflinching labour and an earnest desire for Truth. . . . I pray God, in whose name and to whose glory I undertake this work, to grant me in it, above all, the earnest love and patient toil after historical truth.[7]

As these passages suggest, Green's choice of subject matter derived from his religious thinking and troubled relationship with the Church of England, and he entered the task with a almost Christian sense of mission. Yet it must also be remembered that he was deeply influenced by the ferment in the world of science. He had accepted Darwinism and even exulted in the discomfiture of orthodox Christians. While it would not be until the end of the 1860s that the corrosive effects of the new science on his fundamental beliefs would make it impossible for him to continue his clerical career, the effects were already painfully evident. Another factor propelling him toward a history of the people was his interest in the history of towns, best shown in his articles on Oxford. Municipal liberties increasingly appeared to him as the linchpin of English free institutions. The evolution of municipal freedom would provide the underlying institutional unity against which the broader cultural patterns of national life could be played out.

Biography was also to play a key role in his "social" history approach. The narrative would turn on key individuals who had resonated with and helped shape patterns of culture and national life. This approach is evident in his 1862 paper on Dunstan, in which the medieval cleric is made to function as a representative of a broad, humane Christianity as well as an active forger of English national consciousness. The emphasis on such individuals, many of them intellectuals, also assisted in Green's slighting of kings and other traditional leaders.

As he neared the end of his clerical career, Green had refined his notions to a general history of the English people. He now sought a publisher. In 1862 he had secured an introduction to Alexander Macmillan through Boyd Dawkins,[8] and he was thereafter a frequent visitor to Macmillan's home at Tooting. The publisher's son George described his father's feeling about Green as well as his own reaction on first meeting him around 1867 at a gathering that also included Charles Kingsley:

> My father always liked his friends to know each other. He had already, it seems, seen a good deal of Mr. Green in London, and had taken a great fancy to him, being struck, as no one could help being, by the brilliance and vivacity of his conversation. Two of us children were sitting in the drawing-room that Saturday evening counting the moments till Mr. Kingsley should come in. But when the door at last opened there appeared a small slight man with a bald head and slight stoop, the brightest, keenest brown eyes and a gentle ingratiating manner. The smallness, what seemed the insignificance, were all that struck one at first, but he had not talked for five minutes before we were absolutely fascinated. He began about handwriting, *apropos* of some MS. that was lying about, and then got on to Freeman's *Old English History for Children*, telling us how it came to be written and what delightful stories there were in it—all in that charming vivid manner that no words can describe.[9]

At the end of 1869 Green set forth his plan to Macmillan:

> I propose to condense into a volume of 600 pages the history of the English people which I contemplated undertaking on a far larger scale. The work

would serve as a school-manual for the higher forms, and as a handbook for the universities, while in a more general sense it might I think supply a want in our literature—that of a book in which the great lines of our history should be fixed with precision and which might serve as an introduction to its more detailed study.

The book would be strictly a history of *England,* in which foreign wars and outer events would occupy a far more subordinate position than they generally do, and in which the main attention would be directed to the growth, political, social, religious, intellectual, of the people itself. Thus men like Aidan and Bede would claim more space than the wars of the Anglo-Saxon kingdoms; and Spenser, Shakespeare, and Bacon would stand as prominently forward as the defeat of the Armada or the death of Strafford.[10]

Before he could proceed, Green needed money. Having resigned his living, he was forced to rely for his income entirely on churning out articles for the *Saturday Review.* This left little time for his great project. His friends, led by Stopford Brooke, quietly organized a scheme of assistance. Brooke wrote to Macmillan asking him to contribute something, as well as appealing to Freeman, Stubbs, and Bryce. With Macmillan's assistance and other of Green's friends chipping in, something on the order of £100 was raised, buying Green the precious time to commence his scholarly labors. A further advance was secured when Green assigned the copyright to Macmillan for a payment of £450, noting that the book would represent "not merely a year's good work but the result of ten year's reading and thought." Macmillan agreed to pay him £350 in installments before publication and the additional £100 upon the sale of 2,000 copies.[11] When the book surpassed the most optimistic hopes of both author and publisher by selling 8,000 copies just in the first few months, Macmillan generously destroyed the contract in which Green had assigned his copyright, substituting a royalty agreement that was to produce a handsome income for many years.[12]

In undertaking his research, Green conducted a fair amount of archival work in addition to reading all the secondary works, chronicles, and other published documentary authorities. From Oxford he reported to Freeman that he "got into the City archives—saw the charter of John, and the Old English copy (as I take it to be) of the Charter of Henry III.; some autograph letters of William of Wykeham, etc."[13] At Lincoln he fell in with a local antiquary, who had made copies of the corporation charters and other civic documents. These were placed at Green's disposal.[14] He also visited the archives at Caen in Normandy, though he had to report there was not much of use to him there.[15]

The notebooks he kept of his reading and archival research are models of clarity, and include drawings of topography, architecture, and town layouts. Some parts, especially in the notebooks kept on his travels through Normandy, are in good French. Among the various research notebooks, ten relate directly to the *Short History*, although some of the material could also have been used on the Angevins book. The labels on the front covers have come off most of them, but two are headed: "Social England, 1142–1147" and "The Church, 1147–1154." The first of these has a large section on forests, subdivided into sections on foresters, metalworking, stone houses, trade in carved stone, woodland, pannage, trees, forest service, and essarts.[16]

Green did not confine his scholarly attention to English and Norman history. During his travels to Italy he made a point of studying Italian municipal history, in order to provide some comparative framework for his study of English towns. He was struck by how far advanced the Italians were in writing good urban history. "We have much to do in England," he told Freeman. "I made a start with my first paper on Oxford." Furthermore, he found the medieval Italian city a much more civilized environment than its northern counterpart. Teutonic freedom, he wrote to Freeman, tended to be narrowly political, while in Italy it was "a development of the whole man,—political, intellectual, religious, artistic."[17]

A keen sense of place and the overriding importance of geography in history was a marked feature of Green's approach to historical research. This was derived in part from his scientific interest in geology, as well as his rambles and field work with Dawkins in Somerset. Part of his research for the *Short History* was therefore on foot, notebook in hand. Illustrative of Green's graphic sense of place was his description of Ebbsfleet in Kent. As the place where Hengest and Horsa were said to have led their band ashore, it was considered sacred ground by Green, Freeman, and other good Teutonists. It also was hallowed by its traditional association as the landing spot of Augustine and his fellow missionaries in 597. After carefully reconnoitering the spot, Green wrote to Freeman:

> Ebbs-fleet is a little lift of higher ground on the brink of Minster Marsh,—a mere gravel bank with a few homesteads clustered on it, cut off from the sea nowadays by a meadow and a sea-wall. But the scene has a sort of wild vast beauty about it,—to the right the white curve of Ramsgate cliffs and the crescent of Pegwell Bay,—far away to the left over the levels of Minster Marsh, where the smoke-wreaths dispersing the thin brooding mist tell of Richborough and Sandwich, the dim distant line of the cliffs of Dover and Deal. As

one walks away from the sea, one follows the road which must have been Hengest's and Augustine's along the little gravel-ridge north-eastward to the chalk uplands above Minster, and then there breaks on one a noble view of the great belt of sea round Thanet, and far away over the marshes the tower of Canterbury.[18]

By April 1870, he had completed the first chapter, but it was slow, laborious work, and the end of the project seemed remote. As he told Freeman:

> I have finished the first chapter of Little book, and Macmillan is going to set it up in type—so that one may have a guide to go by. Don't think me idle about it or other things—I do some bit of work every day, but work is very hard when one is weak and disheartened. Moreover I have put a great deal of work into what I have done and have rewritten it again and again to get it to my liking.[19]

By August of that year, he had completed and submitted the first two chapters. But his editor at Macmillan's, George Grove, found the material overly detailed and difficult for a popular readership, and Green was in a quandary. He noted that he had an obligation to fulfill his promise to Macmillan for a history directed to general readers, yet meeting Grove's objections seemed to involve making the book simplistic and dull, "leaving out 50 per cent of the matter I have packed so tight, and chattering more diffusely over the rest." He lamented: "I am almost sure I *can't do* this. If not—then I shall at once begin my *Angevin Kings*." At least, he observed, the project had conditioned him to the daunting challenge of writing a book ("which kept me dawdling so long over the Angevins"), and he could now tackle the more specialized project.[20]

In spite of Grove's negative assessment, Macmillan strongly supported the project, and Green was convinced to stick to "Little Book." The work progressed very slowly, and it was not until August of 1871 that he had finished the third chapter, grousing to Freeman: "It is in fact, done as I am doing it, very hard and bothering work, and involved (especially in the Literature parts) a good deal of fresh reading."[21] Yet he was more and more convinced that the social and cultural approach he was taking was the right one, contrasting it with the narrowly political concerns of his friends. Freeman had sent him the proofs of his *General Sketch of European History*, a school text. After reading it, Green reported: "The 'facts' are there, and the 'dates' are there, but the history isn't. When I was a boy, I was as 'historical' as most boys, more so than most perhaps, but writing of this sort used simply to paralyse me." Recalling his own negative experiences with such texts in his school days, he asserted that "it is this sort of dry rattle of names and dates that sets boys against history."[22] Whatever the frustrations, therefore, of writing for a general audience, Green had the satisfaction of knowing that his own work had the potential for bringing large numbers of people to an awareness of the excitement and deeper meaning of their history.

Another point on which he challenged Freeman was, ironically, on the issue of great men in history. It must be remembered that Green tended to build his account of society and culture on a biographical structure: Key individuals were made to represent certain trends or characteristics of an era. This was no means confined to literary men or religious figures. In spite of his overall bias against political and military history, Green recognized the decisive importance of certain men in these fields. An example was William the Conqueror, who, because of his role as a subverter of Anglo-Saxon institutions, was not presented favorably in Freeman's account of the Norman Conquest. Green wrote to Freeman criticizing another writer's negative view of William, but Freeman must have felt something of the sting himself: "All that 'hatred' of Duke William—what a sort of herophobia it is! Take him altogether and take him in his time and he is surely among the greatest of men. But great men are always a puzzle to your Philistines—to your 'right and wrong,' your 'truth and falsehood people.'"[23]

This episode shows Green to have been remarkably free from any taint of anti-Norman bias, a marked weakness of most Teutonist historians. In his research on Thomas Becket, he recorded in his notebook all the evidence he could find on Becket's origins. Some writers had depicted Becket as being of good English stock and thus naturally disposed to resist Henry II's "tyranny." In his notebook, Green amassed the evidence supporting the Englishness of Thomas's father, Gilbert Becket, then recorded the contrary evidence, which he found convincing. This included Gilbert's birth into a family of burghers in Rouen, his wife's similar background in Caen, and Gilbert's claim of kinship with the Norman Archbishop Theobald. "No instance," he concluded, "could show better the position of the new colony, pursuing the Norman connexion and Norman policy, leading the way as Normans among their fellow citizens, concives, Londoners."[24] As with his appreciation of the superiority of Italian civic life, Green did not allow his enthusiasm for native English institutions to blind him to the virtues and contributions of Norman immigrants. For all his patriotic instincts, there was always a wider, more cosmopolitan spirit at work.

The organizing principle of the *Short History* is an emphasis on social and cultural history at the expense of political and military accounts. This is exemplified by an oft-quoted passage in the preface, in which Green disparaged "drum and trumpet history":

> At the risk of sacrificing much that was interesting and attractive in itself, and which the constant usage of our historians has made familiar to English readers, I have preferred to pass lightly and briefly over the details of foreign wars and diplomacies, the personal adventures of kings and nobles, the pomp of courts, or the intrigues of favourites, and to dwell at length on the incidents of that constitutional, intellectual, and social advance in which we read the history of the nation itself. It is with this purpose that I have devoted more space to Chaucer than to Cressy, to Caxton than to the petty strife of Yorkist and Lancastrian, the Poor Law of Elizabeth than to her victory at Cadiz, to the Methodist revival than to the escape of the Young Pretender.[25]

Even though this proclaimed shift from political and military history to social and cultural history was rather less dramatic than Green claimed (as Gertrude Himmelfarb has shown by the simple expedient of counting the number of pages assigned to these topics[26]), it was nonetheless significant. It was also deeply satisfying. Writing to Freeman from Italy in 1872, Green was able to report faster progress, noting that in a ten-day period, he had covered the period from the Peasant's Revolt of 1381 to the end of the early English Renaissance in 1520.[27]

His progress may perhaps be ascribed to the warmer climate and more relaxed atmosphere of Italy, where his physician, alarmed at his deteriorating health, recommended that he spend his winters. In Florence, Capri, and finally Mentone, Green found the perfect balm for his troubled spirit as well as his debilitated frame. Carriage rides through the countryside, explorations of villages and old churches, and social visits with English and American vacationers enlivened his Italian sojourns. This included the joys of flirtation. From Florence in 1872, he described himself as being "in the hands of Yankee Gals, who flourish and abound here." He was intrigued to be told that "in Yankee Land a popular preacher gets his £1500 clear, and all curates paid, etc.!" and wondered whether he might be tempted to cross the Atlantic to resume a clerical career: "But then saith my Yankee gal, 'You would have to swallow our canons, you know!' 'Carissima mia,' I reply, 'for £1500 a year I would swallow all the artillery in America.'" Such gallantry was a pleasant counterpoint to his intellectual labors: "I do Little Book all the morning, and lounge in the sunshine all the afternoon, and do dinner and Yankee Gal till I go to bed. *That* is what I call life,—not all that treadmill—aestheticism, big volumes, and tall staircases, into which my blighted existence was rapidly dying."[28]

Thus while at the outset of writing "Shorts" (his alternate nickname for "Little Book"), the going was tedious, Green had warmed to the project considerably. Work proceeded rapidly from 1872. It is true that he found the modern period, especially the eighteenth and nineteenth centuries, considerably less engaging and tended to rush through it. But this was also due to his intense eagerness to see the book in print. He clearly relished the prospect of both impressing and provoking the academic establishment at his university, telling Alexander Macmillan on the eve of publication: "I am *very anxious* that it should be out *before I go to Oxford in the middle of November*. I hope you can make sure of this."[29]

The *Short History of the English People* was published in November 1874, generating widespread admiration and only limited censure, in Oxford as well as the rest of the country. The admiration was not confined to those who shared Green's passionate sense of the need to restructure the past. Those who still looked to history for inspiration, excitement, drama, and instruction found ample rewards in Green's work. Battles and kings were still there, even though they had to share the stage with less exalted folk and less turbulent events. Green's narrative gifts, his vivid picture of times past and lives lived, his finely wrought sense of place, and above all, his profound belief in the majesty of the English people, carried all before it.

For Green, as for all good Teutonists, English history commenced in the fifth century, with the Anglo-Saxon migrations. Roman Britain was dismissed in two pages. The rude but vigorous institutions of the premigration Angles and Saxons are described admiringly, especially their primitive egalitarianism. The landing of Hengest and his followers at Ebbsfleet in the Isle of Thanet in 449 was for Green a solemn event: "No spot in Britain can be so sacred to Englishmen as that which first felt the tread of English feet."[30] Yet for all the reverence embedded in that statement, and the loving detail heaped on the place of landing, the chapters that follow are by no means uncritical of the Anglo-Saxon peoples or their institutions. Not only were many kings bloodthirsty aggressors, but there was considerable social inequality, with a growing class of slaves. The saving grace of early English society was its freemen, who perpetuated in the new land self-government in their "tuns" and "hams": "Each had its moot-hill or sacred tree as a centre, its "mark" as a border; each judged by witness of the kinsfolk and made laws in the assembly of its freemen, and chose the leaders for its own governance, and the men who were to follow headman or ealdorman to hundred-court or war."[31]

The Anglo-Saxon monarch singled out for praise in Green's account is, not surprisingly, Alfred the Great. While approving the king's military skills and key role in paving the way for a unified England, he reserved the highest praise for Alfred's intellectual endeavors. Green described at some length royal support of education and the patronage extended to intellectuals, concluding with the king's role in the great expansion of the Anglo-Saxon Chronicle. If English history conceived as a sequence of events began with Hengest, history as an intellectual discipline got its true start with Alfred: "The writer of English history may be pardoned if he lingers too fondly over the figure of the king in whose court, at whose impulse, it may be in whose very words, English history begins."[32]

Another Anglo-Saxon accorded favorable treatment is Dunstan, and for similar reasons. As in Green's 1862 paper, the tenth-century cleric is portrayed as a major force in English religion, government, and culture. As Archbishop of Canterbury for sixteen years during the vigorous reign of Eadgar, Dunstan wielded great secular as well as ecclesiastical power. Since the reform of learning was the Primate's special interest, Green deemed him worthy of the highest approbation.[33]

Yet however secure and prosperous was the kingdom of Eadgar, however wise the policies of king and archbishop, it was no golden age to be looked back upon wistfully. On the contrary, the tenth century witnessed growing social inequality, which Green saw as emerging repeatedly throughout English history, undermining the healthy institutions and practices centered in communities of freemen. Arising from a concentration of wealth and a consolidation of political power, the new oligarchy of local grandees and noble advisers to the king grew heedless of national interests. The consequences, especially under weak sovereigns like Ethelred the Unready, were military vulnerability and social tension.

The ensuing period, beginning with the Danish and Norman invasions and continuing through the early Angevin period, was subsumed by Green under the concept of "England under Foreign Kings," the title he gave to Chapter 2 of the Short History. Far from seeing them as an era of national shame (as some of the more extreme Anglo-Saxon enthusiasts regarded it), he viewed these two centuries (1014–1204) as a time of prosperity, generally wise leadership, and revitalization of the older traditions of free self-government. The key to this paradox of rejuvenation through defeat lay in the rise of an urban middle class. A long paragraph near the beginning of Chapter 2 so well sums up Green's approach to this period that it needs to be quoted in full:

Under Dane, Norman, or Angevin, Englishmen were a subject race, conquered and ruled by foreign masters; and yet it was in these years of subjection that England became truly England. Provincial differences were crushed into national unity by the pressure of the stranger. The same pressure redressed the wrong which had been done to the fabric of national society by the degradation of the free landowner at the close of the preceding age into a feudal dependent on his lord. The English lords themselves sank into a middle class as they were pushed from their place by the foreign baronage who settled on English soil; and this change was accompanied by a gradual elevation of the class of servile and semi-servile cultivators which gradually lifted them into almost complete freedom. The middle class which was thus created was reinforced by the upgrowth of a corresponding class in our towns. Commerce and trade were promoted by the justice and policy of the foreign kings; and with their advance rose the political importance of the trader. The boroughs of England, which at the opening of this period were for the most part mere villages, were rich enough at its close to buy liberty from the Crown. Rights of self-government, of free speech, of common deliberation, which had passed from the people at large into the hands of its nobles, revived in the charters and councils of the towns. A moral revival followed hard on this political developement [sic]. The occupation of every see and abbacy by strangers who could only speak to their flocks in an unknown tongue had severed the higher clergy from the lower priesthood and the people; but religion became a living thing as it passed to the people themselves, and hermit and friar carried spiritual life home to the heart of the nation at large. At the same time the close connexion with the Continent which foreign conquest brought about secured for England a new communion with the artistic and intellectual life of the world without her. The old mental stagnation was broken up, and art and literature covered England with great buildings and busy schools. Time for this varied progress was gained by the long peace which England owed to the firm government of her kings, while their political ability gave her administrative order, and their judicial reforms built up the fabric of her law. In a word, it is to the stern discipline of these two hundred years that we owe not merely English wealth and English freedom, but England itself.[34]

This passage tells us a great deal about Green's basic scheme of English history: While self-rule was natural to the English people, it was constantly threatened by an emergent oligarchy. Periods of foreign domination had a salutary function in equalizing the conditions of the people and unifying them to recover their liberties. But it was no Old Testament "scourge of God" concept that Green applied to the Normans and others. They are depicted as having brought with them many positive goods: more efficient institutions, a keener sense of the importance of public law, and a richer, more cosmopolitan culture. Implicit in Green's account is the notion that Anglo-Saxon England, even at its highest levels of cultural attainment, was a provincial backwater.

Normandy and the Normans received particularly favorable attention. Green began by sketching a verbal portrait of the Norman countryside and its people, drawing on the experience of his own travels through Normandy. He concluded: "The very look of the country and its people seem familiar to us; the peasant in his cap and blouse recalls the build and features of the small English farmer; the fields about Caen, with their dense hedgerows, their elms, their apple-orchards, are the very picture of an English countryside."[35] William, duke of Normandy is praised for his temperament and achievements: "The full grandeur of his indomitable will, his large and patient statesmanship, the loftiness of aim which lifts him out of the petty incidents of his age, were as yet only partly disclosed. But there never was a moment from his boyhood when he was not among the greatest of men."[36]

As these passages make clear, Green was no uncritical admirer of Anglo-Saxon England freedoms, and neither did he accept the "Norman yoke" theory of history, a belief still common among nineteenth-century popular radicals. It is also plain that he valued cultural vitality as much as political freedom. While he believed there was some connection between the two, he was far from denying that a vibrant culture often thrived under far from admirable political institutions, or that some eras of free self-government were culturally barren.

The creative fusion of races and cultures was exemplified for Green by William of Malmesbury. Of Norman and English parentage, the twelfth century historian is portrayed as a leading light of a cultural revival that produced a vibrant secular literature. Another scholar singled out for praise is Matthew Paris, whose chronicle of the events of John's age is depicted as an early example of a people's history: "His point of view is neither that of a courtier nor a churchman, but of an Englishman, and the new national tone of his chronicle is but an echo of the national sentiment which at last bound nobles and yeomen and churchmen together into a people resolute to wrest freedom from the Crown."[37] Yet another heroic intellectual was the Welsh-Norman scholar Gerald de Barri (Giraldus Cambrensis), admirable for his audacity, irreverence, and willingness to challenge the king. As with Matthew Paris, Green succumbed to the temptation of finding in Gerald an essentially nineteenth-century spirit, writing "just the sort of letters that we find in the correspondence of a modern journal." The same is said to apply to the political pamphlets, in which Gerald's "profusion of jests, his fund of anecdote, the aptness of quotations, his natural shrewdness and critical fearlessness and impetuosity that made him a dangerous assailant even to such a ruler as Henry the Second."[38]

It is not by accident that these attributes sound rather like those that Green might have imputed to himself. He was projecting himself back into English history, infusing his own persona into the medieval intellectuals (mostly secularized clerics) he chose to highlight. In the process, the influence of these men of letters was exaggerated. Not only are they said to have made monarchs tremble, but, Green asserted, these writers were the architects of a new mental alertness throughout English society that made possible the recovery of liberty and self-government. Indeed, the Great Charter itself is declared to be the consequence of their labors: "It is no mere accident that the English tongue thus wakes again into written life on the eve of the great struggle between the nation and its King."[39]

This assertion, however, remains undemonstrated, for the following two sections mark an abrupt shift into a fairly conventional political and biographical story of the fight for Magna Carta. Interposing itself between this section and what might be thought a natural follow-up on the Barons' War against Henry III is a chapter on the universities. Then there is a return to the political and military struggles in the following chapter, with an abrupt shift back to cultural matters in a chapter on the friars. These sharp oscillations between culture and politics are managed with a minimum of transitional passages, which betray an obvious preference for the cultural chapters. The first sentence in the chapter on universities is: "From the turmoil of civil politics we turn to the more silent but hardly less important revolution from which we may date our national education." The opening of his discussion of the friars offers an even stronger declaration: "From the tedious record of misgovernment and political weakness which stretches over the forty years we have passed through, we turn with relief to the story of the Friars."[40]

Green's attitude toward the friars was favorable, yet tinged with disapproval. In the thirteenth century, they are shown as a progressive force, reinvigorating popular religion and university learning alike. As the friars became dominant at Oxford, the scholastic system they fostered was an impressive achievement, but "was soon seen to be fatal to the wider intellectual activity which had till now characterized the Universities." More important for Green, the friars' alleged "strong popular sympathies" were "exerted in the coming struggle between the people and the Crown." Their influence, he claimed, led Oxford University to be in the forefront of opposition to royal policy. More significant, the burghers "on whom the influence of the friars told most directly were the steady supporters of freedom throughout the Barons' War."[41] This assertion of the instrumental role of the friars, however, remained undemonstrated.

In his account of the Barons' War against Henry III, Green shifted to a somewhat conventional political and military narrative, emphasizing the skill and daring of Simon de Montfort, who is depicted as representing a "tide of popular feeling." This sentiment, centered in the towns, is characterized by Green as a "democratic spirit." Seeing the lack of baronial supporters, Simon summoned to his parliament the knights and burgesses, many of whom, Green claimed, embodied the new popular impulse.[42] Once again, however, the historian provided more rhetorical flourishes than hard evidence. As so frequently happens with Green's claims of an intellectual vanguard for political resistance to tyranny, the essential questions were begged.

Moreover, Green adopted an extreme view of the parliament that emerged during Edward I's reign, claiming that it was "absolutely identical with those which still sit at St. Stephen's," yet offering little evidence beyond the fact that a statute of Edward could still be pleaded in court. From this dubious assertion, Green leaped to an even more astonishing conclusion: "From the reign of Edward, in fact, we are face to face with modern England."[43] This was of course a particularly vivid example of Whiggish "presentism." It underscored a liberal descent from not just the thirteenth century, but, because the system of electing parliamentary representatives was through the shire courts, which were in turn said to descend from "our earliest English folk-moots," to the age of Alfred the Great.[44]

In spite of his tendency to glorify medieval burghers and to ascribe modernity to thirteenth-century parliaments, however, Green was well aware of the many setbacks to the people's attempts to govern themselves. As in the earlier chapters describing the eclipse of Anglo-Saxon self-government by a rising class of wealthy thanes, he detailed the development of a rigid class structure in the towns at the end of the Middle Ages, with a closed oligarchy monopolizing political and economic power. This followed close on the heels of the rise of civic institutions with widespread participation by merchants and craftsmen. Green saw the emergence of municipal liberty as one of two revolutions, "almost ignored by our historians," that were "silently changing the whole character of English society." The other revolution was the appearance of "a new class of tenant farmers" that challenged established feudal relationships.[45]

Green's glorification of the rise of a new agrarian class led him to take a sympathetic stance toward the Peasants' Revolt of 1381. He sees the rebels as expressing the basic aspirations of the entire English people, including "their longing for a right rule, for a plain and simple justice, their scorn of the immorality of the nobles and the infamy of the court; their resentment at the perversion of the law in the cause of oppression."[46] The issues raised by Wat Tyler's revolt stirred the historian deeply, not only for past injustices but for current ones as well. Around the time he was working on this section of the *Short History*, he wrote to Freeman: "Socially I look upon England as wholly feudal and barbarous. When I see your Somerset peasantry trembling before your county magistrates, I thrill with anger."[47] Characteristically, however, Green viewed the aggrieved rural masses as needing the inspiration of the men of ideas to stir them to action. In the fourteenth century, this function was fulfilled best by the radical priest, John Ball: "Mad as the landowners called him, it was in the preaching of John Ball that England first listened to a declaration of natural equity and the rights of man."[48]

For all his sympathy with radical revolution, however, Green was torn. Recognizing the cultural vitality of court life, its receptiveness to the freshening currents of the creative spirit wafting into England from Italy, he was drawn to strictures on the puritanical narrowness of medieval proponents of the lower orders. Nowhere was this shortcoming so evident as in the case of William Langland. For all of Langland's earnestness, "there is not a gleam of the bright human sympathy of Chaucer, of his fresh delight in the gaiety, the tenderness, the daring of the world about him, of its picturesque sense of even its coarsest contrasts, of his delicate irony, of his courtly wit."[49] This friction between the historian's social and political sympathies on the one hand and his identification with the great literary figures of England's past on the other created a tension in his work that continued in later sections of the *Short History*. This would be most visible, as we shall see, in his treatment of seventeenth-century Puritanism.

In the chapter following the Peasants' Revolt, Green showed his marked distaste for the long feudal reaction, the suppression of Lollardy, the Wars of the Roses, and the near-extinction of self-government under closed oligarchies in the towns. As he remarked: "There are few periods in our annals from which we turn with such weariness and disgust as from the War of the Roses."[50] Even this bleak period could boast the appearance of printing in England, and Green devoted a full eight pages to William Caxton and the spread of literature.[51] With the introduction of Caxton, his interest quickened, particularly since there was a greater abundance of major literary figures on which to anchor his account. The spread of the Renaissance to England also meant a livelier and freer intellectual climate. Green clearly relished writing about this period, and the opportunity it afforded to foreground the men of letters. He taunted Freeman that his friend "would stare to see seven pp. devoted to the Wars of the Roses, and fifteen or sixteen to Colet, Erasmus, and Tommy More, 'Great Tom,' as he ought to be called,—however, so it is." He went on to describe the section on the New Learning, along with the previous ones on the Peasants Revolt and on the Towns, as "by far the best things I have done yet."[52]

Another reason for his heightened interest in the New Learning was that it was a natural lead-in to the section on the Reformation. By giving this title to an entire section of the *Short History*, Green was breaking from the powerful Victorian tendency to see continuity in the English church before and after the reign of Henry VIII. By no means was this view confined to the "apostolic succession" enthusiasts spawned by the Oxford Movement. Freeman shared fully in it, and denigrated Green's emphasis on discontinuity. As with the other numerous areas of disagreement between them, Green did not hesitate to make a spirited response. It was only necessary, he argued, to compare English religion in 1480 and 1580. The changes were fundamental, and not confined to institutional structure, for "looking strictly as an historian to the religious opinions of the English people at the two epochs, I see a change even greater than the outer constitutional change in the aspect of the Church—and I know no name for this change but the same one of the Reformation."[53]

Green's viewpoint was probably doubly galling to Freeman because it seemed to align his friend with the interpretations of Freeman's arch-nemesis, James Anthony Froude. Green had earlier attempted, without success, to dissuade his older friend from persisting in the protracted and obsessive feud.[54] But any comparison between Green and Froude was superficial. Froude's twelve-volume *History of England from the Fall of*

Wolsey to the Defeat of the Spanish Armada (1856–70) was an ardently Protestant account in which Henry VIII was praised for creating a national church and for forging a powerful English state.[55] Green, while agreeing on the importance of the break with Rome, ascribed more importance to diffuse religious impulses and to key religious reformers than to the king. Furthermore, he strongly disapproved of the centralized despotism that developed under the Tudors. Any suspicion that Green was aligning himself with Froude was laid to rest by his introduction to the section of Chapter 6 devoted to Thomas Cromwell. As with all the sections in the book, Green headed it with a "List of Authorities" in lieu of footnotes. This one began: "Mr. Froude's narrative . . . , though of great literary merit, is disfigured by a love of paradox, by hero-worship, and by a reckless defence of tyranny and crime. It possesses, during this period, little or no historical value."[56]

For Green, the rapid rise of royal authority amounted to nothing less than a "New Monarchy,"[57] and could be dated to 1471, with the Yorkist King Edward IV's victory over the Lancastrians in the War of the Roses. It was made possible only by the decay and disarray of those forces that had served as an effective counterweight to monarchy: the baronage, the church, and the towns. English government from Edward through Elizabeth was thus for Green an aberration. Like the Norman conquest, it was a period of powerful, often ruthless kingship. But, like Norman government, it produced conditions that led to fresh constraints, principally the New Learning and the Reformation. The latter was important chiefly as providing an environment in which free discussion could shift England back to its constitutional track: "The real value of the religious revolution of the sixteenth century to mankind lay, not in the substitution of one creed for another, but in the new spirit of inquiry, the new freedom of thought and of discussion, which was awakened during the process of change."[58]

"Arbitrary taxation, arbitrary legislation, arbitrary imprisonment were powers claimed without dispute and unsparingly exercised by the Crown."[59] Such was Green's description of Henry VIII's reign, and he ascribed these excesses entirely to one man, Thomas Cromwell. Indeed, "the years of Cromwell's administration form the one period in our history which deserves the name which men have given to the rule of Robespierre. It was the English Terror."[60] Such a harsh and extreme characterization was followed, however, by a delineation of a far from unattractive personality. Cromwell, Green declared, "never struck uselessly or capriciously," while in person he was "a generous, kindly-hearted man, with pleasant and winning manners which atoned for a certain awkwardness of person, and with a constancy of friendship which won him a host of devoted adherents."[61] This fascination with the personal details of men of power owed more to Carlyle (and even Froude) than Green would have likely acknowledged, and saved his account from the conventional pieties of Whig constitutional history.

Queen Elizabeth held a similar fascination for Green. A lengthy section on her personality is a superb portrait of a devious, supremely intelligent woman whose political genius lay in patience, dispassionate analysis, and a firm grasp of detail: "She had a finer sense than any of her counselors of her real resources; she knew instinctively how far she could go, and what she could do. Her cold, critical intellect was never swayed by enthusiasm or by panic either to exaggerate or to under-estimate her risks or her power."[62] Yet while Green admitted that these qualities were largely responsible for preserving the country during a period of protracted crisis, he considered her to have been untouched by the noblest currents of the age. The flowering of literary genius during the Elizabethan period owed nothing to Elizabeth, according to Green. It was with an obvious sense of relief that he turned from his account of England's great naval victories to the real glories of the age:

> As yet the interest of Elizabeth's reign had been political and material; the stage had been crowded with statesmen and warriors, with Cecils and Walsinghams and Drakes. Literature had hardly found a place in the glories of the time. But from the moment when the Armada drifted back broken to Ferrol, the figures of warriors and statesmen were dwarfed by the grander figures of poets and philosophers.[63]

The historian considered Elizabethan drama the highest cultural attainment of the age, and exulted in its popular origins: "It was the people itself that created its stage."[64] This topic provided full scope for Green's sense of delight in the raw energy and irrepressible spirits of Londoners of all classes:

> Rude as the theatre might be, all the world was there. The stage was crowded with nobles and courtiers. Apprentices and citizens thronged the benches in the yard below. The rough mob of the pit inspired, as it felt, the vigorous life, the rapid transitions, the passionate energy, the reality, the lifelike medley and confusion, the racy dialogue, the chat, the wit, the pathos, the sublimity, the rant and buffoonery, the coarse horrors and vulgar bloodshedding, the immense ranging over all classes of society, the intimacy with the foulest as well as the fairest developments of human temper, which characterized the

English stage. . . . The people itself brought its nobleness and its vileness to the boards. Wild, reckless, defiant of all past tradition, of all conventional laws, the English dramatists owned no teacher, no source of poetic inspiration, but the people itself.[65]

This breathless litany of traits and images, characteristic of Green at his most rapturous, is followed by details of the wild, irreverent lives of dramatists like Marlowe. In regard to Shakespeare, he carefully noted the almost complete lack of sources, yet averred that the poet's work is "instinct throughout with English humour, with our English love of hard fighting, our English faith in goodness and in the doom that waits upon triumphant evil, our English pity for the fallen."[66]

Shakespeare's life was of particular interest to Green because it stood at the meeting point of two great epochs. The age of the Renaissance was passing into the age of Puritanism. This transition was of crucial significance to the historian, and his attitude toward the dawning era of godliness was deeply ambivalent. He praised the sterner Protestantism for "invigorating and ennobling life," yet simultaneously condemned it for "hardening and narrowing" it.[67] Green's ambivalence toward Puritanism is an important key to his overall interpretation of history, in which the tension between lofty religiosity and a vibrant secular culture fueled the halting progress of the English people. The teleology implicit in Green's scheme was thus a good deal more complex than a Whiggish advance to freedom, or to the Victorian constitution. It was a move toward holism, to a union of the spiritual, cultural, and material. And because this coming together of disparate elements was incomplete in his own day, might indeed remain forever a yearning, there was none of the smugness usually associated with Whig constitutional teleology. As he expressed it several years later to his future wife:

> What I protest against is mere asceticism, a blindness to what is really beautiful and pleasurable in life, a preference for the disagreeable as if it were in *itself* better than the agreeable, above all a parting of life into this element and that, and a contempt of half the life we have to live as if it were something which hindered us from living the other half.

He went on to express the hope that mind, soul, and body would "all harmoniously develope together—neither intellectualism nor spiritualism, nor sensualism, but a broad humanity."[68]

The importance that he attached to Puritanism and to the great political and religious struggles of the Tudor-Stuart era can be seen in the space devoted to it. Nearly 30 percent of the *Short History* is given to the period 1540 to 1660, far more than to any period of similar length.[69] Three lengthy chapters, on "The Reformation," "Puritan England," and "The Revolution," are thus the real centerpiece of the book. This alone distiguishes Green from the medievalists Freeman and Stubbs, who did not care to venture much into modern history and whose attitudes toward Puritanism were decidedly negative.[70] Stubbs, moreover, was to caution sternly in his annual Regius Professorship lecture in 1876 against the tendency "to dwell unnecessarily on, or to choose for exaggerated illustration, those periods which are connected most closely with the questions and controversies of today." The chief example he provided of this failing was undue attention to the struggle of Puritanism and absolutism.[71] It was precisely because Green believed that the issues in the great political and religious struggles of the seventeenth century echoed loudly in his own day that he devoted so much attention to them.

Green began his account of Puritanism by denouncing the extreme fanaticism and intolerance of the Presbyterians, beginning with a sharp attack on the Elizabethan Thomas Cartwright, whose "bigotry was that of a medieval inquisitor."[72] The real Puritans comprised nothing less than "three-fourths of the Protestants of England,"[73] and their leaders were figures like John Hampden and John Pym. These men, Green wrote, had no deep-seated objection to Episcopacy, and accepted the Presbyterian system with great reluctance and out of political necessity.[74] Even this moderate Puritanism, however, had its down side. While applauding the simplicity, tenderness, and love of learning among most of the godly, Green decried their growing rigidity:

> A temper which had thus lost sympathy with the life of half the world around it could hardly sympathize with the whole of its own life. Humour, the faculty which above all corrects exaggeration and extravagance, died away before the new stress and strain of existence. The absolute devotion of the Puritan to a Supreme Will tended more and more to rob him of all sense of measure and proportion in common matters. . . . Life became hard, rigid, colourless as it became intense.[75]

Thus, an otherwise unexceptional Whiggish account of the triumph of liberty over political and ecclesiastical tyranny is presented contrapuntally with a treatment of the conflicts within the mental culture of the Stuart regime's enemies. And while John Pym is, not surprisingly, accorded highly favorable treatment, it is as much for maintaining his equitable temper and breadth of human spirit as for his vigorous leadership of the parliamentary opposition.[76] On the royalist side, Archbishop William Laud and Thomas Strafford are predictably vilified, but Charles I receives a somewhat better-balanced assessment. On the one hand, Green wrote of "the strange mixture of obstinacy and weakness in [Charles's] character, the duplicity which lavished promises because it never purposed to be bound by any, the petty pride that subordinated every political considera-tion to personal vanity or personal pique."[77] Yet he also absolved the king from any plan to abolish Parliament, noting that Charles possessed "neither the grander nor the meaner instincts of a born tyrant."[78]

A similar balance is evident in his treatment of Oliver Cromwell, though the overall picture was more favorable. Possibly in reaction against Carlyle's adulation of the Lord Protector as a heroic man of destiny, Green's treatment is cool and measured. Cromwell is praised for his toler-ant, moderate Puritanism, yet criticized for the high-handedness of the fi-nal years of his regime. The care that Green took with this portion of the book, as well as his determination to offer a fresh interpretation of Cromwell, can be seen in a letter to Freeman in January 1874. Noting that his characterization of the Lord Protector was a new one and that Stubbs had already declared the book too "fanciful," he described the extreme pains he had taken

> to avoid being fanciful here, and amongst other things read all his letters and speeches *twice through* to make sure of things. Cromwell seems to me nei-ther the ambitious hypocrite nor the "government genius" which people on one side or the other try to make him out, but a very right-meaning and able man who got with quite honest intentions into a false position and had not political genius enough to clear out of it.[79]

Cromwell's rise to command the parliamentary army and his victories over the Royalists are seen as producing a great watershed in English his-tory: "Modern England, the England among whose thoughts and senti-ments we actually live, began however dimly with the victory of Naseby."[80] While Cromwell was the enabler, however, it was the men of the New Model Army who forged this modern consciousness in their in-tense debates over the kind of society they wanted to emerge from the war. The Levellers are thus Green's principal heroes, men whose valor and determination established the agenda for all subsequent constitutional discourse: "For the last two hundred years England has been doing little more than carrying out in a slow and tentative way the schemes of political and religious reforms which the army propounded at the close of the Civil War."[81]

If Green identified the rise of Parliament during Edward I's reign as one turn toward modernity and the battle of Naseby as a second, the Stuart Restoration was yet another:

> From the moment of the restoration we find ourselves among the great currents of thought and activity which have gone on widening and deepening from that time to this. The England around us becomes our own England, an England whose chief forces are industry and science, the love of popular freedom and of law, an England which presses steadily forward to a larger social justice and equality, and which tends more and more to bring every custom and tradition, religious, intellectual, and political, to the test of pure reason.[82]

This statement reflects the radical nature of Green's Whiggishness, for "social justice" is a concept far in advance of the thinking of a Macaulay or a Hallam, for whom limited government, equality before the law, and a prudent advance toward greater political participation were the sufficient elements of a wise constitution. Moreover, Green's insistence that modernity involves bringing "every custom and tradition . . . to the test of pure reason" presses against the outer limits of normal Whig discourse, which has embedded in it a measure of Burkean restraint and reverence for the long-established.

His declaration that the Restoration marked the arrival of modern England offered an excuse to devote less attention to the eighteenth and nineteenth centuries. Having lingered over the Tudor and Stuart periods, he felt impatient to complete the book. As he wrote later to Freeman: "The truth was that when I reached 1660 I had to face the fact that the book must have an end, and that I *must* end it in about 800 pp."[83] In spite of his eagerness to be finished with the book, the last chapters of the *Short History* are not without interest. While literature does not receive nearly the attention it had in earlier parts, the political and military narrative, at least through the end of the Napoleonic Wars, is accurate and interesting. There are excellent discussions of the leaders of the age, especially William III, Robert Walpole, and William Pitt the Elder. However, there are some glaring critical and stylistic lapses, especially in the section on the American Revolutionary War. Green's account of the period is vitiated by his extreme antipathy for George III:

> In ten years he reduced government to a shadow, and turned the loyalty of his subjects at home into disaffection. In twenty he had forced the American colonies into revolt and independence, and brought England to what then seemed the brink of ruin. Work such as this has sometimes been done by very great men, and often by very wicked and profligate men; but George was neither profligate nor great. He had a smaller mind than any English king before him save James the Second. He was wretchedly educated, and his natural powers were of the meanest sort. Nor had he the capacity for using greater minds than his own by which some sovereigns have concealed their natural littleness. On the contrary, his only feeling towards great men was one of jealousy and hate.[84]

This negative assessment was thrown into relief by being followed by an effusion of praise for George Washington worthy of Parson Weems.[85]

At the outset of the modern period Green had announced that science and industry were the most important topics, yet he gave relatively little space to them. He admitted to Freeman that industry "is dust and ashes to me,"[86] and its neglect is therefore not surprising. But science, in which he did have a considerable interest, is not treated as fully as one might expect. There is extensive coverage of religion throughout the eighteenth century, including fourteen pages given to Wesleyanism and its effects. The scientific revolution of the seventeenth and early eighteenth centuries, on the other hand, receives just ten pages.[87] Readers look in vain for any real discussion of science after Newton. Even Darwin, who had exercised a profound influence on Green's thinking, is passed over in silence.

The many political movements and events of the previous hundred years that lent themselves to a radical interpretation are also, with few exceptions, ignored. The last popular movement Green treated sympathetically in the *Short History* is the Wilkesite agitation of the 1770s. The protests of the Middlesex followers of John Wilkes, together with the associated movement of Yorkshire freeholders, "proved that Parliament, whether it would or no, must soon reckon with the sentiments of the people at large."[88] Apart from brief asides about the "blind panic" of the repressive measures passed by Parliament during the French Revolutionary War, practically the whole of the treatment of the period 1793 to 1815 is given over to diplomatic and military events.[89]

The period since 1815 receives the scantiest treatment of all. There is not even a separate chapter but rather a brief "Epilogue" with a lame introductory statement: "With the victory of Waterloo we reach a time within the memory of some now living, and the opening of a period of our history, the greatest indeed of all in real importance and interest, but perhaps too near to us as yet to admit of a cool and purely historical treatment."[90] Leaving aside the question of how "cool and purely historical" is Green's treatment of Puritan England, there is evidence that he had originally planned a much fuller treatment of the nineteenth century. In a letter of December 1871 to Freeman he had outlined his plan for the post-Waterloo period:

> 1. Canning—show the new tone which came over politics, and especially over our European relations, and continue our foreign policy, wars, etc. to the present time. 2. Colonisation—history of Australia, emigration and the like—to the same date. 3. Constitutional Reform, from Catholic Emancipation to the last Reform Bill. 4. Commercial reform, taking all one can of commercial growth by the way, with Free Trade, and doing kootoo [sic] to Peel. 5. Intellectual progress, popular education, the reforms of schools and universities, advance and generalizing character of science as in Lyell and Darwin,—religion in the philanthropy of the Evangelicals, the rise of the "Catholic" High Church folk, science producing religious liberalism,—literature reflecting all these various tendencies of the age, especially the economical and historical, our romance, humorists, poets.[91]

Had this scheme been adhered to, especially section 5, the *Short History of the English People* might have had a concluding chapter of the same power and vibrancy as its central core.

NOTES

1. LJRG, 209.
2. Green to Freeman, n.d. [1869], LJRG, 240.
3. E. A. Freeman, *History of the Norman Conquest* (Oxford: Clarendon Press, 1867), 1, xii.
4. Green to Freeman, n.d., LJRG, 151.
5. E. A. Freeman, "John Richard Green," *British Quarterly Review* 155 (July 1883): 69, 74.
6. Green to Dawkins, 11 Sept. 1862, LJRG, 103.
7. LJRG, 104.
8. *Life and Letters of Alexander Macmillan*, ed. Charles L. Graves (London: Macmillan, 1910), 183–84.

9. Ibid., 292–93.

10. Green to Alexander Macmillan, December 1869, *Letters to Macmillan*, selected and edited by Simon Nowell-Smith (London: Macmillan, 1967), 117.

11. Ibid., 119–20.

12. Charles Morgan, *The House of Macmillan, 1843–1943* (London: Macmillan, 1944), 107.

13. Green to Freeman, n.d. [May 1868], LJRG, 193.

14. Green to Freeman, n.d., [June 1868], LJRG, 194.

15. Green's notebook of 1867, in B.L. ADD. MS. 40,169, fo. 7.

16. B.L. ADD. MS. 40,172, fos. 13–18.

17. Green to Freeman, 20 March and 17 Nov. 1871, LJRG, 296, 309.

18. Green to Freeman, 3 Feb. 1870, LJRG, 243.

19. Green to Freeman, n.d. [April 1870], LJRG, 250.

20. Green to Freeman, August 1870, LJRG, 255–56.

21. Green to Freeman, n.d. [Sept. 1871], LJRG, 306.

22. Green to Freeman, 27 June 1871, LJRG, 303.

23. Green to Freeman, n.d. [1870], LJRG, 247.

24. B. L. ADD. MS. 40,172, fo. 233.

25. SHEP, 1: xxiv.

26. Gertrude Himmelfarb, *The New History and the Old: Critical Essays and Reappraisals* (Cambridge, Mass: The Belknap Press of Harvard University Press, 1987), 152–53.

27. Green to Freeman, 11 Oct. 1872, LJRG, 331.

28. Green to the Rev. Isaac Taylor, 5 Oct. 1872, LJRG, 328–29.

29. Green to Alexander Macmillan, n.d. [1874], Macmillan Archives, B.L. ADD. MS. 55058, fo. 58.

30. SHEP, 1: 12–13

31. SHEP, 1: 25–26. In the unrevised one-volume edition, after "leaders" it reads "among the 'eorls' for peace or war" (shep, 12). This change was in response to critics who claimed the original wording suggested an overly democratic character to the early folk-moot.

32. SHEP, 1: 98.

33. SHEP, 1: 103–10.

34. SHEP, 1: 119–21. Some stylistic alterations from the unrevised edition (shep, 60).

35. SHEP, 1: 134.

36. SHEP, 1: 139. Very slight stylistic alterations from the unrevised edition (shep, 71).

37. SHEP, 1: 278. In this case, the statement is much more ringing than in the unrevised edition, which has nobles, yeomen and churchmen being bound together simply into "the English people" (shep, 143).

38. SHEP, 1: 224. There are some stylistic changes from the unrevised edition, including the substitution of simply "letters" in place of "lively, dashing letters" (shep, 116).

39. SHEP, 1: 229. Very slight stylistic alterations from the unrevised edition (shep, 117).

40. SHEP, 1: 247, 279.

41. SHEP, 1: 287–88.

42. SHEP, 1: 296.

43. SHEP, 1: 323–24.

44. SHEP, 1: 334–35.

45. SHEP, 1: 368.

46. SHEP, 2: 486. Very slight stylistic alterations from the unrevised edition (shep, 245).

47. Green to Freeman, 14 April 1871, LJRG, 300.

48. SHEP, 2: 483. This sentence in the unrevised edition ends with: "England first listened to the knell of feudalism and the declaration of the rights of man." (shep, 243).

49. SHEP, 2: 494.

50. SHEP, 2: 561.

51. SHEP, 2: 575–84. This was, as Gertrude Himmelfarb has pointed out, only half the space given to the War of the Roses—contrary to what Green claimed he would do in the Preface to the *Short History*. See Himmelfarb, *The New History and the Old*, 152 n.

52. Green to Freeman, 11 Oct. 1872, LJRG, 331.

53. Green to Freeman, n.d., LJRG, 361.

54. Green to Freeman, n.d. [1870], LJRG, 252–53.

55. For Froude's views on the English Reformation, see J.W. Burrow, *A Liberal Descent* (New York: Cambridge University Press, 1981), Chap. 9, esp. 236–40.

56. SHEP, 2: 652.

57. The name he gave to a lengthy chapter. SHEP, 2: 526–651.

58. SHEP, 2: 714.

59. SHEP, 2: 653.

60. SHEP, 2: 675.

61. SHEP, 2: 676–77.

62. SHEP, 2: 737.

63. SHEP, 2: 844.

64. SHEP, 2: 860.

65. SHEP, 2: 860–61.

66. SHEP, 2: 871. Slight stylistic changes from the unrevised edition (shep, 425).

67. SHEP, 2: 875.

68. Green to Alice Stopford, 24 March 1877, LJRG, 450.

69. The period 1742 to 1872, for example, is covered in just over twelve percent of the book.

70. P.B.M. Blaas, *Continuity and Anachronism* (The Hague: Nijhoff, 1978), 191. Blaas goes on to observe that S.R. Gardiner, James Gairdner, and others were unable to convince Green that his intense anti-Royalism was one-sided.

71. William Stubbs, *Seventeen Lectures on the Study of Medieval and Modern History* (Oxford: Clarendon Press, 1887), 53–54.

72. SHEP, 3: 953.

73. SHEP, 3: 967.

74. SHEP, 3: 952.

75. SHEP, 3: 948.

76. SHEP, 3: 1115.

77. SHEP, 3: 1019.

78. SHEP, 3: 1068.

79. Green to Freeman, 23 Jan. 1874, LJRG, 376. Such a measured view clearly places Green at the "modern" end of Kathleen Van Eerde's typology of Victorian attitudes toward Cromwell. See Katherine Van Eerde, "The Uses of History: Cromwell and the Victorians," *Victorians Institute Journal* 15 (1987): 81–102.

80. SHEP, 3: 1176. The modifying phrase, "however dimly," is absent from the unrevised edition (shep, 542).

81. SHEP, 3: 1191.

82. SHEP, 3: 1286–87. Slight stylistic changes from the unrevised edition (shep, 587).

83. Green to Freeman, 18 Jan. 1875, LJRG, 408.

84. SHEP, 4: 1665. Beyond slight stylistic changes, there is also the omission of a sentence that appears in the unrevised edition, after "He was wretchedly educated, and his natural powers were of the meanest sort." In the original there appeared the following: " 'Was there ever such stuff,' he asked, 'as Shakespere?' " (shep, 741).

85. SHEP, 4: 1699–1701.

86. Green to Freeman, 18 Jan. 1875, LJRG, 408.

87. SHEP, 3: 1295–1305; 4: 1607–21.

88. SHEP, 4: 1692.

89. SHEP, 4: 1763–1828.

90. SHEP, 4: 1829.

91. Green to Freeman, 30 Dec. 1871, LJRG, 314.

7. Public Acclaim

Throughout the writing of the *Short History*, Green was beset by doubts as to its reception. More than a year before publication, he had expressed to Freeman his fear that "the book may utterly fail" and that "I ought not to grumble if it does." Still, he was satisfied that he had presented English history in the only way that was "interesting and intelligible" to him. With a nod toward Freeman's own views, he observed that "others may quite fairly feel that, however interesting the attempt to work in literary and moral influences may be, it is safer and less confusing to stick to a purely political mode of viewing things." He also feared that some might find it superficial, others picturesque, and still others partisan.[1]

Green had little cause for concern, for the great majority of the reviews were positive, some of them glowing. His friends came through for him, in spite of their reservations about the structure and emphasis of the *Short History*. Freeman's review appeared in the *Pall Mall Gazette* in January 1875, less than two months after publication. While the review noted Green's sometimes extravagant metaphors, slighting of military history, and disregard for conventional chronology, it was highly favorable.[2] Green wrote to thank him for it, observing: "I have never seen a really grander instance of resolve to look at a book from the author's and not the reviewer's point of view, or a finer appreciation of modes of treatment which may happen to differ from one's own."[3] In his reply, Freeman could not resist telling him: "Perhaps if it had not been Johnny Green who had written the book, I might have enlarged more fully on certain features of it." The older man went on to point out that he could always give a fair review to a book very different from his own, while Green could not—an obvious reference to Green's critical reviews of his *Norman Conquest*. He concluded: "I always told you that you and I, Stubbs, Bryce, anybody else, will each have his own way—that each will do it best by doing it his own way, and that he should be judged by that standard. Remember this another time."[4]

Another historian reporting favorably on the book in spite of some reservations was Samuel Rawson Gardiner, writing in the *Academy*. Gardiner, a lecturer (soon to be professor) at King's College, London, had already established a solid reputation as a specialist in seventeenth-century England and would later achieve eminence with his magisterial history of the Great Rebellion. Gardiner noted some factual errors, questioned Green's treatment of the Civil War, and criticized the scanty coverage of the period after the Restoration. But he declared that the *Short History* "stands alone as the one general history of the country, for the sake of which all others, if young and old are wise, will be speedily and surely put aside."[5] Even more fulsome praise, without any reservations, came from J. A. Grant in the pages of *Blackwood's Edinburgh Magazine*:

> [W]e don't know how to express ourselves about this book in ordinary words. It is simply the ideal history we have been looking for since ever we knew what history was—the simple, straightforward, rapid narrative, clear and strong and uninterrupted as a vigorous river, carrying you on with it in an interest too genuine and real to leave you any time to think of style—yet with a style which is perfectly adapted to the purpose, neither florid nor rigid, neither ornamental nor austere, but, far better than either, unconscious, like the voice of a man who has so much to say that he entirely forgets how he is saying it—a grand condition of natural eloquence.[6]

The book also found favor in the United States, due no doubt in part to Green's highly positive account of the American Revolution and his antipathy to monarchy and nobility. Henry Adams, professor of history at Harvard and editor of the *North American Review*, had already met Green in London and was as impressed by the book as he had been by the man: "It is difficult to speak of this book in any other terms than those of unqualified praise. Its learning, its style, its imagination, and, almost above all, its sound common sense, are most remarkable. . . . Mr. Green cannot be ranked among contemporary English historians second to any one but Macaulay himself."[7] Quoting extensively from the *Short History*, Adams praised Green's demonstration of the Anglo-Saxon roots of free government, but found the sections on the "New Learning" and the "New Monarchy" the most interesting. The only critical note he sounded was on the brevity of coverage after 1700, and certain errors in presenting American history. He concluded his review: The advance of historical knowledge and the steady application of sound historical method may diminish the authority and value of Mr. Green's work as a mere statement of fact or theory, but nothing can ever take away its calmness of judgment, its elevation of tone, or its beauty of style."[8] Adams chose not to include his more extensive criticsms in the review, but grumbled privately that the book "swarms with inaccuracies which are quite inexcusable. . . . He seems to have written much without verifying from original sources."[9]

The book proved extremely popular with American readers, but the absence of a copyright treaty with the United States meant that Green received no royalties. Like other British authors, he was appalled at the lost income, but did manage to see some humor in the situation: "I am musing gloomily on the Pirate Copy which has arrived from New York [published by Harpers], gorgeous in form, and margin, and type, a fine book, but a Felon! As I look on it my dream of a brougham fades away, and I fall back on the chance of a market-cart to jog through life with."[10]

In Germany, Reinhold Pauli (1823–82), professor of history at the University of Göttingen, published a thoughtful and partly critical review essay in *Historische Zeitschrift*.[11] Pauli had spent a number of years in England, and had produced a biography of Alfred the Great and a translation of John Gower's *Confessio Amantis*. The third and final volume of his *History of England since Waterloo* was published in 1875. Known and highly respected in English historical circles, his reputation was enhanced among academic liberals for his having been demoted from a professorship at Tübingen for an article criticizing the political regime in Württemberg. Green shared in this admiration and was therefore deeply gratified at Pauli's lavish praise of him as a man "with a sensitive and richly honed intellect who is, above all, a superb stylist."[12] Pauli especially commended Green's treatment of literature and his vivid, sympathetic depiction of the Peasants' Revolt. But he also pointed out numerous errors, faulted Green for not having consulted Ranke's history of England, for using Gardiner only fitfully, and for the shallowness of his coverage of recent history.

Pauli's review, like Adams's and Gardiner's, was, on balance, a positive one. There were, of course, some severely negative reactions, the most important of which appeared in the *Athenaeum*, the *Dublin Review*, *Fraser's Magazine*, and the *Quarterly Review*. The first part of the *Athenaeum* review was favorable, praising Green's breaking with the practice of periodizing English history by reigns and declaring the book to be highly readable. It then turned critical, not on questions of detail but on overall approach, in effect indicting the *Short History* for pushing a "politically correct" line. The reviewer claimed that Green

assumes throughout a didactic, dogmatic position. He does not seem to have it in view to stimulate thought, but rather to furnish a set of correct opinions. You would say he does not investigate history in order to generalize from it a system of political truth, but, on the contrary, that he tries the acts and characters presented in history by some political system already made. And what is this political system? It is a kind of residuum produced by taking the opinions fashionable just now at present among educated Englishmen, and removing from them the excesses produced by active adhesion to a party, and the narrowness produced by want of knowledge of other countries and other ages. It is a very respectable system, but we suspect a philosopher would question every article it contains.[13]

This thoughtful charge was far more telling than the Catholic *Dublin Review*'s claim that Green was biased against the papacy.[14] The Dublin critic also claimed that Green's book was plagued by numerous errors, for the details of which readers were referred to a recently published review in *Fraser's Magazine*. The author of this painstaking two-part critique was James Rowley, a teacher of history and English literature at a public school in Monkstown, near Dublin. His review carried the provocative title, "Mr. Green's Short History of the English People: is it trustworthy?" He began by declaring that he had eagerly awaited the *Short History*, planning to use it as a text for his students. Dismayed to find a multitude of errors in the first chapter, he had gone through the entire volume with extraordinary care, checking references, noting inconsistencies, misspellings, and blatant factual errors. In his two review essays, Rowley listed well over 100 of these.[15] His intention, he claimed, was to warn unsuspecting teachers who, like himself, might be planning to use the *Short History* as a school text.

Of the listed errors, the majority were trivial, some were simple misprints, and some were not mistakes at all. Green was quick to recognize that there were some genuine mistakes and corrected them in subsequent editions. But there was a good deal more at work here than a conscientious schoolmaster vetting a potential manual for his pupils. Throughout his essays, Rowley came repeatedly to the defense of Froude, whom Green had impugned in his lists of "Authorities" at the beginning of certain chapters. It was suggested to Green by John Morley, who had turned down the review for the *Fortnightly*,[16] that Rowley's real motive was "not so much to avenge Truth as to avenge Froude, and so he has turned what might have been a useful criticism into a personal attack."[17]

His friends consoled him over this onslaught. Stubbs wrote to urge him "to take advantage of Rowley's insolent criticism to make the book more perfect." With characteristic frankness, Stubbs added that he wished that "our views in this and in more important matters were more in unison, so that I might feel more 'solidarity' with little Book than I do." However, he reassured Green: "The structure of the book is untouched by the attack, and the structure was . . . the strong point of it."[18] Freeman's response, while sympathetic, also included a reiteration of his belief that it was best to periodize history by reigns. They had already clashed on this point, Green writing defiantly to Freeman in 1872: "I *won't* divide by Kings, a system whereby History is made Tory unawares and infants are made to hate History."[19]

There had also been a sharp disagreement between the two men over a proposed short history of France in a series that Freeman was editing for Macmillan. He originally wanted Green to write the volume, but they quarreled when Green insisted on doing the book his way instead of just "telling the facts" as Freeman stipulated.[20] Green appealed to Macmillan, asserting that he could "only undertake the book on the distinct understanding that in all matters of arrangement, of treatment, and of detail I should be left wholly to myself."[21] Freeman, however, was adamant that the project be assigned to another author, declaring flatly that Green's plan to pattern a history of France after the *Short History of the English People* "would not suit my purpose."[22]

One of the issues at stake in this exchange was the nature of one's readership and the author's relationship with the public. Regarding the criticisms of the *Short History* by Rowley and others, Freeman could not resist chiding Green for his sensitivity to them, suggesting that such concerns were unworthy: "My own position is this: On the whole, allowing for human infirmity, I satisfy myself and those for whose opinion I really care, and I stand much better with the 'vulgar public' than I ever expected to stand." He concluded by observing that he cared "very much for everything that you and Stubbs and a few more say; very little for what anybody else says, good or bad."[23] If there was more than a touch of jealousy in Freeman's comment, it also expressed a gap between "amateur" and "professional," the former longing for favorable reviews and brisk sales, the latter writing increasingly specialized monographs for a small academic readership.

There were also important political dimensions to much of the criticism directed against the *Short History*. Rowley's critique had gone deeper than the noting of factual errors. In the conclusion of his second essay, he addressed Green's slighting of military history, which, he claimed, "is the only side of history in which intelligent lads will or can take an interest." "Talk to them," he continued,

> in straightforward forcible language of Harold and his huscarls rolling back again and again the tide of Norman chivalry at Senlac, or lying, the night after, a confused heap of carnage across the portals of their land; of the Ironsides raising the hymn of thanks and praise at the foot of the Doon Hill; of Lord Charles Hay's column blasting its way with gunpowder into the centre of the French position at Fontenoy, and their interest never flags: talk to them of the principles of the Constitution, of waves of human progress and the forces that set them in motion, and few of them keep up more than a show of attention. They are so made, and we must deal with them as they are.[24]

There was a good deal more in Rowley's assertion than a preference for "drum-and-trumpet" history or a debate over pedagogy. Green hotly refuted the notion that schoolboys could only be induced to take an interest in the nation's past by recounting deeds of arms, and the subsequent success of the *Short History* as a school manual proved him right. At stake was a fundamental disagreement about history and history's role in forming social values and political allegiances. For conservatives like Rowley, military history was not just exciting, it was a crucial component of English patriotism, inspiring all ages and classes to embrace values like honor, duty, and deference to established institutions. To denigrate it, as Green so blatantly did, was to undermine the very foundations of English society.

This line of reasoning was made more explicit in J.S. Brewer's review in the *Quarterly Review*. Brewer was a lecturer at King's College London, an institution that had earlier rejected Green's application for a position because of his "notorious broad-churchism."[25] As a noted historian, archivist, and editor of the *Calendar of State Papers of Henry VIII*, Brewer's lengthy critique[26] carried some weight. Pointing to the astonishing success of the *Short History* (32,000 copies sold within the first year), Brewer insisted that Green had a heavy responsibility to ensure that the volume was accurate and well balanced. While he did mention a few of the factual errors noted by Rowley, the heart of Brewer's review was a spirited reply to Green's attack on military history. He was particularly incensed that warfare had been characterized as "mere butchery" in the *Short History*, and proceeded to ask how the country "would have obtained its colonies, its Indian Empire, its internal consolidation; without war, its national strength and unity; its proud and vigorous independence; its moderation, promptitude, courage, and endurance."[27] He also denounced Green's disdain for monarchy and aristocracy, called him a "partisan of Wilkes, Beckford, and Junius," and concluded by asking:

> Is this a history, we ask, to be put in the hands of the young and incautious? Is it from this they are to learn wisdom and moderation, to form just and equitable judgments of past events, or of the great actors of times that are gone? Is this the teaching by which they are to estimate rightly the deeds of kings, the worth of an aristocracy, and the beneficial effects of order and religion? We think not.[28]

A more sweeping indictment along similar lines appeared in a pamphlet by the Rev. James Baker, the chaplain of Winchester College, who complained of Green's radical bias, his adulation of Pym, and vigorous espousal of popular rights. He found Green's assault on the Church of England deeply offensive, along with the vilification of George III. To this critic, the *Short History* was nothing less than an attack on the English constitution.[29] Clearly, criticisms like those of Baker, Brewer, and Rowley, while in the minority, did represent a significant segment of conservative British opinion. It should also be noted that even some of Green's supporters by no means shared wholeheartedly in his radical perspectives. This was certainly true of Freeman, Stubbs, and Gardiner.

The great majority of the readers of the *Short History* appear to have been delighted, including many of the leading literary figures of the time. Just a fortnight after publication, George Eliot wrote to Macmillan:

> I have read it aloud to Mr. Lewes and it has given us many happy hours—such as good work always secures to those who come under its influence. Can anyone recall a history which is an equal example of condensation accompanied with fine judgment in selection? so that the brevity, instead of stinting the reader, serves to instruct him the more fully by fixing his attention on the characteristic lives—the true logic—of the history, and saving him from that waste of brains to which he is condemned by the sprawling flabby style of the historic writing into which we all of us have a melancholy acquaintance. Mr. Green's work seems to me a great contribution to the well-being of his countrymen—giving a vivid sense of the national past to a mass of readers who would hardly get it from other sources.[30]

Lord Tennyson requested a copy of the book from Macmillan, adding "I hear it much praised."[31] And James Bryce wrote directly to Green: "Your book even surpasses expectation. It is wonderfully bright fresh animated stimulating; how far always right I can't judge, but of its insight, its literary quality, of its vitality there will be and can be no question."[32]

To ensure that the public was informed of the opinions of such eminent figures, Green helped devise the advertising copy. He sent to his publisher extracts from the reviews and comments, with explicit instructions on how these should be used for the advertisement on the back cover of the *Pall Mall Gazette*, including the precise order of the blurbs: 1. Prof. Pauli in . . . the Historische Zeitung [sic] says. 2. Prof. Stubbs in a letter to the publisher says. 3. Prof. Bryce . . . 4. Prof. Brewer . . . 5. Prof. Henry Morley . . . 6. Mr. E.A. Freeman . . . 7. Mr. S.R. Gardiner says . . ."[33] It is noteworthy that these included favorable extracts from mixed or even unfavorable reviews, as in the case of Pauli and Brewer. He also listed the professors first, with the German historian coming before the others. Green obviously had a flair for publicity, commenting at the end of his letter: "I think this will do more to meet the Fraser article [Rowley's] than a thousand little replies."[34]

Although Green chose not to reply to Rowley, he did quietly undertake some revisions. The reprintings that were required due to brisk sales gave him the chance to correct the numerous errors Rowley and others had pointed out. He also took the opportunity to make some stylistic changes here and there, along with mainly cosmetic alterations in the titles of a few chapters and sections of chapters. One such change was to Chapter 8, section 6. Originally called "The Tyranny, 1629-1640," it acquired the inoffensive title of "The Personal Government, 1629-1640." This was mainly a response to Gardiner, but the content of the section was left virtually unchanged, so that the picture of Charles I's tyrannical government remained intact.

Suddenly in possession of a reputation and a sizable income, Green was eager to follow up this success with new ventures. Macmillan, who was making far more money from the *Short History* than was ever anticipated, was quick to encourage him, especially in projects that offered the prospects of a large readership. Green wanted to capitalize quickly on his fame by publishing a volume of his *Saturday Review* articles. He may have been influenced by John Morley, who had done this a decade earlier.[35] In *Stray Studies from England and Italy*, which appeared early in 1876, Green's historical articles were outnumbered by the light-hearted middles, bearing titles like "Buttercups," "Hotels in the Clouds," and

"Children by the Sea." Freeman was aghast at the publication of such lightweight fare:

> But, O my Johnny, you don't know how I grieve over that square book [the shape of the 1876 edition]. It's all very well making jokes; but don't make them at your own cost. I suppose there is a kind of fun in incongruity; but 'tis too bad to put that Cockney stuff, which seems to have come from the lowest depths of the Daily Telegraph, alongside the really good things that are with it. They ought never to have been in the Sat. Rev.; but to reprint them in a book. . . . How could you write it? How can you preserve it? To me it is nauseous in itself, and further nauseous as unreal. . . . *Do call the thing in*, at whatever the cost.[36]

Green, however, stood his ground, defending with spirit the volume's emphasis on light-hearted pieces:

> I took it that most people would say what you say about the lighter papers in Square Book. But I resolved to have one book at least to my own taste when I have to write volume after volume in compliance with other people's taste; and as, rightly or wrongly, I think "Children by the Sea" the most perfect literary thing I have ever done, and have no sort of sympathy with the feeling which puts social essays below historical volumes, or Addison below Gibbon.[37]

Most readers of the *Short History* would have been as astonished as Freeman to know that Green thought "Children by the Sea" the best thing he had ever done. Published in the *Saturday Review* on 31 August 1872, it is a seemingly frivolous, sentimental account of children frolicking at the seaside.[38] Yet it can also be seen as an intensely personal testament, with a libertarian fervor similar to that which animates the *Short History*. Based in part on his experiences in bringing the boundless pleasures of an "away-day" each year to the deprived children of his East End parish, it also recalls his own childhood striving for freedom and joy. Moreover, it reflects a pronounced inner tension between the serious and the irreverent, between devotion to duty and what Freeman would later call the "monkey element" in Green's personality.[39]

Having satisfied his "light-hearted" side with *Stray Studies*, Green turned to more serious writing projects. He had often declared that once "Shorts" was done, he would turn his attention to "Big Book." As late as 1873, this still meant the long-deferred scholarly follow-up to Freeman's study of the Norman Conquest, carrying the tentative title of "History of the Great Charter." This plan was the one Freeman had long been counting on his protégé to undertake. The projected three-volume work would not be as original as "Little Book," he noted, "but people measure one very much more by the size of one's book than by the intrinsic value, and you must publish in 'three volumes octavo' to be a great historian."[40]

Yet by 1875, he had turned away from the idea of a sequel to Freeman. Instead he began to work intensively on the centuries before the Conquest, the same ground Freeman had covered in his magisterial four-volume work. Green assured his mentor that he would not challenge his views directly, even when they sharply differed, as in the interpretation of Harold and William. He wrote Freeman that he had just gone carefully again through the *Norman Conquest*, with particular attention to Freeman's laudatory treatment of Harold and the house of Godwin:

> It is a great comfort to have their side put as thoroughly as it ever can be in your book; I feel that I know now all that can be said against the views I hold, and the fact that reading and re-reading what you say I still feel their case to be so weak gives me some sort of hope that I am not being misled by mere "fads" and one's natural ingenuity. It certainly does seem to me that the success of William was due mainly to the long-nursed ambition of Godwine and his house. But though I have read and re-read every word of your big volumes and am ever turning back to them, I have made up my mind to make no reference to you in any points where we disagree, but only where we agree. I will give my authorities, but I will take my chance of people's saying, "On this point he has not weighed what Mr. F has said," rather than enter into a controversy with a master and a friend.[41]

Coupled with Green's assertiveness in challenging Freeman was a pronounced enthusiasm for his new project. Less than three months after the publication of the *Short History*, he told Freeman that he was considering not going to Italy with the Macmillans, as he was "bitten with my Big Book and want to go on with it."[42] He also believed he was a more mature and disciplined historian, having learned "a will and capacity to work at periods I don't like as much as periods I do." Portions of the *Short History*, he admitted, were "shameful bits of work" such as "the page in which I hurried over Henry the Fourth." Such lapses, he declared, were "the real fault of the book, its inequality of treatment, its fitfulness and waywardness—not the faults the Rowleys were down on."[43] He also proclaimed the new work would be free of the fatal "essayism" and "jerkiness" that plagued the earlier book.[44] Furthermore, he was using some new sources, most notably *Beowulf*. He had ignored the great Anglo-Saxon poem in the *Short History*, but for the new work he incorporated its vivid imagery and projection of early English life, exulting to Freeman: "How folk can have neglected Beowulf as they have done I can't conceive. . . . One gets out of it a world of knowledge about them, not only about their life and warfare, but their art, their civilization, above all their moral feelings."[45]

Green continued to labor on the project for another two years before abruptly laying it aside in 1877 in order to take up an expanded version of the *Short History*.[46] He always planned to return to the more scholarly undertaking, however, and managed to do so during the last three years of his life. Thus, much of the material he wrote during the 1870s was to be included in his final two books, *The Making of England* (1882) and *The Conquest of England* (1883).

The reason for turning to an expanded version of his popular history was financial. It is not coincidental that he laid the early England book aside and undertook the much more lucrative project on the eve of his marriage. Published between 1877 and 1880 as *The History of the English People*, the four-volume book made predictably less stir than his first. Containing large sections of the earlier work and little change of scope, content, or emphasis, it was widely viewed as an expanded version of the *Short History*. The one glaring defect of "Little Book" that might have been rectified in "Big Book," namely the absurdly short coverage given to the nineteenth century, was not corrected. Or rather, it was "corrected" by stopping at 1815, omitting the much-maligned Epilogue to "Shorts." Still, the new book had reasonable sales, was politely received, and, Green hoped, would confer greater scholarly prestige by dint of its multi-volume format. To that end, he sent copies to leading figures like John Morley, W.E.H. Lecky, Reginald Palgrave, Robert Lowe, and James Bryce. Lowe replied: "I consider it by far the most valuable contribution to the history of England which has yet been made and am glad to think that it is as appreciated as it deserves."[47]

There were other projects to absorb his energies in these years, some of them actively promoted by his publisher. Eager to capitalize on the fame of his best-selling author, Alexander Macmillan encouraged Green to press forward with plans hatched as early as 1870 for various publishing projects of a popular nature. The *Short History* was already being widely adopted as a school text, supplanting the *Student's Hume*. Green's name as editor of a new series of school books or popular reading matter would guarantee substantial sales.

In 1870, while he was still in the initial stages of writing the *Short History*, Green agreed to edit a biographical series for Macmillan. His original list of subjects shows the range of his thinking, embracing political, military, and religious leaders, prophets, adventurers, philosophers, scientists, and literary figures:

1. Gotama Buddha and Confucius. 2. David. 3. Pericles. 4. Socrates. 5. Alexander. 6. Hannibal. 7. Caesar. 8. Constantine. 9. Mohammed. 10. Charles the Great. 11. Hildebrand. 12. Dante. 13. Columbus. 14. Michael Angelo. 15. Luther. 16. Bacon. 17. Cromwell. 18. Newton. 19. Voltaire. 20. Mozart. 21. Napoleon. 22. Goethe. 23. Abraham Lincoln.

He sought to enlist James Bryce for Charlemagne, Goldwin Smith for Lincoln, and Freeman for Caesar. These men proved less enthralled than Green at the prospect of £250 for books that they felt would do little for their reputations.[48] In 1874 he was also turned down by Benjamin Jowett and Max Müller, the latter objecting to "any history of human progress being summed up in biographies at all—ideas not men."[49] With the great success of the *Short History*, however, it proved easier to line up major authors. Over the next several years, Macmillan published numerous primers under Green's editorship. Among the authors were Mandell Creighton (*Rome*), E.A. Freeman (*Europe*), Stopford Brooke (*Milton* and *Shakespeare*), George Grove (*Geography*), and William Gladstone (*Homer*).

That Green was motivated by a straightforward desire for increased income is clear. He had never been indifferent to money, even when he had given it away to the needy during his years of service as an East End clergyman. His involvement in the struggle over his uncle's legacy shows a healthy respect for financial matters and a determination to secure his just due. For those with professorships or independent means, writing primers or popular biographies might have seemed less attractive. But Green, who was still in the process of building a secure income, could not afford to be so disdainful. He also hoped to marry and felt he could not do so without reasonable financial security. Beyond this, of course, he believed ardently in popularizing history, and thus such writing was crucially important. It would do nothing for his professional standing, but it would foster a broad advance in historical literacy.

Green also hoped that some of the other popular works might have some of the radical impact of the *Short History*. The most intriguing scheme was a plan for a "People's Bible." In the travel notebooks he kept during 1872, several pages are given over to a sketch of the project, which was to be edited by himself and Stopford Brooke. Near the top of the sketch, he wrote: "Controversy avoided, but general plan from that of new criticism."[50] He divided the "General Method" section into critical, historical, and geographical subdivisions, with himself slated to write the historical part. Following the scriptural text was to come a section of notes, the historical segment of which was to be written by A.P. Stanley. He had not yet decided on someone for the geographical notes, but those on "Manners, etc." were to be assigned to the anthropologist E.B. Tylor (1832–1917). The "Exegesical and Literary" notes were to be taken from the writings of authors like Maurice and Brooke, supplemented by passages from Goethe. Near the bottom of this page of his notebook, Green wrote: "Get Tyler—need anthropological notes, Huxley scientific."[51]

By injecting the new Biblical criticism forcefully into the lives of ordinary people, such a project would have been a major breakthrough, and obviously would not have avoided controversy. On the contrary, it almost certainly would have drawn even more fire from conservatives than did the *Short History*. Green was reluctant to give up on the scheme. As late as 1878, while admitting to his publisher that "Biblical criticism is unsuitable for Primers," he went on to ask whether Macmillan might "consider the suitability of the subject for treatment in a larger form?"[52] The plan remained unrealized, but his tenacity shows the importance he attached to publishing a work comparable to the *Short History* in its impact on popular beliefs.

In addition to these various potential means of magnifying his public voice, Green also had to consider his relationship to the emerging historical profession. Had he simply written a popular school manual with little professional substance? It was clear that well-established historians, even those who had praised the book, had major misgivings. At a time when historical scholarship had already begun to move in the direction of specialization, how much significance could be accorded to a general history written in a popular tone? Beset by doubts on these points, he was attempting to work out his relationship to the university system (especially Oxford) and to the emergence of a professional historical journal in England.

His attitude toward Oxford was complex. On the one hand, he did serve for a time as Examiner in the School of Modern History and thus had an official function. He also maintained a certain affection for the university, observing that, with all its oddities, Oxford provided a "wide toleration and charity to the social intercourse of thinkers."[53] Yet he continued to harbor considerable bitterness toward Jesus College. On a visit there in 1868, he was forcefully reminded of the shallowness and hypocrisy he had encountered as a student: "Do you know, when I was at Oxford last term, the dons asked me to dinner and Common Room, and positively *crawled*. One brute who bullied me into an illness years ago told me I was 'an honour to my College,' and God knows what! And then you wonder that I despise Welshmen!"[54] In spite of this animus, he was elected an honorary fellow of Jesus College in 1877.[55]

Such marks of distinctions by the academic establishment did not open any real prospect for a professorship. Green was far too radical in his views, not just about the university, but the church, the throne, and the peerage, to be acceptable as a member of the faculty. Furthermore, he had failed to establish a reputation as a specialist in a particular field, a qualification that was becoming increasingly important in professorial appointments. Neither is it clear that he would have accepted one had it been offered. He much preferred his life of active scholarship and the public acclaim that went with it. He also greatly preferred living in London, remarking that "there are a thousandfold better lectures to be got in London than in Oxford."[56] There was the additional important factor of his health, and the need to spend his winters in Italy.

The historical review project was of considerable interest to Green. Germany and France had already established such journals, providing historians with an important forum for criticism, new interpretations, the publication of shorter documents, and other functions crucial to the advance of the profession. In 1866, Green had begun working on a plan for such a publication with A. W. Ward (1837–1924), Professor of History and English Literature at Manchester. They were anticipated by James Bryce, however, who had already approached Alexander Macmillan. When the men conferred, a major disagreement surfaced. Macmillan was thinking of an annual digest, while Bryce wanted the traditional scheme of a quarterly and Green hoped to see a more popularly pitched shilling monthly. Bryce was eager to secure Stubbs as editor, but Green seems to have been less enthusiastic.[57]

Among others whom Green approached was Mark Pattison (1813–84), a leading proponent of the research ideal at Oxford.[58] While he hoped to bring Pattison on as a contributor, he told Macmillan that "it is on young writers we shall very much to rely."[59] He had earlier hinted at this desire to give preference to himself and those of his generation when he noted that "one of the difficulties would be what to do with the Stanleys and Kingsleys."[60] Freeman was excited about the prospects, but Green, after conferring with his publisher, had to tell him:

> I saw Macmillan on my return and found him cooled about the *Historic Review.* The new organization of the *North British,* with its wonderfully good summary of the historical literature of the quarter, and the appearance of the *Academy,* certainly cut into our original plan. Moreover, thinking quietly over it in Switzerland, I doubted whether the sum Macmillan offers would really do—it would only give a modicum for papers, and nothing for editing. And again Bryce and Ward must come to much clearer terms as to the work they will undertake or I must hold back. It is far too big a job to start without clearly seeing one's way. So you will see one need not think just yet of papers.[61]

A couple of months later he informed Macmillan that Bryce was "disheartened" by the delay, but that he still hoped to see the journal launched, with an emphasis on appealing to general readers.[62]

Macmillan was skeptical about the financial viability of the project and convinced that the only hope of success lay in securing a good editor. Green was Macmillan's choice, but he had to beg off for reasons of ill health, telling Dawkins that the plan might still be salvaged if a good editor could be found.[63] Green wanted Bryce to take the lead, but there remained important differences between them on the scope, content, and tone of the new journal. A fundamental disagreement was over Green's plan for the focus of the journal to be on the historical background of contemporary problems. As he told Freeman:

> As to the "Chronicle of Contemporary Events" I stand a bit alone, Macmillan doubting its commercial value, Bryce its historical. As to the latter that will settle itself, if as I hope I can induce Bryce himself to take it [the editorship]. My firm belief is that nothing is more wanted than an accurate account of the real current history of the day, done with some literary skill; where the events shall be given, if not in the ultimate relation to each other and the world which only time can reveal, yet at any rate in some sort of relation to each other, and with the amount of light which a serious historical student from his knowledge of the past can throw on their character and value.[64]

While Green's delicate health was a factor in turning down the editorship, this was also the time he was heavily involved in the *Short History,* and he did not wish to be distracted with the enormous burdens of editing a new journal. Once his book was published, however, Green did push the project again. Freeman wrote to him in 1875: "I rejoice in your success. How you do sell. I rejoice too if there be a chance of Hist. Rev."[65]

It was Green's renown that helped make the project possible, and this time he was interested in the editorship. In 1876, he again urged Macmillan to press forward, telling him that Bryce and Ward still wanted a scholarly journal like those in Germany and France, "a purely scientific organ of historical criticism and means of information as to the progress of historical study at home and abroad."[66] Green, while reconciled to the idea of a quarterly rather than a shilling monthly, still argued strongly for a popular review built around contemporary issues. This should be accomplished, he told Macmillan,

> (1) by including in each number an elucidation of some pressing subject of the day from a purely historic point of view (e.g. in the present state of the Turkish question, a detail of the internal history of Turkey, its reforms, etc., from the Crimean War till now; or should questions affecting the Church come into prominence an examination of the relative weight of the Church and the Non-conformist bodies at each stage in our history from the Reformation); (2) by inserting in each number careful and philosophical biographies of persons of contemporary eminence; (3) by claiming for historic treatment the outer history of literature, science, etc., in their direct relations to national life; and (4) by closing each number with a summary of European events during the quarter, done by some semi-political semi-scientific person like Grant Duff.[67]

The priority he assigned to the Turkish question, rapidly becoming the most contentious of the day, shows how politicized the new journal would have been under Green's editorship. It is also clear that he envisioned the review as a forum for his radical religious views. Alongside his history of the people and a still-hoped-for "People's Bible" would go a "People's Historical Review." He was realistic enough, however, to see the immense obstacles in the way of such a publication. This was not only due to the opposition of conservatives and moderates to his radical views, but to the doubts of many historians about his professional credentials. As he told Macmillan:

> I do not possess that confidence of historic scholars which the editor of such an organ *must* possess. I should be looked upon then by the bulk of them as a person imposed on the review by the unhappy necessity of securing a publisher, and as the representative not of the scientific but of the non-scientific element within it.[68]

It is very likely that Macmillan himself shared in some of these misgivings; at any rate, the plan was allowed to die. When it was resurrected a decade later, three years after Green's death, it took the form Bryce had wished to see. The *English Historical Review* was established in 1886 under the editorship of the eminently respectable and professional Mandel Creighton. From the outset, it featured narrowly focused articles written by specialists for other specialists, with little evident interest in contemporary issues. Green's concern about the lack of popular interest in a professionally oriented historical journal is borne out by the circulation figures of the review, which remained at 1,000 or less for the first forty years of its existence.[69] An ironic twist to this aspect of professionalization is that while the "amateur" Green considered payment essential, from the outset contributors to the *English Historical Review* were unpaid. As Philippa Levine has noted, this economic necessity was justified by the professionals on the ground that "their motives were purer than those of the cash-conscious trader."[70]

Green thus lost out in his attempt to forge a new historical journal that would be at once popular and politically engaged. During these years, however, he also sought to influence the course of events by taking an active and highly visible part in the political agitations of the day.

NOTES

1. Green to Freeman, 16 Sept. 1873, LJRG, 358–59.
2. *Pall Mall Gazette*, 18 Jan. 1875, 11–12.
3. Green to Freeman, 18 Jan. 1875, LJRG, 407.
4. Freeman to Green, 21 Jan. 1875, Jesus College MS. 201, J 49/5.
5. *Academy* 6 (1874): 601.
6. *Blackwood's Edinburgh Magazine* 108 (July 1875): 90.
7. *North American Review* 121 (1875): 216.
8. Ibid., 223–24.
9. Henry Adams to Sir Robert Cunliffe, 31 Aug. 1875, *Henry Adams: Selected Letters*, ed. Ernest Samuels (Cambridge, Mass.: Belknap Press of Harvard University Press, 1992), 137.
10. Green to Olga von Glehn, 21 June 1875, LJRG, 419.
11. *Historische Zeitschrift* 34 (1875): 205–11. I am deeply indebted to my former student and good friend Ursula Marcum, Ph.D., now the assistant editor of *Central European History*, who gave generously of her time and expertise in providing me with a translation of Pauli's review.

12. Ibid., 206. "Mit einem feinen und reich gebildeten Geist und vor Allem mit einem vollendeten Stilisten."

13. *The Athenaeum*, 6 March 1875, 323.

14. *Dublin Review* 77 (1875): 303–41. In this review, the *Short History* was linked with Ranke's *History of England*, which was likewise condemned for its hostility to the Catholic Church. Green later claimed that "Catholics generally say I use them fairly; and I have made acquaintance with both Manning and Acton through their sense of this fairness, which is like pleasing both the lion and the lamb." Green to Freeman, 7 Feb. 1878. Jesus College MS. 202, J 49/6.

15. *Fraser's Magazine* 12 (Sept. and Dec. 1875): 395–410, 710–24.

16. Robert Livingstone Schuyler, "John Richard Green and His Short History," *Political Science Quarterly* 64 (1949): 341.

17. Green to Freeman, 2 Sept. 1875, LJRG, 421.

18. Stubbs to Green, 16 Dec. 1875. W.H. Hutton, *William Stubbs, Bishop of Oxford* (London: Archibald, Constable, and Co., 1906), 104.

19. Green to Freeman, 30 Dec. 1872, LJRG, 340. Freeman was still trying in 1876 to persuade his friend of the error of his ways: "A King is at any rate a finger-post that shows you the way, and with your system I often lose it." Freeman to Green, 23 Jan. 1876, Jesus College MS. 202, J 49/6.

20. Green to Freeman, 30 Oct. 1873, LJRG, 364.

21. Green to Alexander Macmillan, 19 Sept. 1873, Macmillan Archives, B. L. ADD. MS. 55,058, fo. 32.

22. Freeman to Green, 5 Nov. 1873, Jesus College MS. 201, J 49/5. Yet Freeman allowed the author of the history of Scotland in his series somewhat more latitude: "I believe it is somewhat enlarged and enlivened by sticking in stories." Freeman to John Hill Burton, 16 Jan. 1873, Burton MSS., National Library of Scotland, MS. 9399, fos. 213–14.

23. Freeman to Green, 5 Sept. 1875, E.A. Freeman Archives, John Rylands Library, FA 1/8/44.

24. *Fraser's Magazine* 12 (Dec. 1875): 724.

25. Green to Dawkins, 2 Feb. 1869, LJRG, 227.

26. *Quarterly Review* 141 (1876): 285–323.

27. Ibid., 288.

28. Ibid., 321, 323.

29. James Baker, *An Oxford Attack on our English Constitution exposed in a Review of "A Short History of the English People" by the Examiner in the School of Modern History, Oxford* (Winchester: J. Wells, 1875).

30. Mrs. Lewes to Alexander Macmillan, 10 Dec. 1874, uncatalogued MS., Green MSS., Jesus College.

31. Tennyson to Macmillan, 11 Jan. 1875, uncatalogued MS., Green MSS., Jesus College.

32. Bryce to Green, n.d., uncatalogued MS., Green MSS., Jesus College.

33. Green to Mr. Crick, 10 Sept. 1875, Macmillan Archives, B.L. ADD. MS. 55,058, fos. 75–76. The ellipses are Green's.

34. Ibid., fo. 76.

35. Morley published one collection of his *Saturday Review* articles as *Modern Characteristics* in 1865 and another as *Studies in Conduct* two years later.

36. Freeman to Green, 26 March 1876, Jesus College MS. 202, J 49/6. Original emphasis.

37. Green to Freeman, 18. March 1876, LJRG, 429.

38. SSEI, 143–52.

39. Freeman to Dawkins, 12 March 1883, Uncatalogued MS., Green MSS., Jesus College.

40. Green to Olga von Glehn, 2 Aug. 1873, LJRG, 356–57.

41. Green to Freeman, 21 Dec. 1876, LJRG, 443.

42. Green to Freeman, 13 Feb. 1875, LJRG, 411.

43. Green to Alice Stopford, 26 May 1877, LJRG, 464–65.

44. Green to Alice Stopford, 2 Feb. 1877, LJRG, 445.

45. Green to Freeman, 21 March 1875, LJRG, 412.

46. Green to Alice Stopford, 28 May 1877, LJRG, 465.

47. Acknowledgments from Morley, 7 Dec. 1877; Lecky, 15 Nov. 1877; Palgrave, 4 Dec. 1877; Lowe, 22 Feb. 1878; Bryce, 8 Nov. 1877. Uncatalogued MS., Green MSS., Jesus College.

48. Green to Freeman, n.d. [1870], LJRG, 249.

49. Green to Alexander Macmillan, n.d. [1874], Macmillan Archives, B.L. ADD. MS. 55,058, fo. 60.

50. B.L. ADD. MS. 40,170, fos. 14–15.

51. Green consistently misspelled his name as "Tyler."

52. Green to George Macmillan, 22 Sept. 1878, Macmillan Archives, B.L. ADD. MS. 55,058, fo. 170.

53. Green to Louise von Glehn, n.d. [1869], LJRG, 242.

54. Green to Freeman, 19 Aug. 1868, LJRG, 198.

55. The following year he was awarded an honorary LL.D. degree by Edinburgh University. LJRG, 388.

56. Green to Olga von Glehn, 10 March 1871, LJRG, 290.

57. Green to Freeman, 28 Jan. 1867, LJRG, 172–73.

58. See Anthony Grafton, "Mark Pattison," *American Scholar* 52 (1983): 229–36.

59. Green to Alexander Macmillan, 25 May 1869, Macmillan Archives, B.L. ADD. MS. 55,058, fo. 2.

60. Green to Freeman, 28 Jan. 1867, LJRG, 173.

61. Green to Freeman, [Nov. 1869], LJRG, 324.

62. Green to Alexander Macmillan, 4 Feb. 1870, Macmillan Archives, B.L. ADD. MS. 55,058, fos. 12–15.

63. Green to Dawkins, 5 March 1870, LJRG, 246.

64. Green to Freeman, 27 April 1872, LJRG, 317.

65. Freeman to Green, 21 July 1875, Freeman Archives, John Rylands Library of Manchester University, FA 1/8/37.

66. Green to Alexander Macmillan, 15 June 1876, LJRG, 433.

67. Ibid., 434

68. Ibid., 436.

69. Doris Goldstein, "The Organizational Development of the British Historical Profession, 1884–1921," *Bulletin of the Institute of Historical Research* 55 (1982): 183.

70. Philippa Levine, *The Amateur and the Professional: Antiquarians, Historians, and Archaeologists in Victorian England, 1838–1886* (Cambridge: Cambridge University Press, 1986), 174.

8. Political Beliefs and Involvements

Readers of the *Short History* can have had but few doubts about the author's political persuasion. Informed throughout by an advanced liberalism, the book was markedly critical of monarchy, aristocracy, and the traditional authority of the Church of England. A substantial minority of his readers no doubt shared these opinions, for the 1870s was a decade in which republicanism and the campaign to disestablish the Church reached a high-water mark. Most of his readers had a greater attachment to the country's hereditary institutions, but given the vigor of Green's prose and the powerful sense of the majesty of the English people that it projected, relatively few allowed his political bias to detract from their pleasure. The subversive nature of the book was, indeed, one of the qualities conservatives considered most alarming. Green's talent for disseminating radical values to the public in an attractive package gave him considerable potential power. It is with this potential in mind that the evolution of his political principles must be considered.

As we have seen, the anti-establishment bent of Green's boyhood beliefs carried over into later life. He had been an outsider and critic at Oxford, and as a young clergyman had railed against the restrictive ways of the ecclesiastical hierarchy. During his early clerical career, he was a spirited advocate of the liberal point of view, but with a narrow focus: the great debates of the 1860s over theology and Church governance. It was the Church Liberal Association rather than the Liberal Party that drew his energies. As a *Saturday Review* writer he took a somewhat cool, distanced view of national politics, and did not hesitate to make Gladstone a recipient of the "Reviler's" sarcasm. In 1867 he could applaud the remark made by Stubbs in his inaugural lecture as Regius Professor: "I don't want to teach you to be a Tory or a Whig—but whichever you are, be a *good*

Whig or a *good* Tory."[1] And as late as 1869, for all his animus against Oxford, he contrasted the atmosphere of the university favorably with the shallowness of political parties:

> The real peril of our days is not that of being wrong, but of being right on wrong grounds; in a liberalism which is a mere matter of association and sentiment, and not of any consistent view of man in his relation to society; the Liberalism of the daily papers, I mean, and of nine-tenths of their readers; a Liberalism which enables the *Times* to plead this morning for despotic government in Greece, or Froude to defend the rack. And with all its oddities [Oxford] seems to give a wide toleration and charity to the social intercourse of thinkers; Comtist and Romaniser laugh together over High Table and are driven by the logic of fact from the shallow device of avoiding one another as "fools" or "madmen."[2]

In spite of these concerns about the Philistinism of popular politics, Green became increasingly partisan as the decade came to a close. Lord Palmerston's death and the Second Reform Act created exciting new possibilities for the reform of state and society. Moreover, his own waning religious faith made theological debates seem irrelevant, while his decision to abandon his clerical post removed the exhausting preoccupation with ministering to his flock. Political involvement thus became a compelling course of action just as he was taking up his pen to write the *Short History*.

It was not only developments in Britain that propelled him toward greater political activism, but also European events. The most important of these was the Franco-Prussian War. Like most Englishmen, Green took a dim view of the French Emperor, Napoleon III. The vainglorious posturing of their leader, he thought, brought out the worst characteristics of the French. Like other Teutonists, he tended to view favorably the creation of a united Germany, in spite of some misgivings about Bismarck's methods. Thus, when hostilities erupted in 1870, Green reported to Freeman that "the spirit in Germany is wonderfully good." Carried away with enthusiasm at the prospect of French humiliation, he proclaimed: "I hope when the war is over they will just lock up all France—turn it into a gigantic National Asylum and keep every man of 'em in a strait-waistcoat."[3] With the abdication of the hated Emperor, however, Green, like many English liberals, experienced a change of heart. Now that Napoleon III was gone, he told Freeman, "France remains vain, ignorant, insufferable if you will, but still with an infinite attraction in her, at least to me. There is a spring, an elasticity about her, a 'light heart' that has its good as well as its bad side, a gaiety, a power of enjoyment, which Europe can't afford to miss." Although willing to describe the German triumph as "victories of truth and right and intelligence," he denied the right of Germany to annex Alsace, because it was "French to the core."[4]

This partial change of heart did not persuade Freeman, who continued to glory in the German victory. An even wider gap between the two men's views developed with the emergence of the Paris Commune. For Green, this was a pivotal event. As Paris, in the final days of the war, was convulsed by a radical republican revolution that defied German armies and French conservatives alike, Green was deeply stirred. Here before his eyes was the playing out of a great drama of municipal liberty: an embattled city proclaiming a new dawn of human equality and dignity. He wrote excitedly to Louise von Glehn (the future Mrs. Mandell Creighton):

I hope you are "Red" in your French sympathies and don't follow the *Times* and the English papers in their rabid attack on Paris. Things have gone a long way beyond its original demands, but it is well to remember that these were simply for the self-government which every English town has. . . . At any rate, is not this Paris a wonderful spectacle of a government of artizans, governing ably, preserving order, and with property and life as safe as in Regent Street?[5]

After the bloody suppression of the Commune by the Versailles government, Green described to Dawkins how the forces of reaction were keeping all the burned buildings in ruins "by way of keeping up the 'Red spectre' to frighten the bourgeoisie into conservatism." Surely, he continued, "there was something nobler even in the ends of the Commune than in this shopkeeper's 'order' of M. Thiers."[6]

To Mary Arnold (the future Mrs. Humphry Ward) he described himself as a "Communist," that is, an admirer of the Paris Commune. This letter is tinged with a note of republicanism that was to become such a marked feature of British radicalism of the 1870s. Registering his repugnance at the outpourings of sentimental loyalty to Queen Victoria occasioned by the Prince of Wales' serious illness, he exclaimed: "I am glad that the Prince is better, if only that his recovery will deliver us from a deluge of that domestic loyalty which believes the whole question of republicanism solved by the statement that the Queen is an admirable mother and that her son has an attack of typhoid."[7]

In addition to his ideological sympathy with the Communards, Green had also been deeply shaken by the appalling carnage of the conflict. His hatred of warfare became more intense as a result. Traveling through Germany in the autumn of 1870, he was horrified to see large numbers of wounded coming back from the front. Haunted by the image of an ashen-faced young German soldier who had been shot through the shoulder, he wrote angrily to Freeman:

> Pleasant for you folk who "rejoice in war" as the Psalmist says, but I am a poor weak-nerved creature who have seen too much human suffering in my time to think the world needs more of it than God gives it, and all the telegrams and bunting and guns in the world won't make me forget that white boy's face at Köln.[8]

It was experiences like this that prompted him to describe warfare as "butchery" in the *Short History*.

This deeply felt disdain for militarism extended also to great-power politics and diplomatic maneuvering. He became increasingly contemptuous of Bismarck's *realpolitik* and Disraeli's foreign adventures as the decade came to a close. Looking to the future, he could see beyond the Eurocentric obsessions of his contemporaries. As he wrote to James Bryce from Italy in 1880:

> Perhaps I am fanciful and "Johnnyesque" in longing to see English politicians rise to a higher point of view than those of the day, in wearying of leaders born seventy years ago, and whose view—however widened by a sympathy with great and free things—is still necessarily bounded by the world into which they were born, or in longing for younger men who will realise the world of *fifty years to come* and let Europe alone sink into its coming littleness! In that greater World, how odd, how ludicrous, will be the spectacle of a Germany and a France, each passed by in the race of nations, still snarling and growling over their little Alsace! To me all these Bismarks [sic] and Dizzys and Andrassys are alike anachronisms, men living in a world which is passing away, and whose mighty schemes and mightier armies are being quietly shoved aside by the herdsman of Colorado or the sheep-masters of New South Wales.

He concluded: "[I]n this dead Rome I gather courage at the sight of another world that is passing away, and I look across the Atlantic and the Pacific to a new world and a better."[9]

Green had his own political leader, Gladstone, in mind as much as Disraeli when he described his longing to sweep the old men from the political stage. His attitude toward Gladstone was not unlike that of other advanced liberals. The Liberal Party leader, by turns pompous, bombastic, and enigmatic, had a way of perplexing those who yearned for sweeping reforms. Green had already chastised him in the *Saturday Review* for his lack of vision during his first Reform Ministry. Green's disenchantment led him to hope for a reverse so that the party might be forced to adopt a more radical posture, such as embracing disestablishment of the Church. Describing himself to Freeman as an "old Radical" and "a worshipper of Joe Hume," he declared as the election of 1874 approached: "I think it would be a good thing for Liberalism if we got a good beating this time and had to form a policy in opposition."[10]

Green got his wish, as Disraeli and the Conservatives were swept into office. As he had hoped, the experience served ultimately to galvanize Gladstone and the Liberals. Partly this was a matter of luck, for an opportune crisis arose in the Balkans. The Conservative government, following the traditional policy of propping up the Ottoman Empire as a bulwark against Russian expansion, found itself faced with a public outcry over Turkish suppression of Bulgarian Christians. The "Bulgarian atrocities" campaign put the Disraeli government very much on the moral defensive and handed the Liberals a potent political weapon.

Gladstone, although reluctant to jump into the fray, eventually emerged as a great champion of the oppressed.[11] The campaign served to propel him back into the leadership of the Liberal Party, which he had resigned after the 1874 defeat. It also brought Green forward as an active public figure in a great political cause for the first time in his life. For all his earlier criticism of Gladstone, Green was disheartened by his resignation, partly because it placed leadership of the party in the hands of the Whigs. As he told Freeman: "It makes me want to carry out my notion of writing a history from 1815 to now, if only to say that I for one love and honour Gladstone as I love and honour no other living statesman."[12] There was an element of exaggeration in this statement—far from expanding his coverage of the nineteenth century in the enlarged version of his history, he eliminated it altogether—but the warmth was genuine.

As Richard Shannon makes clear, the Bulgarian atrocities campaign of 1876 was launched, not by Gladstone, but by journalists like W.T. Stead.[13] The movement drew much of its moral fervor from the Nonconformist community, which reacted with deep shock at the news of Bulgarian Christians being massacred by Turkish mercenaries. Indeed, the intense Christian religiosity of the campaign repelled many secular liberals, notably the Positivists. Frederic Harrison, for example, implored John Morley not to allow the *Fortnightly Review* to be used to "encourage the silly Christian cry of 'down with the Beastly Turk!'"[14] No follower of Comte, Green was undeterred by the Christian zeal of many of the agitators, though he did write dismissively of them as "mere 'Christian sympathisers.'"[15] His own involvement was based on opposition to Disraeli's policy of military bluster against Russia (the champion of the oppressed Bulgarians), an ardent attachment to incipient nationalist movements in the Balkans, and a stout Gladstonian "little Englandism."

In spite of his sympathy with the cause, it is unlikely that Green would have become so deeply involved were it not for Freeman's insistent urging. Freeman had taken an early interest in the Balkan question, visiting Greece and being made a Commander of the Greek Order of the Saviour.[16] He became a vigorous fund-raiser for refugees from Turkish misrule, imploring Green at the end of 1875: "Now you have waxed so rich with royalties, you may give me a trifle yourself, but that is only a trifle; I want you to beg, beg, beg."[17] When Green pleaded that a school in east London he was helping to support prevented him from giving much time or money, Freeman replied impatiently: "So you have a school at 'the East End' which is to hinder your working for my refugees. . . . O man! they want bread and blankets now, in the snow; you can teach A.B.C. or geopolitics either any time."[18]

With the heating up of the public agitation in Britain and the repeated importunings of Freeman, Green was drawn more deeply into the movement by the end of 1876. He agreed to serve on a committee of the Eastern Question Association to draw up a manifesto convening a great meeting that was to be held at St. James Hall, Piccadilly, in December. James Bryce, Stopford Brooke, and William Morris were also members of the committee. Despite the seriousness of their task, Green characteristically saw the humor in the situation, especially having to cowrite a manifesto with Morris, whose devotion to a vocabulary free of Latinisms was even fiercer than Freeman's. Green had earlier registered his dissent from such linguistic puritanism, noting that the "reason I stand a little on my guard as to the 'English' restoration which is going on is that I am afraid we should lose through it certain elements of beauty in style which the mixed texture of our present speech gives us."[19] At a meeting of the committee, he could not resist a joke at Morris's expense. He "insidiously persuaded" Morris that the committee had assigned him to write one of the campaign pamphlets, on the topic of "The Results of the Incidence of Direct Taxation on the Christian Rayah." However, Green sternly warned Morris that "he was forbidden to speak of the 'onfall of straight geld,' or other such 'English' forms. I left him musing and miserable." At the same meeting, he poked fun at Gladstone's suggestion that the Eastern Question Association publish a paper called *The Star in the East*: "I suggested that we should ask him if we could get the Magi to edit it."[20]

The meeting at St. James Hall was held on 8 December 1876, and was one of the defining moments of the campaign. Gladstone spoke to great effect for several hours. Among the other speakers were several historians: Freeman, Bryce, and G.O. Trevelyan. The four general points carried at the meeting were: (1) Turkey was to pay reparations to the Bulgarians; (2) The Muslim population of Bulgaria was to be disarmed; (3) Autonomy for Christians was to be established in Bulgaria; (4) Britain was to cooperate with Russia on the enforcement of these provisions.[21]

Green and others may have been pleased at the outcome, but Freeman saw great danger ahead, especially since British policy was in the hands of the man he detested above all political leaders. He was convinced that Disraeli ("the Jew," as he invariably called him), planned by masterful inaction to goad Russia into taking aggressive action: "Depend on it, the Jew himself means to wait till Russia does something which may give him an excuse for attacking her. This must be stopped beforehand."[22] While Green was persuaded of the necessity of keeping the pressure on the government, he did not share in Freeman's anti-Disraeli rancor. Although he apparently never chided his older friend for his anti-Semitic obsessions, nowhere in his own letters does he refer to the Prime Minister as "the Jew." Green believed that British policy in southeastern Europe was mistaken because it was too narrowly political, not because the Conservative leader was morally depraved.[23] Disraeli, for his part, was an admirer of the *Short History*, and was known to have distributed copies to his friends. Green informed Freeman that "Dizzy has noble points! He reads and gives away 'Shorts.'"[24]

Maintaining his close involvement in the Eastern Question Association, Green fell increasingly under Gladstone's spell. Writing to his future wife in February 1877, he exclaimed:

Last night I met Gladstone—it will always be a memorable night to me; Stubbs was there, and Goldwin Smith and Humphrey Sandwith and Mackenzie Wallace whose great book on Russia is making such a stir, besides a few other nice people; but one forgets everything in Gladstone himself, in his perfect naturalness and grace of manner, his charming abandon of conversation, his unaffected modesty, his warm ardour for all that is noble and good. I felt so proud of my leader—the chief I have always clung to through good report and ill report—because, wise or unwise as he might seem in this or that, he was always noble of soul. He was very pleasant to me, and talked of the new historic school he hoped we were building up as enlisting his warmest sympathy. I wish you could have seen with what a glow he spoke of the Montenegrins and their struggle for freedom; how he called on us who wrote history to write what we could of that long fight for liberty! And all through the evening not a word to recall his greatness amongst us, simple, natural, an equal among his equals, listening to every one, drawing out every one, with a force and a modesty that touched us more than all his power.[25]

It was uncharacteristic of Green to become so captivated by anyone, but Gladstone in the fullness of his powers could be a formidable charmer. At any rate, Green would return to a more measured appraisal after the heat of the Eastern Question had abated.

Through the first part of 1877, Green worked passionately at the cause, for the Russian declaration of war against Turkey in April threatened to bring Britain into the struggle. At one point he even wished for a British defeat in the war he was certain Disraeli was planning:

I am afraid we are drifting into war—into war on the side of the Devil and in the cause of Hell. It will be terrible to have to wish England beaten. . . . I love England dearly. But I love her too much to wish her triumphant if she fight against human right and human freedom.[26]

He was increasingly caught up in the public agitation, which reached a climax at a great meeting in Birmingham at the end of May. Gladstone was the principal speaker at this gathering on 31 May, which drew an estimated crowd of 30,000. Replying to Conservative charges that the members of the Eastern Question Association were long on sentiment and short on knowledge, the Liberal leader pointed to the presence of the country's leading historians in its ranks. To prolonged applause, he cited the names of Freeman, Froude, Carlyle, Stubbs, and Green.[27]

While Green was gratified at such public marks of esteem from his political chief, his characteristic skepticism was beginning to reassert itself. The day after the meeting, he wrote to Freeman expressing his satisfaction that they had both been praised by Gladstone, but noted that he was "more interested in the Western than in the Eastern results of this Birmingham movement." It would, he hoped, end not only in the recon-

struction of the Liberal Party, "but in a new system of political party altogether, with principles gathered from the general opinion of all who belong to it rather than given from above by a knot of oldish gentlemen who
sit on the 'front bench.'"[28] The reference here was to a hoped-for recon-
struction under Joseph Chamberlain, who had developed a new type of
radical political organization at Birmingham ("the Caucus"), which he
sought to extend to the whole country through his National Liberal Feder-
ation. Gladstone, as part of his struggle against the old-line Whigs in the
party, appeared to give Chamberlain's organization his blessing, but there
was a clear underlying tension.[29] What, after all, was Gladstone in the
final analysis but one of Green's "oldish gentlemen" of the front bench?
Chamberlain, born just a year before Green, was of his own generation,
and had earlier expressed markedly republican sentiments to the radicals
of Birmingham.[30]

In addition to Green's chafing at elderly leaders and traditional political hierarchies, he was hoping to end the crisis without British military
intervention. Lacking Freeman's visceral hatred of Disraeli and tendency
to idealize the victorious Russians, Green longed for a negotiated settlement. As he wrote to Freeman:

> How I wish English folk, Libs and Tories alike, would take it for a "new de-
> parture." Neither party has much to reproach the other with in Eastern mat-
> ters: both might now forget the past and unite to build up a Christian power
> on the Bosphorus, whether as a new nation, or as a bulwark against Russia—
> what matters?[31]

In the end, peace was maintained, but not in the way Green hoped. It was
rather through Bismarck's convoking the Congress of Berlin at which
Disraeli, through military threats and skillful diplomacy, led the powers to
a settlement that stripped Russia of most of its gains. In order to maintain
a barrier against Russian expansion, Turkey was left in unfettered control
of a portion of Bulgaria. Thus the Eastern Question of the 1870s, for all of
the sound and fury of public agitation, was temporarily resolved by great-
power politics. The unfulfilled nationalist yearnings of the Bulgarians and
other Balkan peoples were left to fester, with ultimately catastrophic results.

Green was disappointed, but not nearly to the extent of those for
whom the agitation had been nothing less than a great moral crusade. Not
only had he begun to weary of the protracted crisis, but his former impatience with conventional politics and leaders had reemerged. In spite of

the ardor with which he had carried on his part in the movement, in the end it was eclipsed by his disgust with the structures and leadership of British politics. This distancing had a personal dimension, in the form of a partial cooling toward Gladstone. While Green recognized that Gladstone still had an important role to play, a mocking tone had crept back into his attitude. Bryce told him in June 1878 that Gladstone insisted, against all scientific evidence, that Homer's description of an "outer sea" might be correct, since northwestern Europe had once been under water. When Bryce replied that this had happened many millions of years before, Gladstone exclaimed: "Oh, if you believe geologists with their millions and trillions of years, I have done."

Relaying this story to Freeman, Green observed: "Surely it is strange and marvellous that he should be believing that the Alps and Pyrenees were being deposited in the sea-bottom in the time of Homer! But do not tell this abroad lest the daughters of the Philistines rejoice and make merry over our old Hero."[32] This was more characteristic of Green's iconoclastic disposition, and can be compared to the earlier lessening of his adulation for Stanley and Freeman. None of this was as pronounced as his adolescent reaction against older authority figures, especially his uncle. The mature John Richard Green was confident of his powers and convinced of the importance of his contribution to the writing of history. While continuing to hold men like Stanley, Freeman, and Gladstone in high esteem, he was unwilling to persist in a deferential posture.

Not only did Green find his independence compromised by political involvement, but he was impatient of the limited horizons of even the most advanced reformers and agitators. His frustration was best expressed in a despairing letter to Freeman on English politics, in which he complained that the Liberals were "but half-an-inch in front of the Whigs and . . . the Whigs but an eighth of an inch in front of the Tories." He concluded: "The only questions I care for are questions fifty years ahead and which I shall never live to see even discussed, such as the entire revolution of our higher education, Oxford and Cambridge having previously been ground into powder and the place thereof sown with salt and left as a place for dragons."[33]

If a desire to maintain a critical independence and frustration over the restricted vision of his contemporaries partly account for the lessening of Green's political engagements, there was a more personal explanation. In 1877, at the height of the Bulgarian agitation, he married Alice Stopford. For the remaining six years of his life, he devoted himself to this intensely fulfilling emotional and intellectual partnership, and to the creation of historical works that, he hoped, would have more enduring value than the *Short History of the English People.*

NOTES

1. Green to Freeman, n.d. [1867], LJRG, 178. Original emphasis.
2. Green to Louise von Glehn, n.d. [1869], Bodleian Library, MS. English Letters, e. 48, fo. 80; LJRG, 242.
3. Green to Freeman, n.d. [1870], LJRG, 257–58.
4. Green to Freeman, 31 Aug. 1870, LJRG, 259–61.
5. Green to Louise von Glehn, 6 March 1871, LJRG, 288.
6. Green to Dawkins, n.d. [Oct. 1872], Jesus College MS. 200, J 49/4. This letter is printed in LJRG, 325, but Stephen was unable to decipher the word "order."
7. Green to Mary Arnold, 19 Dec. 1871, LJRG, 311.
8. Green to Freeman, 31 Oct. 1870, LJRG, 266. The telegrams referred to announced the French surrender at Metz, at which news the cannons at Mainz thundered a salute.
9. Green to Bryce, n.d. [1880]. Quoted in H.A.L. Fisher, *James Bryce* (New York: Macmillan, 1927), 1: 172–73. Original emphasis.
10. Green to Freeman, 24 Jan. 1874, LJRG, 377–78.
11. See R.T. Shannon, *Gladstone and the Bulgarian Agitation in 1876*, 2nd edition (Hassocks, Sussex: The Harvester Press, 1975).
12. Green to Freeman, 18 Jan. 1875, LJRG, 409.
13. "[F]ar from being a decisive agent, Gladstone was practically carried into the agitation by others." Shannon, 90. Ann Pottinger Saab, in her *Reluctant Icon: Gladstone, Bulgaria, and the Working Classes* (Cambridge, Mass.: Harvard University Press, 1991), explores more fully than Shannon the mass-movement aspects of the agitation, and sees it as having a more decisive effect on the nature of the Liberal Party.
14. Harrison to Morley, 17 Sept. 1876, quoted in Martha S. Vogeler, *Frederic Harrison: The Vocations of a Positivist* (Oxford: Clarendon Press, 1984), 133.
15. Green to Freeman, 1 Dec. 1876, LJRG 441.
16. Freeman to Green, 21 July 1875, E. A. Freeman Archives, John Rylands Library of Manchester University, FA 1/8/37.
17. Freeman to Green, 19 Dec. 1875, E. A. Freeman Archives, John Rylands Library of Manchester University, FA 1/8/50a.
18. Freeman to Green, 12 Jan. 1876, Jesus College MS. 202, J 49/6.
19. Green to Freeman, 7 Jan. 1875, LJRG, 404. In this letter, he quoted a lengthy passage from Portia's "quality of mercy" speech in the *Merchant of*

Venice, noting Shakespeare's skillful interweaving of Latinisms with Anglo-Saxon root words.

20. Green to Freeman, 1 Dec. 1876, LJRG, 441.

21. Shannon, 258–62.

22. Freeman to Green, 19 Feb. 1877, Jesus College MS. 202, J 49/6.

23. "The sympathies of peoples with peoples, the sense of a common humanity between nations, the aspirations of nationalities after freedom and independence, *are* real political forces; and it is just because Gladstone owns them as forces, and Disraeli disowns them that the one has been on the right side, and the other on the wrong in parallel questions such as the upbuilding of Germany or Italy." Green to Alice Stopford, 23 Feb. 1877, LJRG, 447.

24. He went on to point out the irony of having both Gladstone and Disraeli as enthusiastic readers. Green to Freeman, 22 Jan. 1878, LJRG, 472.

25. Green to Alice Stopford, 2 Feb. 1877, LJRG, 446.

26. Green to Alice Stopford, 7 May 1877, LJRG, 460.

27. *The Times*, 1 June 1877. Gladstone's exalting of sentiment over calculation echoed Green's belief, which he expressed to Alice Stopford on 23 May: "I like to see the cynics of the clubs and the hard-headed Whigs growling at 'sentiment' while 'sentiment' is making nations." LJRG, 464.

28. Green to Freeman, 1 June 1877, LJRG, 466.

29. Saab, *Reluctant Icon*, 146–50.

30. Philip Magnus, *Gladstone: A Biography* (New York: Dutton & Co., 1964), 207.

31. Green to Freeman, 7 Feb. 1878, Jesus College MS. 202, J 49/6.

32. Green to Freeman, 24 June 1878, Jesus College MS. 202, J 49/6.

33. Green to Freeman, 21 Dec. 1876, LJRG, 443–44.

9. Marriage and Final Works

John Green had long yearned to marry. The loss of his adored sister Adelaide, as well as the separation from his mother following his father's death, had created an emotional void within him; even the adolescent flirtations of his undergraduate years were expressive of an abiding loneliness. During the interval between taking his Oxford degree and becoming a clergyman, he had rushed into an ill-advised engagement to a young woman in Somerset, a difficult situation from which he was extricated through the good offices of Boyd Dawkins.[1] His passionate devotion to Jane Ward during his tenure as a young curate made her early death a particularly wrenching loss. Through the dark days of his waning faith and failing health in the East End, Green clung to the prospect of marriage, telling Dawkins in 1864: "It seems to me (I am old at twenty-six) that there is very little worth the longing for in life but a bonnie wee wife and crowing bairns."[2] His financial straits as well as his tubercular condition led him to defer this dream, but with his deep emotional and physical needs unsatisfied, he became involved in the guilt-provoking sexual relationship referred to at the end of Chapter 4.

This liaison precipitated a severe personal crisis from which Green was rescued, or so he came to believe, by the friendship of Louise von Glehn. Her father was a wealthy German merchant, her mother Scottish. The family lived at Sydenham in south London, and their home at Peak Hill became a haven of safe domesticity and intellectual stimulation for Green. Among the regulars at Peak Hill were the artist William Holman Hunt, the musical authority and Macmillan editor George Grove, and the Talmudic scholar Emmanuel Deutsch.[3] Louise, who grew into a cultivated and beautiful young woman, became Green's special confidante. Louise's moral principles were apparently rather more orthodox than those of her skeptical, freethinking parents. Green, hinting at his own dark secret, told her on the eve of his marriage to Alice Stopford how she had been his salvation:

> Your mention of the old days at Peak Hill brings them back to me with a strange vividness! What an odd circle it was of men with how different destinies! Well, that memory of the earnest, resolute girl who came into the midst of it with her love of knowledge and love of right, "young" certainly but *not* "very foolish," because there is no wiser thing in the world than the love of those two things, that memory is one of the pleasantest of all that time, as it is assuredly one of the *best*. It was a great crisis in my life, Louise, though none of you then knew it; I stood on the very brink of a moral wreck; and if I was saved, perhaps the steady right-mindedness of a certain Louise von Glehn, moving amidst that sceptical self-indulgent circle, with her resolute spirit of love and duty, had more to do with it than she knew.[4]

He developed a similarly enduring but less intense friendship with Louise's younger sister, Olga.[5]

Green's interest in Louise von Glehn seems to have had a romantic component, but as an impecunious clergyman, he was in no position to seek the hand of a wealthy young woman. Moreover, being a clergyman was a psychological barrier to the kind of passionate physical relationship he wanted in marriage, and was a factor in his ultimately abandoning clerical life. "A parson's wife," he wrote to Dawkins in 1866, is "suggestive of tracts, beef tea, and good works. Heaven deliver me! However, Heaven seems extremely likely to."[6] The same frustrating sense that his profession was an obstacle to a fulfilling life is evident in a letter to Edward Denison in 1868, in which he described a conversation in a railway carriage with "a charming little maiden of 17 who pratted to me of everything in heaven and earth, with a great many 'Mr. Greens' in every sentence." When he mentioned always carrying a book with him, her reply was: "Oh yes . . . I suppose it is the Bible." It was, in fact, the *Physiologie du goût*,[7] and Green wondered dishearteningly: "Are these the thoughts of little maidens concerning parsons—are we ideals with perennial Bibles in our pockets?"[8]

Leaving the clerical profession and seeking his fortune as a writer were thus motivated in part by a strong matrimonial urge, but it would be a long time before this was possible, and the sometimes desperate state of his health made it seem extremely unlikely. In January 1871, he defined to Olga von Glehn the satisfactions of marriage as "the trust, the self-sacrifice, the quiet daily growth of affection, the strange, sweet sense of a double life, of a life at last more than double, multiplied a thousandfold by the new child-faces, enlarged and enriched with every new responsibility or peril." But, he lamented, "even if I live on (and I am not so well again)—all this is lost to me."[9]

Just two months later came the shock of Louise's engagement to Mandell Creighton. He mustered a warm response to her announcement, but there is evident disappointment in his assertion that "happy as I am about it—and *indeed I am on all grounds most happy*—there is always a shadow of dread about a friend's marriage, and I have too few real friends to care to lose *one*." He expressed the wish that their friendship would "remain just as warm and true as ever, although you will have some one else now to treat you to 'wise conversation.'"[10] The feeling of deprivation was powerful, for Green had delighted not only in intense and free-ranging discussions of books and ideas with Louise, but also in sharing his profound love of music and art. She also experienced a sense of loss, and recalled with deep affection many years after his death:

> When he took me to the National Gallery and talked to me about the pictures, I felt as if for the first time I was learning really to look at pictures. Nothing was dead to him, everything lived, and his sympathy and vitality made it possible for him to communicate to others something of what he saw and felt.[11]

Green's relationship with Louise von Glehn shows how he had come to value intellectual companionship with women, a considerable advance over his earlier views. Another woman with whom he developed a close connection was Mary Arnold, whom he met in 1867, at the time of her engagement to Humphry Ward. She later described their friendship as developing into a "literary partnership," with Green constantly encouraging and advising her. "'Anyone can read!' he would say; 'anybody of decent wits can accumulate notes and references; the difficulty is to *write*—to make something.'"[12] There was nothing patronizing in Green's statement, for when he undertook to edit a series of primers for Macmillans, he agreed to let her try writing the one on English poetry. But he insisted on the highest standards, and after reading her initial twenty-page effort told her, in as kindly a fashion as possible, that she would have to give it up. The primer, enlarged to one on English literature, was turned over to Stopford Brooke.[13] She was deeply mortified by the incident, but it apparently had the salutary effect of forcing her to become more exacting in her writing. And two years later he was urging her forward with her plans for a book on Spain.[14]

By the end of 1873, as the publication of Green's book approached and his health improved temporarily, he began planning seriously to marry. It is not clear, however, that he had anyone particular in mind, and Freeman chided him: "You are a cool fellow to talk calmly of being married in the early summer, as if it was a thing which might be done at any moment, an 'indifferent official act,' after the manner of Froude and King Harry."[15] This plan, whether or not a specific bride was intended, came to nothing. Despite the stunning literary and financial success Green achieved by 1875, it would be another two years before he married.

Green had first made the acquaintance of Stopford Brooke in 1865, but nearly ten years elapsed before he met Brooke's cousin, Alice Stopford. While Brooke was, like Green, a liberal clergyman increasingly alienated from the Church of England, Alice had been relatively sheltered from free-thinking influences. The Irish Protestant Stopfords boasted a number of notable figures in the Church of Ireland. Her grandfather was Bishop of Meath and her father was Archdeacon of that see. Born in Kells in 1847, Alice was raised in a moderately Evangelical household; duty and discipline were stressed, but there was also room for decorous amusement.[16] The loose financial dealings of an uncle left the family saddled with debt, so that material conditions declined sharply during Alice's childhood. Nonetheless, it seems to have been a happy household, which she recalled in later years with affection.

Upon her father's death in May 1874, Alice and her sister, Louisa, moved with their mother to Chester. Mrs. Stopford was a difficult character—much more intensely Evangelical than her late husband and firm in her conviction that women had little need of books other than devotional ones. Earlier, Alice had struggled to teach herself the rudiments of German, Greek, and metaphysics, producing severe eye strain that plagued her the rest of her life. She had also managed to attend physics lectures at the College of Science in Dublin. The opportunities for such endeavors were severely limited at Chester, so she labored over a novel that proved unpublishable. Alice's spirit remained undimmed through this trying period. She had a lively, quick mind and an irreverent sense of fun reflected in her avid reading of *Punch*. She and her sister were able to travel around England and Ireland visiting relatives, and to undertake some excursions to the Continent. Whatever the difficulties of her situation, Alice Stopford was a resourceful, spirited young woman, and more than a match for her strong-willed mother.

It was while visiting Stopford Brooke and his family in London in December 1874 that she met John Green. The *Short History* had just been published, and its author was an even more animated conversationalist than usual. Alice noted his views carefully in her diary, and he was a frequent caller at the Brooke home in Manchester Square for the remainder of her stay.[17] While attracted to Green, she entertained some doubts because of his heterodox views on religion, and there does not seem to have been much contact for the next two years. By the end of 1876, they were seeing each other again, her scruples evidently overcome. Mrs. Stopford loomed as a potential obstacle to the match, however, and Green had to convince her that Alice's soul would not be placed in jeopardy by marrying him. In his initial letter, he concentrated on his financial and physical condition, telling that he could reckon on at least £1000 a year from his royalties. He was candid about his health: "I shall never be a strong man, and I may be a short-lived man."[18]

On the far touchier question of religion, he wrote to Mrs. Stopford a few days later:

> I believe that life with me, a life of real happiness and affection, will take from her much of the stress and strain under which her mind has of late been dwelling on religious difficulties; but not that it will take from her love of religion or her seeking to know what is spiritually true. In that seeking to know the truth we are one; and if our conclusions in some ways differ, this still leaves the sense of a common loyalty to Truth itself, of a common earnestness in the seeking after it.[19]

Far from being reassured by this letter, she tried to stop the match. But when she formally refused her assent to "a marriage which was not based on an identity of religious sentiments," Green replied that it was Alice's decision to make. Mrs. Stopford bowed to the inevitable, and the wedding plans went forward. Alice wrote to her sister that her betrothed had "great stores of affection, all the more from having long been pent up."[20] The intensity of his feelings, and their link to the emotional deprivation of his childhood, are well expressed in a letter to Alice three months before their marriage: "Dearest, you know how dependent I am on your love. There are moments, moments of weakness and weariness, when I feel like a little child and [illegible] cry for the sense of your arms around me."[21] Even in this emotional state he was able to mock his own anxieties in a letter to Olga von Glehn:

I see the ring is already on her finger! . . . Oh, Olga! may you never know what it is to be wedded against your will. Matrimony, once my fondest dream, is now my nightmare. In fact slavies sport in fancy round my bed— they flourish tiny brooms and dustpans, and call me "Father." I wake from horrid visions that *She* is mine, and I cannot give her a month's warning. Pray for me; and when you come again *storm* my stairs whether she will or no. How I would fly into your arms—if it were only proper—and hail you as my Deliverer.[22]

After their wedding in June 1877, the couple lived in a flat over a decorator's shop at 25 Connaught Street, just north of Hyde Park. Green had rented it the previous December, probably in anticipation of his marriage, and quickly made the four rooms "daintier and prettier than the rooms of old."[23] The "rooms of old" were his bachelor quarters at 4 Beaumont Street, Marylebone, where he had lived during the writing of the *Short History*. The association of the Marylebone address with his most famous work would, decades later, lead the London County Council to commemorate its site with a blue plaque, even though the residence had long been demolished. In the autumn of 1877, John and Alice moved to 50 Welbeck Street, and in 1880 finally settled at 14 Kensington Square, a comfortable Georgian house with a small garden. By that time, however, they were forced to spend a major portion of each year in Italy because of his worsening tubercular condition.

From the outset, the marriage was extremely happy. In January 1878 John Green wrote to Macmillan from Paris:

I can't tell you what a change and rest this new life is. The old work-worry is drifting away, and the holy day [holiday] feeling coming on fast. All my pleasure is doubled in little wifie: her care and thoughtfulness, her bright sociable temper, her clever talk and vivid interest, brighten everything. What a wonderful gift God gave me in life.[24]

He took Alice on a visit to Oxford, showing her his old haunts at Magdalen College, but refusing to set foot within Jesus College. They also went on a tour of historic sites in Britain, and called on Lord Tennyson at Aldworth. On parting, the Poet Laureate said to Green: "You're a jolly, vivid man, and I'm glad to have known you; you're as vivid as lightning."[25]

Thanks to Alice's vigorous assistance, Green was even more productive in the final six years of his life than in the preceding period, in spite of failing health. Between 1877 and 1880 he was writing the four-volume

History of England, and Alice was immensely helpful in researching, transcribing, checking references, and conducting business correspondence. Similar efforts on her part made possible the flurry of additional primers that were published under Green's editorship during this period. His work on this series had begun earlier in the decade, and he was able to boast to Alice shortly before their marriage that he had already produced nine primers selling about 100,000 copies a year, and that twelve more were on the way, by such authorities as Max Müller, Stopford Brooke, John Seeley, George Grove, F.J. Furnivall, and himself.[26] Green's contribution was to have been a primer of English history, but his enthusiasm for it quickly waned. In spite of Macmillan's urging, he was determined to write something more than "a good book which will sell."[27] It was this same concern to create only works that might have enduring value that led him to decline an offer from John Morley to do an article for the *Fortnightly Review:* "I don't grudge the years I spent on 'the Saturday' and other things—in some ways it was not bad training—but after all one ought to concentrate oneself on what may last further than on what *must* pass away."[28]

Although eager to press on with his plans to write additional serious history books of lasting value, Green was also determined to increase his income through editing primers and undertaking other publication projects with Macmillan. As he told Freeman, there were "heaps of such books which bring in £50 a year as regularly as clockwork," though he admitted that Alice was possibly right when she said he had a "Primer-fit."[29] In February 1879 Green signed no fewer than six contracts with Macmillan.[30] Three were for his services as editor—of Historical and Literary Primers, a Classical Writers series, and a Periods of English History series. His royalties for these were to be one-thirtieth of the price. He also renewed the contract on his *Stray Studies from England and Italy*—his collection of "middles" from the *Saturday Review.* One contract was for a new book that he would co-write with Alice on the geography of Britain. Finally, he agreed to produce a single-volume history of England composed of an anthology of selections from major historians.

Readings from English History was published in 1879 and reflects the same concern Green had shown in "Little Book" and "Big Book" for liveliness, readability, and a popular tone. He chose the most vivid passages from the works of thirty-three authors, including Freeman, Lingard, Froude, Macaulay, Palgrave, Brewer, Kingsley, Gardiner, Scott, Southey, and Samuel Smiles. French historians were represented by Michelet, Thierry, and Guizot; the Americans by Bancroft and Motley.[31] Green wrote the preface and introduction, as well as connective paragraphs between each selection. In the preface, he declared that while the study of English history was spreading rapidly in schools, it was still considered "hard, dry, and uninteresting," a perception the volume was intended to correct.[32] There was more of his own work than that of any other author. The following selections were taken from the *Short History:* The Early Englishmen, Dunstan, Blending of Conquerors and Conquered, John and the Charter, Expulsion of the Jews, The Peasant Rising, Joan of Arc, Caxton, Translation of the Bible, Protestant Martyrs, Shakespeare's Early Life, Milton, Charles II, *The Pilgrim's Progress,* Marlborough at Blenheim, Whitefield and Wesley, and Waterloo. Of a total of eighty-two selections in the book, twenty-nine are from the period between the Peasants' Revolt and Oliver Cromwell, an emphasis similar to that in the *Short History.* Another similarity to "Little Book" is the biographical emphasis of forty of the selections.

Also published in 1879 was the book he wrote with his wife, *A Short Geography of the British Islands.* It was a school text that aspired to do for geography what the *Short History* had done—infuse drama and interest into a field of study most pupils considered dry and onerous. John Green wrote the introduction to the volume, and proclaimed in his opening sentence: "No drearier task can be set for the worst of criminals than that of studying a set of geographical textbooks such as the children in our schools are doomed to use." He denounced conventional texts, with their endless and formidable tables of heights, areas, and populations, as "mere handbooks of mnemonics" designed to torment students. Against this forbidding methodology Green offered an approach that relied on narrative structure and literary power: "Geography, as its name implies, is an 'earth-picturing,' a presentment of earth or earth's surface in its actual form, and an indication of the influence which that form has exerted on human history or human society."[33]

The close connection between geography and history was a key feature of the book, though it was more pronounced in the sections on England and Wales written by John Green than in those on Scotland and Ireland by Alice. In his introduction to the book, Green laid considerable stress on the importance of geographic knowledge to historical understanding:

> History strikes its roots in Geography; for without a clear and vivid realization of the physical structures of a country the incidents of the life which men have lived in it can have no interest or meaning. Through History again Poli-

tics strike their roots in Geography, and many a rash generalization would have been avoided had political thinkers been trained in a knowledge of the earth they live in, and of the influence which its varying structure must needs exert on the varying political tendencies and institutions of the peoples who part its empire between them.[34]

This sense of the crucial effects of the natural environment on human development, which had been evident in the *Short History*, was to be even more pronounced in his penultimate book, *The Making of England.*

Green considered the *Readings* and the *Short Geography* to be likely money-makers and of some importance in furthering his views about history. Still, he was vexed by the reflection that he was widely regarded as a popularizer, and not taken altogether seriously by the emerging professional specialists. His sense of humor still served him well in these matters, as can be seen in a letter he wrote to Freeman while honeymooning in the north: "Your name is known unto the ends of the earth, while mine is unknown even in Scarborough. The doctor who visits me here is innocent of the Short History or of its author, and seeing it on the table noted blandly 'Ah same name as yours! is it a nice book?' "[35]

In 1881, Freeman, writing from Baltimore, was able to assure him of his great popularity in the United States: "You will be glad to hear that we are all, you, I, Bryce, Stubbs, much honoured on this side of the river Ocean. . . . Everybody says that you are mightily read and run after."[36] But popularity alone no longer sufficed, for Green knew that it was for the *Short History of the English People,* a general work that some considered simply a lively school manual. The impulse to leave a solid, unimpeachable work of scholarship as a legacy remained compelling.

By 1879, he was able to declare that he had "a satisfactory income, the best of wives, and a happy home; while my health, which so long troubled me, seems now to be fairly restored."[37] The restored health proved an illusion; later that year his tubercular condition was tormenting him again, requiring the couple to spend more and more time abroad. Still, with Alice's care and assistance, and by carefully husbanding his strength, he might hope to achieve unqualified admission into the ranks of the leading historians.

The only other publishing venture he allowed to intrude during these last years was an edition of Joseph Addison's essays. Ever since his schoolboy fascination with Addison's Walk in Oxford, Green had been a devotee of the great essayist. The witty skewering of pomp, power, and pretentiousness in Addison's work was exactly to Green's taste. Equally important, the essays were genuinely popular in tone. As Green remarked in the introduction: "Literature suddenly doffed its stately garb of folio or octavo, and stepped abroad in the light and easy dress of pamphlet and essay. Its long arguments and cumbrous sentences condensed themselves into the quick reasoning and terse easy phrase of ordinary conversation."[38]

Green noted that Addison was a clergyman but remarkably free of any bigotry. He excluded from the collection all of Addison's political, moral, and theological essays, asserting that what was left was Addison's "large and generous humanity."[39] The essays Green chose to print were social satire, not unlike his own middles from the *Saturday Review*. They included Sir Roger de Coverley, Tattler's Court, Stateswomen, Humors of the Town, Tales and Allegories, Court of Honour, Country Humour, and Humours of Fashion.

Having honored a long-term source of inspiration and celebrated his own journalistic moorings by publishing the Addison volume, Green was at last free to turn to his final scholarly labors. Freeman, who had been so disappointed in 1875 when Green had turned his back on the long-deferred study of the Angevins in favor of one on early England, no longer entertained any hope that Green might some day return to it. The Angevins project had already been turned over to Kate Norgate (1853–1935), a young protégé of Green whom he had met a few months before his marriage. Using some of Green's research materials, Norgate would labor on her book for over ten years before it was finally published in 1887. Green gave generously of his time and advice, encouraging Norgate to work hard at visualizing the scenes and settings of history, for it is "only by seeing things ourselves that we can make others see them." For all the importance of source criticism and a skeptical, balanced approach to the past, Green told her, the most important quality was imagination. It was therefore necessary to "dwell upon these names till they become real to us, real places, real battles, real men and women—and it is only when this reality has struck in upon us and we 'see' that we can so describe, so represent that others see too." Seize upon certain key characters, he continued, "let your mind play on them, write them when you feel they are real and life-like to you, do not be afraid of exaggeration or over-rhetoric (that is easily got rid of later on), but just strive after *realization* and you will write history."[40] But he was never doctrinaire in his counsel, telling her in a subsequent letter full of specific suggestions that "these are simply hints to help you, for you will have to work in your own way, as we all have."[41]

It was quite natural for Green to return to the early England project that he had abandoned several years earlier. By the time work commenced on *The Making of England* and *The Conquest of England*, the Greens were ensconced in their comfortable house at 14 Kensington Square. In spite of his declining health and a demanding scholarly regimen, they kept one of the liveliest salons in London. Mrs. Humphry Ward recalled later that

> the pretty house in Kensington Square was the centre of a small society such as England produces much more rarely than France. Mr. Lecky came—Sir Henry Maine, Mr. Freeman, Mr. Bryce, Bishop Stubbs sometimes, Mr. Stopford Brooke, and many more. It was the talk of equals, ranging the widest horizons, started and sustained by the energy, the undauntedness of a dying man. There in the corner of the sofa sat the thin wasted form, life flashing from the eyes, breathing from the merry or eloquent lips, beneath the very shadow and seal of death—the eternal protesting life of the intelligence. His talk *gave* perpetually. Much of the previous talk of the world has not been a giving but a gathering and plundering talk. . . . But Mr. Green's talk was of the best kind, abundant, witty, disinterested; and his poet's instinct for the lives and thoughts of others, his quick imagination, his humorous and human curiosity about all sorts and sides of things made pose and pedantry impossible to him. He could be extravagant and provoking; it was always easy to set him on edge, and call up a mood of irritation and paradox. But as he grew happier, as success and fame came to him, he grew gentler and more pliable.[42]

Unacknowledged in this tribute was Alice's role in making their home a magnet for some of the leading Victorian intellects. Far from being merely a dutiful hostess, Alice relished lively company, and her own conversational powers are attested to by the fact that she continued to attract major figures to Kensington Square for many years after Green's death.

Portions of *The Making of England* were written in London, but much of it was composed or compiled in Italy and at various other spots the Greens visited. By 1880, his doctors had warned him that the severity of his tuberculosis made his very survival dependent on seeking out warmer and sunnier climes. Italy had been an annual destination since 1869, so it was natural to extend these winter sojourns. A journey to Egypt in January 1881, however, nearly proved fatal. After surviving a gale that almost sank their ship, the couple arrived in Cairo only to find unhealthy conditions. Proceeding to Luxor, they visited one of the tombs, and Green was badly injured when a rocket, thought by his guide to be a candle, blew up in his hand. In shock and with his arm badly burnt from elbow to fingertips, he had to endure a three-hour return trip in terrible heat. Convalescing in Luxor with the temperature sometimes reaching 115 degrees, he still managed to get some writing done. On the journey home, his life was threatened by bitterly cold weather at Avignon.[43]

After their return to London, Green's physician, Andrew Clark, declared that he had only six weeks to live. Upon receiving this grim news, John and Alice set resolutely to work. It was she who devised the scheme of dividing the work into two separate volumes, with the first (*The Making of England*) able to stand as his final scholarly testament should he die before undertaking the later Anglo-Saxon and Norman period.[44] With the author prostrate and unable even to hold a pen for many weeks, Alice had to take dictation and look up references in addition to her nursing duties. Many of the sections were rewritten numerous times, though some material had been written long before, and some passages were lifted directly from the *Short History*. By late autumn, their labors were at an end, and the book was published in January 1882.

In the preface to *The Making of England* Green described his desire to bring the Anglo-Saxon age to life, so that it would no longer be, as it was for Milton, a story of "mere battles of kites and of crows." He also made reference to Freeman's attempt to dissuade him from the enterprise:

> The remoteness of the events, the comparative paucity of historical materials, no doubt make such an undertaking at the best a hazardous one; and one of the wisest of my friends, . . . the greatest living authority on our early history, warned me at the outset against the attempt to construct a living portraiture of times which so many previous historians . . . had left dead.[45]

Green declared his intention to deploy two kinds of sources that had been all but ignored by previous writers on the subject—archaeolgy and geography. Archaeolgical research, he asserted, often furnished evidence that was "more trustworthy than that of written chronicles," while the terrain itself, "where we can read the information it affords, is, whether in the history of the Conquest or of the Settlement of Britain, the fullest and most certain of documents."[46] If the first of these shows the influence of his friend William Boyd Dawkins, the second was a deep interest of long standing, recently strengthened by working with Alice on *A Short Geography of the British Islands*.

Both kinds of evidence are used throughout the book, though typically to embellish narrative passages based on more traditional sources. In some cases he cautions that the physical record may distort history, an example being the non-survival of the rows of slaves huts alongside the impressive remains of Roman villas in Britain. Here imagination must come into play, for a single wretched hut of the underclass, "in its dark contrast with the comfort and splendor of the mansion itself, would have painted for us far better than a thousand passages from law or chronicle the union of material wealth with social degradation that lay like a dark shadow over the Roman world."[47] More directly, field work could illuminate historic events and processes for which there were no literary sources, especially for the chaotic period of the Anglo-Saxon migrations into Britain:

> If history tells us nothing of the victories that laid this great district [in the north] at the feet of its conquerors, the spade of the archaeolgist has done somewhat to reveal the ruin and misery of the conquered people. The caves of the Yorkshire moorlands preserve traces of the miserable fugitives who fled to them for shelter.[48]

His footnote reference for this passage was to Dawkins's *Cave Hunting.*

Green also treated seriously the effects of geography on Roman Britain and early English history. In the table of contents for the introductory chapter on the Roman period, there are subheadings titled "Its Civilization Hindered by the Physical Character of the Country," "Its Downs," "Its Waste and Fen," "Its Woodlands," and "Effects of this on the Provincials." The chapter on "Conquests of the Engle" begins with a geographical subsection on "The Bulk of Britain Still Guarded by Strong Natural Barriers." That on "Conquests of the Saxons" starts with "Character of the British Coast to the Westward of Sussex" and "The Estuary of the Southampton Water Leads up to Gwent." There are other sections in the body of the same chapter, such as "Original Character of the Ground about London." While these passages are inserted in the midst of more conventional narrative and are sometimes little more than descriptive embellishments, they do represent a signal advance in historical accounts of early England. Freeman and other writers on the topic had not accorded as much significance to geography, and had virtually ignored archaeology.

Some readers of *The Making of England* must have been struck by the familiar ring of certain passages, for Green did not scruple to lift whole sections out of the *Short History,* sometimes altering a few words. The section on the "sacred spot" of Hengest's landing is an example.[49] Others include Augustine's arrival, the ecclesiastical reorganization by Theodore of Tarsus, Baeda's character, and Ecgberht's triumph over Mercia and Northumbria.[50] Other parts had been written years earlier, like the treatment of *Beowulf*.[51] In spite of these borrowings, the great bulk of *The Making of England* was original material, informed by Green's characteristic descriptive and storytelling powers.

As far as the overall interpretation, it was even more ardently Teutonist than the *Short History*. In the preface, he described the age as one "during which our fathers conquered and settled over the soil of Britain, and in which their political and social life took the form which it still retains."[52] If the essence of "Liberal Descent" doctrine is embodied in this passage, it was made much more explicit in a long and reverent section treating the life of the freemen and their active participation in village moots and hundred moots. Green asserted, somewhat solemnly, a direct link between these early English local assemblies and Victorian Parliaments:

> A humorist of our own day has laughed at parliaments as "talking-shops," and the laugh has been echoed by some who have taken humor for argument. But talk is persuasion, and persuasion is force, the one force which can sway freemen to deeds such as those which have made England what she is. The "talk" of the village moot, the strife and judgment of men giving freely their own rede and setting it as freely aside for what they learn to be the wiser rede of other men, is the groundwork of English history.[53]

Similar significance was accorded to the church synods established by Theodore of Tarsus in the seventh century. These, Green claimed, "led the way to our National Parliament; while the canons which these councils enacted, though carefully avoiding all direct intermeddling with secular matters, pointed the way to a national system of law."[54]

The Greens were in Mentone when the book was published and the first reviews began to appear. Alice wrote to Macmillan that her husband was deeply gratified to be getting favorable reviews and was particularly pleased to receive a positive assessment of the book in a letter from Henry Adams.[55] But while Adams did praise Green's lively style, he also chided him, only partly in jest, for his serious devotion to the topic. "The whole Anglo-Saxon history," he wrote, "reads to me like that of the Iroquois and Creeks. We know the kind of animal the archaic man is. That you should devote yourself to them in a spirit of ancestral homage troubles me as though I saw a diamond used to cut slate rock." As for the Anglo-Saxon people, Adams continued: "For some six or seven centuries they muddled their brains with beer and cut each other's throats for amusement, and did not even leave an institution worth preserving, for a rottener society never existed than that which the Normans so easily extinguished."[56]

Green may have been influenced by Adams's views when, two weeks later, he wrote to Freeman to thank him for his review. In a sharp retreat from the positive picture of the Anglo-Saxon age in *The Making of England*, he admitted that he had grown weary of the subject, especially as he approached the end of the volume, and that this made the thought of a sequel increasingly distasteful:

> The truth is the subject tempts me less and less the more I work at it. The more I study the two centuries before Ecgberht, the more I see the old free constitution crushed out by the political consolidation, the old Folk-moot dying with the Folk themselves into the local shire and shire-moot; and by the extinction of the old Ætheling class and the upgrowth of the big kingdoms transformed into a small royal council. After Ecgberht things only grow worse; and closer study of the law and administrative acts convinces me that the conquest was continuous from Hengest to William, that in spite of all the West Saxon brag the Danelagh remained virtually independent from Ælfred to Eadward's day, . . . As I read it the story isn't a pretty one, and the people aren't pretty people to write about.[57]

Yet in spite of these misgivings and his worsening health, he believed that the book was at last earning him that reputation as a serious historian that had so long eluded him: "What has cheered me most . . . has been the reception of 'Making.' I don't mean its sale and the praise of it, but the cessation at last of that attempt, which has been so steadily carried on for the last ten years, to drum me out of the world of historical scholars and set me among the 'picturesque compilers.'" The effort, he noted, "cost me many a bitter hour, but I suppose it is now over."[58]

Green's labors on the book, while taxing his health severely, had not yet proved fatal. Having survived well beyond Sir Andrew Clark's allotted six weeks, he was now hopeful that sufficient time might remain to complete the companion volume. He spent a considerable period after completing the *Making of England* in the autumn of 1881 recuperating in their new winter home, the Villa San Nicolas in Mentone, before starting the preliminary work on *The Conquest of England*. Back in London by late spring of 1882, he began to compile notes for the new work, and by the autumn he and Alice were organizing the final expedition to Italy, where the book would be written. Alice wrote to Macmillan that Green was so eager to press on with the project that during a delay at Nice, he was "covering sheets of paper with notes for his next volume!" She also asked the publisher to arrange to have *The Times* and some of the major reviews (including the *Saturday Review*) sent to them.[59]

They were happy to be back in their sunny villa, though Alice was dismayed by the recent encroachments of tourism and gambling on Mentone: "Our hillside . . . is becoming covered with hotels—alas! And a Casino(!) is threatened close by—so we need not go to Monaco to lose our souls."[60] Green's health had continued to deteriorate, and Alice's duties as both nurse and amanuensis increased accordingly. At one point, disabled by a severe attack of writer's cramp, she had to toil on in awkward and halting fashion with her left hand. Green fought off depression by numerous make-believe activities, such as warming his toes at an unlit hearth, pretending to be in England.[61] Alice recorded that her husband fought so bravely against despair that "meals often turned into festivals and poor little drives and walks became holiday excursions."[62]

Green was torn between his eagerness to finish the *Conquest* and his urge to improve it through frequent revisions. The latter impulse won out. There were numerous changes, even after the book went to press. A clearly exasperated Alice wrote to Macmillan in December 1882:

> Mr. Green is so dissatisfied with it in its present form that he wants to cut it up into new and strange chapters. Whether he will really change it or not, I can't yet say, but he wants at least to make experiments. One would have thought that it had gone through so many changes that there were no more metamorphoses left.[63]

He did decide to make wholesale alterations, requiring the recall of 4,000 copies that had been printed.[64] This was in January 1883, and represented his final burst of creativity and will-power. Thereafter he was too weak to carry on, and the final chapters had to be completed by Alice from his rough notes.

The Conquest of England is less innovative than the *Making of England*—there is no use of archaeological evidence and few references to geography. This is partly because Green was covering the ninth through the eleventh centuries, a period for which there were many more literary sources than for the earlier period. It is also due to the fact that major portions of the book had been written much earlier, just after the publication of the *Short History*. Alice explained in the preface that since her husband was unable to finish the book, she had drawn together the concluding chapters on "The Reign of Cnut," "The House of Godwine," and "The Norman Conquest" from materials he had written in 1875.[65] These chapters, a very detailed and masterfully wrought account of the political machinations and diplomatic maneuvers of the leaders of eleventh-century England, Normandy, and Norway, are the most impressive portion of the book. While they were not Green's last words as a historian since they were written eight years earlier, it is ironic that they constitute the concluding section of his final book. They show that, in spite of his having built his reputation on disparaging the overemphasis on politics in history, he was unexcelled as a political historian.

During the last weeks of Green's life, Alexander Macmillan and his wife, alarmed by Alice's reports of her husband's impending demise, left for Mentone. Established in a nearby hotel, they paid daily visits. Macmillan was struck by the dying historian's still sharp powers of analysis, and later wrote to the archbishop of Dublin, Dr. Trench:

> He could rarely bear more than a few minutes' talk at a time, but every utterance was as clear and vivid as it ever was. When one went up in the morning—our hotel was only five minutes' walk from their pleasant little Villa—he had read the little local paper that gave all the telegrams, and with that marvellous power he had of catching the *vital part* in whatever came before him could tell you all you could learn of importance in the longer, later papers. Thanks greatly to the absolute self-sacrifice of his noble, tender, wise wife, he had little, if any, actual suffering, and the natural sense of decaying physical power was borne with admirable patience. I think he had grown in moral sweetness of late years, and one saw its results in those last weeks.[66]

Others who came to visit Green during his final weeks were James Bryce, Humphry Ward, and Brooke Lambert. By 3 March 1883, he was too weak to see anyone but his wife; four days later he died.[67] To Stubbs, Alexander Macmillan wrote: "No man ever lived, I think, who had more the making of a real historian than he had, because he felt keenly, charitably, largely, humanly, man's works and aims."[68]

Green was interred in the Campo Santo above Mentone, with the simple epitaph he had created for himself years earlier inscribed on the tombstone: "John Richard Green, the historian of the English people. He died learning."[69]

NOTES

1. Green to Dawkins, 2 Oct. 1860, LJRG, 47. He told Dawkins: "I hardly knew how heavy my yoke had been till it was thus once and for ever broken and thrown off. Thanks to you, old boy!"

2. Green to Dawkins, 30 June 1864, LJRG, 149.

3. LJRG, 68.

4. Green to Mrs. Mandel Creighton (Louise von Glehn), 4 March 1877, LJRG, 448.

5. He got Macmillan to hire Olga to do the index for his four-volume *History of the English People*. Green to Alexander Macmillan, 29 July 1879. Macmillan Archives, B.L. ADD. MSS. 55,058, fo. 225.

6. Green to Dawkins, 12 Sept. 1866, Jesus College MS. 199, J 49/3.

7. This popular work by Jean Anthèlme Brillat-Savarin (1755–1826), which has attracted the attention of modern scholars like Roland Barthes, was reprinted often throughout the nineteenth century. Green was probably reading the 1866 edition: *Physiologie du goût: ou, Méditations de gastronomie transcendante; ouvrage théorique, historique, et à l'ordre du jour, dedié aux gastronomes Parisiens* (Paris: Garnier Frères, 1866).

8. Green to Edward Denison, 6 Aug. 1868, LJRG, 196.

9. Green to Olga von Glehn, 9 Jan. 1871, LJRG, 276–77.

10. Green to Louise von Glehn, 6 March 1871, LJRG, 287. Original emphasis.

11. Louise Creighton, "Some Reminiscences of J. R. Green," *Longman's Magazine* 39 (1902): 317–18.

12. Mrs. Humphry Ward, *A Writer's Recollections* (New York and London: Harpers, 1918), 1: 190–91

13. John Sutherland, *Mrs Humphry Ward* (Oxford: Clarendon Press, 1990), 61–62.

14. Green to Mrs. Humphry Ward, 9 Oct. 1876, LJRG, 439–40.

15. Freeman to Green, 20 Nov. 1873, E.A. Freeman Archives, John Rylands Library of Manchester University, FA 1/8/21a.

16. See R. B. McDowell, *Alice Stopford Green, a Passionate Historian* (Dublin: Allen Figgis, 1967).

17. Ibid., 22–23.

18. Green to Mrs. Stopford, 18 Jan. 1877, Green MSS., Jesus College Uncatalogued MSS. The letter is misdated 1876.

19. Green to Mrs. Stopford, 22 Jan. 1877, Green MSS., Jesus College Uncatalogued MSS. A few months later he formally tendered his resignation as a clergyman. Green to Crawford Tait, 25 April 1877, Tait Papers, MS. 97. fos. 128–31, Lambeth Palace.

20. McDowell, *Alice Stopford Green*, 43–44.

21. Green to Alice Stopford, 7 Feb. 1877, Jesus College MS. 233, J 49/6.

22. Green to Olga von Glehn, May 1877, LJRG, 461.

23. Green to Freeman, 1 Dec. 1876, LJRG, 440.

24. Green to Alexander Macmillan, 21 Jan. 1878, Macmillan Archives, B.L. ADD. MS. 55,058, fo. 146.

25. LJRG, 393.

26. Green to Alice Stopford, 20 March 1877, LJRG, 449.

27. Green to Alice Stopford, 5 June 1877, LJRG, 469.

28. Green to Alice Stopford, 26 Jan. 1877, Green MSS, Jesus College MS. 233. Original emphasis.

29. Green to Freeman, 24 June 1878, Jesus College MS. 202, J 49/6.

30. Macmillan Archives, B. L. ADD. MS. 55,058, fos. 206–12.

31. A few days before his marriage, Green attended the memorial service for Motley at Westminster Abbey. In a letter to Alice, Green praised Motley for his ability to "knit together not only America and England, but that older England which we left on Frisian shores, and which grew into the United Netherlands. A child of America, the historian of Holland, he made England his adopted home, and in England his body rests." LJRG, 468.

32. *Readings from English History*, selected and edited by John Richard Green (London: Macmillan, 1879), iii.

33. John Richard Green and Alice Stopford Green, *A Short Geography of the British Islands* (London: Macmillan, 1879), vii.

34. Ibid., xi.

35. Green to Freeman, 10 July 1877, Edinburgh University MS. 35/165, fo. 130.

36. Freeman to Green, 22 Nov. 1881, Jesus College MS. 202, J 49/6.

37. Green to Mr. [Richard?] Castle, 4 Feb. 1879, Lambeth Palace MS. 1735, fo. 124.

38. *Essays of Joseph Addison*, chosen and edited by John Richard Green (London: Macmillan, 1880), vi.

39. Ibid., xxiv.

40. Green to Kate Norgate, 5 March 1877, LJRG, 448–49. Original emphasis.

41. Green to Kate Norgate, 18 June 1877, LJRG, 471.

42. LJRG, 397. James Bryce, describing Stopford Brooke's conversational powers, could think of no higher praise than to observe that he had "as much quickness and fun" as Green. L.P. Jacks, *Life and Letters of Stopford Brooke* (London: John Murray, 1917), 2: 635.

43. LJRG, 398.

44. Ibid., 399.

45. *The Making of England* (London: Macmillan, 1882), vi.

46. Ibid., vi–vii.

47. Ibid., 43–44.

48. Ibid., 64.

49. Ibid., 28.

50. Ibid., 214, 324, 392, 424.

51. Ibid., 155–58.

52. Ibid., v.

53. Ibid., 188.

54. Ibid., 324.

55. Alice Green to Alexander Macmillan, 24 April 1882, Macmillan Archives, B. L. ADD. MS. 55,059, fos. 26–27.

56. Henry Adams to Green, 9 April 1882, Green MSS., Uncatalogued MS., Jesus College.

57. Green to Freeman, 8 May 1882, LJRG, 481–82.

58. Ibid., 482.

59. Alice Green to Alexander Macmillan, n.d. [1882], Macmillan Archives, B. L. ADD. MS. 55,059, fo. 32.

60. Ibid., fos. 30–31.

61. LJRG, 401.

62. Quoted in McDowell, 45.

63. Alice Green to Alexander Macmillan, 16 Dec. 1882, Macmillan Archives, B. L. ADD. MS. 55,059, fos. 28–29.

64. LJRG, 401.

65. *The Conquest of England* (London: Macmillan, 1883), xiv–xv.

66. Alexander Macmillan to Richard Chenevix Trench, 6 April 1883, Charles L. Graves, *Life and Letters of Alexander Macmillan* (London: Macmillan, 1910), 366.

67. LJRG, 401–02.

68. Alexander Macmillan to William Stubbs, 10 April 1883, Graves, 367.

69. Mrs. Humphry Ward, *A Writer's Recollections*, 1: 192; LJRG, 402; Letter from the Rev. W. Fowell Swann, *The Times*, 13 Dec. 1937, 8.

10. Aftermath and Legacy

While most of the obituaries of Green were laudatory, Freeman's struck a critical note. During the last year of Green's life, Freeman had begun to adopt a markedly critical, peevish tone, for which Macmillan had reproved him, likening it to "always flicking a horse going uphill."[1] Freeman's obituary of Green was discerning in its stress on the importance of his Oxford boyhood and resulting lifelong devotion to the spirit of municipal liberty.[2] He also invoked, with obvious affection, his recollections of "little Johnny Green" at Magdalen College Grammar School and the pleasure of being reintroduced in 1862 to the unknown but brilliant young clergyman and scholar. Much of Freeman's article, however, had a bitter tone. He clearly felt a keen disappointment, even a sense of betrayal, at Green's refusal to become his protégé and take up the project on the Angevins.

In Freeman's eyes, Green's rejection of his mentoring role was compounded by the younger man's insistence on making political history secondary to broader social and cultural currents. Still smarting over Green's review of his *Norman Conquest* fifteen years earlier, Freeman noted: "He said many brilliant, many sharp, many true things; but he never got over the temptation, one most dangerous for a reviewer, to judge everything by himself. He unconsciously thought that every man was bound to do his work in his, John Richard Green's, way."[3] There was also a lingering resentment at being neglected by Green following the great public acclaim for the *Short History:* "He never visited me after 1875; I never could get him to stir. . . . I sometimes saw him in London; but he was now grown famous and was sought after; it was not so easy as in the old times to get him by himself or in the company of common friends only."[4] Neither could Freeman resist calling attention to the "waywardness and capri-

ciousness" of Green's views of established institutions and to his willingness to sacrifice accuracy in order "to make a good story still better."[5]
Overall, it was a petulant, mean-spirited obituary from the pen of Green's
supposedly closest friend, and was thrown sharply into relief by being
immediately followed in the same issue of the *British Quarterly Review*
by a judicious assessment of Green's work by the geographer J. Scott
Keltie (1840–1927).[6] It also stands in sharp contrast to the handsome
tribute paid by Stubbs in his final lecture as Regius Professor on 8 May
1884:

> For twenty years he and I were close friends; with countless differences of
> opinion, we never quarreled; with opposite views of the line of history and of
> the value of character, we never went into controversy; his letters were a de-
> light and honour to me; I believe that my visits were a pleasure and in some
> way a comfort to him. In the joint dedication of his book I confess that I re-
> ceived a compliment which I place on a level with the highest honours I have
> ever received.[7]

The passage of time failed to soften Freeman's attitude; it was still
evident four years after Green's death, when he reviewed Kate Norgate's
England under the Angevin Kings in the *English Historical Review*.[8] Norgate dedicated her book "to the memory of my dear and honoured master
John Richard Green." In his review, Freeman observed: "In many things
indeed, she has improved on her master; her work, if less brilliant, is im-
measurably more sound. There are no signs in her of the inborn caprice
and love of paradox which make Green's writings dangerous to those who
have to take things on a modern writer's word."[9] There is as much space
devoted to Green as there is to Norgate in the review, and it is characterized by the same sense of betrayal that informed the obituary: "Speaking
for myself, I would give up all that he actually wrote—save a great deal in
the 'Making' and some things in the 'Conquest of England'— to have the
Angevin history which he once promised me, and which would assuredly
have been a masterpiece indeed."[10] As late as 1889, Freeman was still not
able to forgive Green's harsh judgments on the monarchy and the Church
hierarchy: "Johnny Green . . . had ever a mocking vein, which did not
do."[11]

Freeman's criticisms of Green were naturally offensive to Alice, but a
rupture in their relationship was already developing over her attempts to
secure all of Green's letters for a planned published collection. The problem arose when both Freeman and Dawkins refused to turn over a number

of Green's letters. Since Alice had their letters to Green, she was aware of the gaps and pressed them to provide the omitted material. She got S. R. Gardiner to act as an intermediary, but he had to report that the men refused out of concern that Alice would be shocked by the revelations of "all the temptations and trials of early life" and "falls before temptation"—the reference to Green's sexual improprieties while an East End clergyman.[12] Later, Gardiner lamented that he had ever revealed anything to her and thus caused a great deal of pain: "It was almost dragged out of me by my having to account for Freeman's refusal to allow her to see the letters, when I was negotiating about them."[13]

There the matter rested until Freeman's death in 1892. Since Freeman's family wished to publish his letters, Alice now had considerable leverage in the form of Freeman's many letters to Green, which were in her possession. When his daughter Margaret Evans (wife of the archaeologist Arthur Evans), attempted to secure her father's letters, Alice refused, asserting that she had a very good reason, "as you can judge if you know the *whole* story of what has happened with regard to the correspondence and the position in which I have been placed."

At this juncture, Kate Norgate was employed as a go-between, but without success. Her meeting with the Evanses was "very painful" to Margaret, and the dispute over the correspondence went unresolved.[14] Dawkins also remained unmoved by Alice's appeals to send her Green's letters in their entirety. He would provide only verbatim copies, "with the exception of certain blanks which had better remain blank." When Alice tried again, Dawkins urged her not to press him to fill in the blanks "of a correspondence written in the frankest and most outspoken confidence of a youthful friendship and relating to many living people."[15]

The result of this impasse was the unfortunate suppression of vital documentary material relating to the lives of two of the leading historians of the Victorian age, which certainly contained important information on other persons and events. The omission is bad enough in Green's case, but at least in the collection of letters edited by Leslie Stephen, a large number of Green's letters to Freeman and Dawkins were included. Indeed, had all her husband's letters been returned to her, Alice would certainly not have printed any of the ones she most wanted to see. She was being advised to omit "private and intimate exchanges of views as to persons (and occasionally things) rather *too* personal (at all events for years) of being published."[16] In the case of Freeman, the situation is worse, since Alice Green steadfastly refused to return any of his letters. In the two volumes of collected letters edited by W. R. W. Stephens and published in 1895, there is not a single letter from Freeman to Green, even though it is likely that he wrote more letters to Green than to any one else.

Struggling to bring to print as complete a collection as possible of Green's correspondence represented only a small part of Alice's literary endeavors. During the first decade or so after his death, she emerged as an author in her own right, publishing historical works that showed the influence of her late husband. She and Kate Norgate were the most immediate transmitters of his legacy. Norgate's influence was more modest, though arguably she was the better historian; the numerous studies of the Angevins, many of them biographical, which she produced before her death in 1935, had a limited impact. Her work was too scholarly for a popular audience, and yet was never fully accepted by the academic establishment.

Alice was involved in collecting and publishing Green's essays as well as in editing and revising subsequent editions of the *Short History*. This included the illustrated four-volume edition of 1892–94, which fulfilled its author's long-held desire. Her vigorous initiatives and business acumen helped ensure that the first three editions of the *Short History* sold 326,000 copies, while the illustrated edition sold 50,000. She also helped to arrange for the numerous foreign translations that appeared before the end of the century: Italian in 1884, French in 1885, German in 1889, Russian in 1891, and Chinese in 1898. But her own written work also served to transmit her husband's legacy. Her first book, a biography of Henry II, was published in 1888. She was asked to undertake it, in spite of the skepticism of Mandell and Louise Creighton,[17] by John Morley as part of the Twelve English Statesmen series he was editing for Macmillan.

The opening line of Alice's book evoked John Green's passionate insistence that commoners, not kings, were the real shapers of England's glory: "The history of the English people would have been a great and noble history whatever king had ruled over the land seven hundred years ago."[18] Thereafter, however, the book settled down into a rather conventional biography, which was politely received[19] but made little impact. Her second effort was more provocative. In *Town Life in the Fifteenth Century* (1894), she focused squarely on an issue that had been so central to her late husband—the periodic emergence of civic oligarchies and the suppression of popular government.[20] Mandell Creighton told her that her book was a "worthy successor to Mr. Green's work, and carries on his spirit into a detailed treatment of a particular epoch in a way which is sure to be fruitful."[21]

While this book marked her as a direct intellectual heir of John Richard Green, it was to be her last on English history. Thereafter, she turned out a succession of ardently nationalist histories of her native land, starting with *The Making of Ireland and its Undoing* (1908). She returned to Ireland at the end of World War I, living in Dublin through the travails of the Anglo-Irish War (she was listed as a "suspect" by British authorities) and the Irish Civil War. Recognition of her important role in stimulating the historical knowledge and national pride of the people of Ireland through her books and public lectures came with her appointment to the Senate of the Irish Free State. She died in 1929.

In an interview in 1921, Alice Green reflected on how her husband's inspiration had shaped her work on the history of the Irish people: "No one could come in contact with Mr. Green without a deepened sense of how free peoples should rightly live both as regards themselves and their neighbors."[22] It was fitting that his legacy should be applied so directly in Ireland, for he had once planned to write a history of that country as well as a biography of St. Patrick.[23] Furthermore, as James Bryce observed, Green's sympathy for national movements embraced Ireland and "made him a Home Ruler long before Mr. Gladstone and the Liberal Party adopted that policy."[24]

The vital function that Alice's work served in Ireland was not as necessary in England partly for the reason that John Richard Green's popular influence was still very much alive there. A cheap edition of the *Short History* remained in print and, given the brisk sales in the first years of its publication, large numbers of reasonably priced used copies were available. Libraries were another important resource. Working-class readers drew as much inspiration from Green's work as did middle-class readers, as an examination of the reading habits of early Labour Party MPs makes clear. In 1906 the *Review of Reviews* published a survey of Labour MPs, seeking to discover which authors had proved most influential in their development. As the editor noted in the introduction, none of the forty-five parliamentarians who responded had been at Oxford or Cambridge: "What culture they have they obtained from the chapel, from that popular university the public library, or still more frequently from the small collection of books found in the homes of the poor."[25] Among the historians mentioned by the respondents, Green was second only to Macaulay. Moreover, Green's *Short History* was frequently on the assigned reading lists for classes sponsored by the Workers' Educational Association.[26]

When the copyright lapsed on the *Short History*, the publishing house of J.M. Dent brought out a two volume edition for Everyman's Library, using the original 1874 text and incorporating a lackluster account of events from 1815 to 1914 by R.P. Farley to replace Green's brief appendix.[27] A variety of updated versions have appeared since. Everyman's Library, with its mass-produced, inexpensive editions of out-of-copyright works, was aimed at non-elite readers, among whom the *Short History* had found favor all along. In addition to Green, the nineteenth-century historians of England published by Dent in this series were Carlyle, Froude, Hallam, and Macaulay. Together they might be said to represent the distilled essence of popular historical scholarship on England. It is their books, rather than the monographs of the professional scholars, that have been a major force in shaping whatever historical understanding may be said to reside among non-academicians. Historical writers of the twentieth century with a comparable impact include such diverse figures as G.M. Trevelyan, J.L. and Barbara Hammond, Arthur Bryant, and Winston Churchill. Professional historians are not without some popular influence, of course, though it has necessarily been mediated by several layers of the educational hierarchy, and thus attenuated, simplified, and distorted— even at the middle levels of educational attainment. At the lower end it is probably nonexistent.

While Freeman's harsh assessment of Green's work was partly determined by an intensely personal sense of disappointment at having his protégé abandon the project he had marked out for him, there was another factor at work: the disdain of a "professional" historian for an "amateur" and popularizer. By the 1880s, history was securely lodged in university curricula and about to undergo rapid development as an academic specialization. Freeman was appointed Regius Professor of Modern History at Oxford on Stubbs's retirement from the chair (to become Bishop of Chester) in 1884. Freeman and others in the emerging historical profession of the late nineteenth century—the professors, the researchers, the indefatigable toilers in archives and fashioners of learned monographs— were apt to find the *Short History* too "literary" and wanting in scholarly rigor. An example of this attitude can be seen in the obituary of Green written by Samuel Rawson Gardiner. Seemingly a generous tribute that lacked the personal pique of Freeman's reflections, Gardiner's account yet carries a patronizing tone:

> Anyone who writes history knows of the frequent searches into authorities, the necessity of running off, even when proof sheets are in hand, to the

record Office or the Museum to verify a reference suspected to have been wrongly made. How could an invalid weakened by disease do all this? How could he stop to master the latest teaching of ethnology, or to study some new work on constitutional law, or to make himself at home in the political science of Bacon or Burke? His work has to be done in haste with what intellectual furniture he has, lest death should overtake him in doing that which, if it had been possible, he would willingly have delayed for another ten or fifteen years.[28]

Furthermore, the work of the professorial scholars, based on massive research in primary sources and concerned with political and constitutional issues, projected a sense of the majesty of England's historic institutions and avoided the harsh, mocking tone Green had used toward English monarchs and social elites. Stubbs, an ardent admirer of Ranke, set the tone in medieval constitutional studies, and his work was carried forward by such disciples as T.F. Tout, J.H. Round, and Reginald Poole.[29] Typical of the new approach was the publication by Longmans in 1905 of a twelve-volume *Political History of England* under Poole's editorship.[30] Each volume was written by a specialist in the period, an approach already taken by Lord Acton in the *Cambridge Modern History,* which also had a political emphasis. Publications were increasingly designed to be read only by fellow professionals, often in the form of heavily footnoted articles in the new *English Historical Review.* Under the new dispensation, a single-volume history of England by one man did not pass muster, especially when written with a social and cultural emphasis, based on chronicles and literary materials rather than archival sources, and informed by irreverent criticisms and populist values.

It is true that at the level of undergraduate education, the universities did not on the whole become bastions of narrow professionalism, for the consolidation by the tutors of their control over the curriculum helped ensure that history would continue to be taught within a framework of humane letters.[31] But this tradition, with its emphasis on the cultivation of gentlemen preparing to take up prominent positions in government, the empire, the Church, and the professions, had similar political and constitutional preoccupations. And the history purveyed by the dons was as reverential toward established institutions as that written by the professorial scholars. For all the tensions between the amateur and professional currents in the world of Victorian and Edwardian learning, in the end they served many of the same functions. P.B.M. Blaas has noted the connections between the rhetoric of academic professionalism and the cult of "national efficiency" at the turn of the century.[32] Furthermore, as Gareth Stedman Jones has pointed out, the consensual, conservative nature of historical scholarship in Britain acted as a potent barrier against Marxist, Weberian, and other comprehensive interpretive frameworks that were becoming dominant on the Continent by the beginning of the twentieth century.[33]

Not that Green went altogether unhonored by the academic establishment. On 5 June 1909, many of the luminaries of the historical profession turned out for a ceremony commemorating the fiftieth anniversary of his taking a degree without honours at Jesus College, Oxford. Alice Green had presented a stone tablet inscribed in Latin, which was placed over the staircase in the back quadrangle leading to Green's room. It is still there, though partially overgrown. Green's alienation from his college did not go unacknowledged during the proceedings. In the opening speech, the Vice Chancellor of the university, Dr. T. Herbert Warren, stated that Green, like many men of genius, "lived to a certain degree in a state of discontent and revolt."[34] The Principal of Jesus, Sir John Rhys, admitted that the dons of the 1850s were incapable of meeting the challenge of a student of Green's quality: "Therefore they left him on the whole to pursue his own predilections in the matter of study; that fact stands distinctly to their credit. I fear that we have fallen back since that time, for the Jesus dons of the present day would have allowed him no such freedom"[35]

Among the many historians and scholars present were J.B. Bury, Paul Vinogradoff, A.L. Smith, H.A.L. Fisher, T.F. Tout, A.V. Dicey, and C.H. Firth, the Regius Professor of Modern History at Oxford. Mr. and Mrs. Humphry Ward were also on hand, as was William Boyd Dawkins. Firth (1857–1936) gave the handsomest tribute to the *Short History*, noting that it was still the most widely read history of England and that it had influenced him deeply: "It came out just before he left school, just when he was beginning seriously to think of studying history, and it seemed to him a new revelation to one whose notions of early history were derived from the arid pages of the student's Hume."[36] James Ford Rhodes, the American "amateur" historian and author of the highly regarded *History of the United States from the Compromise of 1850*, reported that Green was more widely read in America than any historian save Macaulay.[37] He could have added that the *Short History* had outsold other historical works in the United States during the final decades of the nineteenth century.[38]

At the luncheon, a number of letters were read (including a telegram from James Bryce at the British Embassy in Washington) and speeches were delivered by Dawkins, Tout, Bury, Fisher, Humphry Ward, and A.L.

Smith. Alice Green gave the most moving tribute, explaining why her husband, while fascinated by all of human history, had confined his attentions to his own country:

> England represented to him the best hope of human freedom. His love of England was indeed based on his passion for liberty. The history of the English people commended itself to him because he there saw the struggle for liberty carried on by the people itself, a people endowed with the very genius of freedom.[39]

While the other speeches given that day were probably as sincere as Alice's, it should not be taken to indicate that the world of professional scholarship had embraced Green's methodology or ideology. On the contrary, by 1909 there had been a considerable increase in the level of specialization and fragmentation in historical studies. A scholar like C.H. Firth might nostalgically recall the impression made on him in his youth by the sweep and verve of the *Short History*, but was much more comfortable writing monographs like *Cromwell's Army* (1902) or *The House of Lords during the Civil War* (1910). Works such as these, or the tightly structured, massively documented legal and institutional studies produced by historians like Tout, Poole, Maitland, and their successors, were the new currency of academic respectability.

The academic historians who were apt to feel the greatest appreciation of Green were men like J.A.R. Marriott (1859–1945) or the eminent Tudor historian A.F. Pollard (1869-1948), whose professional duties kept them in close contact with a wider public. From 1887 to 1920, while teaching history at Worcester College, Oxford, Marriott lectured in the university extension delegacy. His lucid and forceful style made him one of the most popular teachers in the program, and his books bear the mark of the popularizer rather than the research scholar. In 1937, for the centenary of Green's birth, Marriott contributed an article to *The Times* praising Green and citing the *Short History* as one of the great classics of English history. Noting that his own treasured copy of the first edition was before him as he wrote, he recalled his first meeting with his tutor in his student days at New College, Oxford. When questioned about his previous work in history, Marriott proudly produced his copy of the *Short History*, which had been recently published. "Oh, Green," said his tutor with a contemptuous shrug, "Green got a Third, and deserved it." But, as Marriott noted, he found out afterward that his tutor had been wrong: "The Third in Law and History was awarded not to J.R., of Jesus, but to T.H. of Balliol (who had of course already got his first in Greats). Thus do legends arise!"[40]

Pollard was, like Green, a Jesus College man (a first-class in modern history, 1891) who became a professor of constitutional law at University College, London and Director of the Institute of Historical Research. In the latter position, he was responsible for producing a number of doctorates in history, and must be therefore accorded a crucial role in the professionalizing of the discipline. Moreover, his own written work was a good deal more scholarly than Green's, or indeed Marriott's. Yet Pollard was profoundly influenced by Green, for example, adopting and extending his concept of the "New Monarchy."[41] He also was President of the Historical Association, which, with its inclusiveness and attention to the needs of history teachers at the secondary level, reflected many of Green's ideals. In 1916 the Association took over the struggling journal *History*. Pollard became its editor and was successful in keeping its tone more popular than that of the *English Historical Review*, a distinction still evident today.

It was probably no accident that the lead article of the first issue of *History* under Pollard's editorship urged that Green's approach be applied to imperial history. Its author was Sir Charles Lucas (1853–1931), a writer on imperial questions and a former official in the Colonial Office who had originally delivered it as a speech to the Historical Association.[42] Lucas transmitted his interest in Green to his protégé A.P. Newton (1873–1942), Rhodes Professor of Imperial History at the University of London from 1920 to 1938.[43] Newton, a conservative imperialist, believed that the greatness of the *Short History* lay in its depiction of England as a "living organism," something he aspired to do for the British Empire.[44] Green's influence on the conservative practitioners of imperial history is ironic considering his own Gladstonian "little Englandism."

Most academic scholars, however, were put off by what they considered the superficiality and feeble documentary foundations of the *Short History* (or even *The Making of England*). Moreover, many found Green's ardently egalitarian tone somewhat old hat, perhaps a trifle embarrassing. This included even those who were politically to the left, for among the tenets of the new professionalism they embraced was a studied avoidance of the kind of moralizing judgments and caustic criticisms that characterized Green's writing. A drier and seemingly more objective "scientific" mode of discourse tended to displace literary concerns and rhetorical flourishes. Considering the importance of the shift that was underway regarding subject matter, style, interpretive frameworks, and readership of historical works, it is difficult to accept without qualification Rosemary Jann's assertion that "the transition from 'literary' to professional history was less a break than a continuum in which, by and large, the demands of professionalism accommodated themselves to the assumptions underlying 'literary' history rather than vice versa."[45]

Recently, Christopher Parker, decrying the advent of "conservative realism" in historical studies at the end of the nineteenth century, notes that the new institutional studies lacked any organicism or holism. The result, as he observes, is that "history lost its national Whig myths and found nothing with which to replace them. As a positive force in the nation's intellectual life history ceased for the moment to exist, and has rarely exerted much power since."[46]

Radical perspectives did emerge in twentieth-century academic history writing, chiefly in the form of Marxism. This undoubtedly invigorated the profession, generating fresh insights and spirited debates while imparting something in the way of a holistic framework to historical studies, though even here the pragmatic quality of British historiography remained dominant. But Marxist historians, with their core belief that England's political and legal structures were emanations of an oppressive economic system, had little chance of becoming genuinely popular in the way that Green had been. For, literary flair aside, the essence of his popularity lay in his ability to harmonize patriotism and radicalism.

Socialist scholars have been unable to recognize Green as in any way a precursor, for his particular social and political values could be easily dismissed as "bourgeois radicalism." It is the "other Green"—T.H. Green (1838–82)—who has been widely seen as a forerunner of modern British socialism for his crucial role in formulating the idealist philosophy and collectivist principles that undergird the New Liberalism. But while J.R. Green was an individualist and libertarian (and hence a "bourgeois radical"), he had labored ardently among the poorest classes, and his credentials as a founder of the settlement movement, which promoted communal values, are as valid as T.H. Green's. In the *Short History*, his iconoclastic approach to many of England's most revered institutions and historical figures did much to prepare the ground for the progressive thrusts of the New Liberalism. Moreover, his insistence that broad popular currents were more important than political and military events should be recognized as an important source of social history, a genre more often than not practiced by leftist historians. Their surprising neglect of Green compounds the irony of his influence among conservative imperialist historians in Britain. In the United States, the *Short History* had a more direct influence on leftist historians, most notably with Charles A. Beard, who, in *The Rise of American Civilization* (1927), sought to do for the American people what Green had done for the English.[47]

Another reason that Green remained largely discredited or simply invisible in British academic circles was the lingering effects of the anti-Victorian reaction of the interwar years. The debunking tendencies of that disillusioned era are represented most brilliantly by Lytton Strachey's *Eminent Victorians* (1918). As far as the historical profession is concerned, the reaction against Whiggery went back to the 1890s, as P.B.M. Blaas has demonstrated, but it became more pronounced after World War I. The most important publication in the process of cutting Victorian scholars down to size was Herbert Butterfield's *The Whig Interpretation of History* (1931). Butterfield found ready assent to his proposition that Victorian scholars, in their smugness, optimism, and complacency, had written history backward. Starting with an assured belief in the superiority of modern British institutions, they had scoured the annals of early England looking for the antecedents of parliament, common law, and modern notions of liberty. Their work, according to Butterfield, was characterized by a naive teleology and anachronistic accounts of earlier times. Green, Freeman, Stubbs, and others were judged guilty of these transgressions against sound modern principles of historical practice, and their work was accordingly devalued.

This anti-Victorian movement was never monolithic and did not preclude a modest revival of interest in the great nineteenth-century historians. In 1948, for example, the medievalist Helen Cam published a thoughtful account of Stubbs's legacy. While admitting that his treatment of the Anglo-Saxon period did not bear close critical scrutiny, she found much of enduring value in his *Constitutional History* and castigated his most severe critics.[48] And in the 1987 Stenton Lecture, James Campbell pointed out that recent scholarship on such topics as Magna Carta and early parliaments tends to support many of Stubbs's interpretations. As Campbell concludes: "When Stubbs writes about liberty, justice, and rights, the national assembly, and constitutional advance, he plainly sets alarm bells ringing in many minds. . . . But much of what he argued about the debt of the English present to the English past is right."[49]

It is unclear whether Stubbs's rising stock might lift Green's with it. If so, there would be an element of irony to it for, as both Stubbs and Freeman recognized, Green's approach to the past was profoundly different. A baneful legacy of Butterfield's analysis is our flattened perspective on nineteenth century history writing. Once most historians of the era are defined by their "Whiggish" approach to the past, important differences are slighted or rendered invisible.[50] It is important to recognize that Green's Whiggishness was not of the assured and celebratory kind associated with a Macaulay or a Stubbs. Green's sense of history was much more strongly marked by an awareness of the tendency for social elites and political oligarchies to form, resulting in the people often being forced to struggle to recover their birthright, sometimes through concerted armed action. He found the British political structure of his own day marked strongly by the same tendencies. Thus, if Green's approach was Whiggish, it was Whiggishness of a particularly radical stripe, whose underlying social dynamic of history turned on a model of class conflict, however imprecise and undeveloped. And while he was a Teutonist, his reverence for early Germanic antecedents was never dominant and certainly did not preclude a more cosmopolitan historical frame of reference, as in his conviction of the superiority of Italian civic culture over that of northern Europe, his deep and finely honed aesthetic sensibilities, and his rejection of the blatant racialist theories associated with Freeman.

Green was thus a unique voice among the historians of the late Victorian period. He imparted a populist impulse to history writing that has had an important impact on writing about the past, even if it has often been unacknowledged. Similarly, his removal of politics and warfare from stage center helped usher in a variety of new approaches in social and cultural history, even if in an immediate sense it was going against the current of the emerging profession, which for a generation or more after his death stressed political, legal, and institutional topics. Above all, he was a superb storyteller and literary stylist, the best of his age. Many professional historians came to disparage style as a mere adornment, even a distraction and obfuscation. The public, however, knew better. Their past was brought to life and their lives were connected directly and vividly to those of the generations before them in the pages of the *Short History*. For them, England became what Green had aspired to make it—a living organism whose evolution explained both its essence and its promise.

None of this should be taken as a lament for the disappearance of a supposed golden age of vigor, clarity, and readability in historical writing, with Green as its most gifted exponent. Neither is it a wholesale criticism of the more specialized scholarly labors of the last century or so. It would be absurd to wish that historical scholarship had not moved beyond the level of the *Short History of the English People*. Thanks to the multitude of detailed studies undertaken during the last century, often in previously unexplored subject areas and deploying new methodologies, we have a deeper, richer understanding of the past than did the Victorians, even if the sheer bulk of scholarship renders much of it unassimilable. It is important to note, however, that some of the new approaches were accepted more readily because Green had already broken with the methodological orthodoxies of his day. At any rate, the transformations in history writing were going on in all academic disciplines, and these complex structural changes in the organization of learning must in some sense be regarded as inevitable.

At the same time, it was not inevitable that such a wide gulf should have opened between the professional and popular worlds, or that such contempt should have been hurled from the battlements of academia at both the authors and readers of popular historical works. While many professional historians have themselves bemoaned the over-specialization and declining literary quality in history writing, most have heedlessly burrowed ever deeper into their esoteric interests, rendering themselves unintelligible not only to the general public but sometimes even to practitioners in other subfields of the discipline. As the *Times Literary Supplement*, in a 1933 article commemorating the fiftieth anniversary of Green's death, noted: "The modern historical specialist may permit himself a supercilious smile at the recollection of the 'Short History' selling vigorously from the railway bookstalls of the seventies, but the joke is by no means wholly at the expense of Green."[51]

NOTES

1. Charles L. Graves, ed., *Life and Letters of Alexander Macmillan* (London: Macmillan, 1910), 364.

2. E. A. Freeman, "John Richard Green," *British Quarterly Review* 78 (July 1883): 119–34.

3. Ibid., 132.

4. Ibid., 133.

5. Ibid., 120, 122–23.

6. J. Scott Keltie, "Some Characteristics of Mr. Green's Histories," *British Quarterly Review* 78 (July 1883): 74–80.

7. William Stubbs, *Seventeen Lectures on Medieval and Modern History* (Oxford: Clarendon Press, 1887), 430.

8. *English Historical Review* 2 (Oct. 1887): 774–81.

9. Ibid., 774.

10. Ibid., 775.

11. Freeman to unidentified correspondent, 1 May 1889, W.R.W. Stephens, *Life and Letters of Edward A. Freeman* (London: Macmillan, 1895), 2: 400.

12. S.R. Gardiner to Alice Green, 30 Nov. 1884, Jesus College MS. 223, J 49/16.

13. S.R. Gardiner to unidentified recipient, 2 Nov. 1892, Jesus College MS. 223, J 49/16.

14. Margaret Evans to Alice Green, 11 Aug. 1892, Alice Green to Margaret Evans, 22 Aug. 1892, Kate Norgate to Alice Green, 28 Oct. 1892, Jesus College MS. 223, J 49/16.

15. Dawkins to Alice Green, 8 Oct. 1892, 18 Nov. 1892, Jesus College MS. 223, J 49/16.

16. Charles Bowen to Alice Green, 2 March 1893, Jesus College MS. 197.

17. R. B. McDowell, *Alice Stopford Green*, 47.

18. Alice Stopford Green, *Henry the Second* (London: Macmillan, 1888), 1.

19. See, for example, *The Athenaeum* 12 (Aug. 1888): 149–50.

20. It was reviewed favorably by James Tait in the *English Historical Review* 10 (Jan. 1895): 157–58.

21. Louise Creighton, ed., *Life and Letters of Mandell Creighton* (London: Longmans, Green and Co., 1905), 2: 107–08.

22. *The Christian Science Monitor*, 13 Aug. 1921.

23. LJRG, 391, 455.

24. James Bryce, *Studies in Contemporary Biography* (London: Macmillan, 1903), 141.

25. "The Labour Party and the Books that Helped to Make It," *Review of Reviews* 33 (1906): 568–82, 568. I am indebted to Professor Jonathan Rose for bringing this important study to my attention.

26. Once again I am beholden to Professor Rose for this information.

27. *Short History of the English People*, ed. L. Cecil Jane, with an appendix by R. P. Farley, 2 vols. (London: J.M. Dent, 1915). Probably in response, in 1916 Macmillan brought out a new, inexpensive edition, revised and enlarged by Alice Stopford Green, with a full 200 pages on the period 1815 to 1914. Her coverage of the preceding century was greatly superior to Farley's.

28. S.R. Gardiner, "Obituary: J.R. Green," *The Academy* 23 (17 March 1883): 186. Gardiner was probably unaware that Green, a year before his death, had approached Lord Acton in a successful attempt to secure from Prime Minister Gladstone a pension for Gardiner in consideration of "the difficulties under which he has done his unremunerative work." Lord Acton to Green, "Most private," Easter 1882, uncatalogued MSS., Green MSS., Jesus College.

29. Doris Goldstein, "History at Oxford and Cambridge: Professionalization and the Influence of Ranke," in *Leopold von Ranke and the Shaping of the Historical Discipline*, ed. Georg Iggers and James M. Powell (Syracuse, N.Y.: Syracuse University Press, 1990), 141–53.

30. Reginald Poole and William Hunt, eds., *The Political History of England*, 12 vols. (London: Longmans, 1905). T.F. Tout wrote one of the volumes.

31. Sheldon Rothblatt, *The Revolution of the Dons* (London: Faber, 1968).

32. P.B.M. Blaas, *Continuity and Anachronism: Parliamentary and Constitutional Development in Whig Historiography and in the Anti-Whig Reaction between 1890 and 1930* (The Hague: Nijhoff, 1978), 228–39.

33. Gareth Stedman Jones, "The Pathology of English History," *New Left Review* 46 (Nov./Dec. 1967): 26–43.

34. *The Times*, 7 June 1909.

35. *The Morning Post*, 7 June 1909.

36. *The Times*, 7 June 1909.

37. Ibid.

38. John Higham, *History: Professional Scholarship in America* (Baltimore: Johns Hopkins University Press, 1983 [first published 1965]), 156.

39. *The Morning Post*, 7 June 1909.

40. J.A.R. Marriott, "A Historian of England. J.R. Green: The Writer and the Man." *The Times,* 10 Dec. 1937, 17.

41. J.P. Kenyon, *The History Men: The Historical Profession in England since the Renaissance* (Pittsburgh: University of Pittsburgh Press, 1984), 203–04. Blaas points out, however, that Pollard had a much more positive view of Henry VIII than Green did, seeing the Tudor monarch's strong government as the key to Parliament's rise. *Continuity and Anachronism*, 287.

42. Sir Charles Lucas, "On the Teaching of Imperial History," *History* 1 (1916): 5–11.

43. Margaret Marion Spector, "A.P. Newton," in *Some Modern Historians of Great Britain*, ed. Herman Ausubel et al. (New York: Dryden Press, 1951), 286–305.

44. Ibid., 298.

45. Rosemary Jann, *The Art and Science of Victorian History* (Columbus: Ohio University Press, 1985), 224. Another recent work stressing the element of continuity is Peter R.H. Slee, *Learning and Liberal Education. The Study of Modern History in the Universities of Oxford, Cambridge, and Manchester, 1800–1914* (Manchester: Manchester University Press, 1986).

46. Christopher Parker, *The English Historical Tradition Since 1850* (Edinburgh: John Donald, 1990), 17.

47. Higham, *History*, 193.

48. Helen Cam, "Stubbs Seventy Years Later," *Cambridge Historical Journal* 9 (1948): 129–47. For an appreciative treatment of his literary qualities, see Robert Brentano, "The Sound of Stubbs," *Journal of British Studies* 6 (May 1967): 1–14.

49. William Campbell, *Stubbs and the English State* (Reading: University of Reading Press, 1989), 13.

50. Thus Patrick Joyce, while recognizing that Green was not typical of the historians of his age, regards him simply as one of the few "school historians" who sought "to rescue the everyday culture and customs of 'the people' from the condescension of posterity." *Visions of the People: Industrial England and the Question of Class 1848–1918* (Cambridge: Cambridge University Press, 1991), 191.

51. *Times Literary Supplement*, 9 March 1933, 153. The reprinting of the article by the *TLS* in 1983 to mark Green's centennial attests to the enduring validity of this observation. *TLS*, 11 March 1983, 251.

Bibliography

PRIMARY SOURCES

Manuscript Materials

Bodleian Library
  MS. English Letters

British Library
  Macmillan Archives
  Notebooks of J.R. Green

Edinburgh University Library
  Letters of Freeman to Green

Jesus College, Oxford
  Green MSS

Lambeth Palace Library
  Green Correspondence
  Tait Papers

National Library of Scotland
  John Hill Burton MSS

John Rylands Library of Manchester University
  E.A. Freeman Archives

Published Materials

Books by Green or Containing Substantial Material by Him

The Conquest of England. London: Macmillan, 1882.

Essays of Joseph Addison. Chosen and edited by John Richard Green. London: Macmillan, 1880.

Letters of John Richard Green. Edited by Leslie Stephen. London: Macmillan, 1901.

Historical Studies. Edited by Alice Stopford Green. London: Macmillan, 1903.

The Making of England. London: Macmillan, 1882.

Oxford During the Last Century, Being Two Series of Papers Published in the Oxford Chronicle and Berks and Berks Gazette During the Year 1859. Oxford: Slatter and Rose, 1859.

Oxford Studies. Introduction by Alice Stopford Green. London: Macmillan, 1901.

Readings from English History. Selected and edited by John Richard Green. London: Macmillan, 1879.

Short Geography of the British Islands. With Alice Stopford Green. London: Macmillan, 1879.

Short History of the English People. London: Macmillan, 1874.

Short History of the English People. Revised and illustrated edition. Edited by Alice Stopford Green and Kate Norgate. London: Macmillan, 1892–94.

Stray Studies. Second series. Edited by Alice Stopford Green. London: Macmillan, 1903.

Stray Studies from England and Italy. London: Macmillan, 1876.

Essays by Green

There is a complete list of all of Green's *Saturday Review* essays and his four essays in *Macmillan's Magazine* in *Letters of John Richard Green,* 500–503. Many of these are reprinted in *Historical Studies, Stray Studies,* and *Stray Studies from England and Italy.* The one essay of Green's that Leslie Stephen failed to list is: "The Revolution in a French Country Town." *Contemporary Review* 7 (March 1868): 416–28.

Works by Green's Contemporaries

Adams, Henry. *Henry Adams: Selected Letters*. Edited by Ernest Samuels. Cambridge, Mass: Belknap Press of Harvard University Press, 1992.

Baker, James. *An Oxford Attack on our English Constitution exposed in a Review of "A Short History of the English People" by the Examiner in the School of Modern History, Oxford*. Winchester: J. Wells, 1875.

Bryce, James. "The Late Mr. John Richard Green," *Nation* 36 (1883): 269–70.

_____. "Edward Augustus Freeman." *English Historical Review* 7 (1892): 497–509.

_____. *Studies in Contemporary Biography*. London: Macmillan, 1903.

Creighton, Louise. "Some Reminiscences of J.R. Green." *Longman's Magazine* 39 (1902): 311–19.

_____. *Life and Letters of Mandel Creighton*, 2 vols, London: Longmans, Green and Co., 1905.

Creighton, Mandel. "John Richard Green." *British Quarterly Review* 155 (July 1883): 66–74.

Dawkins, William Boyd. "Brother Prince." *Macmillan's Magazine* 16 (Oct. 1867): 464–73.

Gairdner, James. "History of the English People." *The Academy* 13 (1878): 405–07.

Gardiner, Samuel Rawson. "History of the English People." *The Academy* 15 (1879): 381.

_____. "History of the English People." *The Academy* 18 (1880): 19.

_____. "Obituary: J. R. Green." *The Academy* 23 (17 March 1883): 186–87.

_____. "A Short History of the English People." *The Academy* 6 (1874): 601–02.

Graves, Charles L. *Life and Letters of Alexander Macmillan*. London: Macmillan, 1910.

Green, Alice Stopford. *Henry the Second*. London: Macmillan, 1888.

_____. *Town Life in the Fifteenth Century*. London: Macmillan, 1894.

"Green the Historian." *London Quarterly Review* 63 (Oct. 1884): 137–56.

Haweis, H.R. "John Richard Green: In Memoriam." *Contemporary Review* 43 (1883): 732–46.

Hunt, William and Reginald Poole. *The Political History of England*, 12 vols. London: Longmans, 1905.

Hutton, W.H. *William Stubbs, Bishop of Oxford*. London: Archibald, Constable, and Co., 1906.

Jacks, L.P. *Life and Letters of Stopford Brooke*, 2 vols. London: John Murray, 1917.

"John Richard Green." *Nation* 74 (1902): 106–07.

"John Richard Green." *Church Quarterly Review* 54 (1902): 282–95.

Keltie, J. Scott. "Some Characteristics of Mr. Green's Histories." *British Quarterly Review* 154 (July 1883): 74–80.

Knight, Charles. *Popular History of England: An Illustrated History of Society and Government from the Earliest Times to Our Own Times*, 8 vols. London: Bradbury, Evans, and Co., 1864.

"The Labour Party and the Books that Helped to Make It." *Review of Reviews* 33 (1906): 568–82.

"The Late Mr. John Richard Green." *Nation* 36 (1883): 269–70.

Maitland, F.W. "William Stubbs Bishop of Oxford." *English Historical Review* 16 (1901): 417–26.

"Memorial to J. R. Green at Oxford." *The Times*, 7 June 1909, 10.

"Mr. John Richard Green." *Saturday Review* 55 (1883): 333–34.

Norgate, Kate. *England Under the Angevin Kings*, 2 vols., London: Macmillan, 1887.

Nowell-Smith, Simon, ed. *Letters to Macmillan*. London: Macmillan, 1967.

"The Oxford School of Historians." *Church Quarterly Review* 59 (1904): 92–127.

Palgrave, Sir Francis. *Truths and Fictions of the Middle Ages: The Merchant and the Friar*, 2nd edn. London: J.W. Parker, 1844.

Powell, Frederick York and Charles H. Firth. "Two Oxford Historians." *Quarterly Review* 195 (1902): 532–66.

Rowley, James. "Mr. Green's Short History of the English People: Is It Trustworthy?" *Fraser's Magazine*, n. s. 12 (1875): 395–410, 710–24.

Stephens, W.R.W. *Life and Letters of Edward A. Freeman*, 2 vols. London: Macmillan, 1895.

Tait, C.W.A. *Analysis of English History, based on Green's Short History of the English People*. London: Macmillan, 1879.

Ward, Mrs. Humphry (Mary Augusta). *A Writer's Recollections*, 2 vols. New York and London: Harpers, 1918.

SECONDARY SOURCES

Addison, W.G. "The Clerical Career of John Richard Green." *Theology* 37 (1938): 203–12.

————. *J.R. Green*. London: Society for Promoting Christian Knowledge, 1946.

Anderson, Olive. "The Political Uses of History in Mid-Nineteenth-Century England." *Past and Present* 36 (1967): 87–105.

Angus-Butterworth, Lionel. "John Richard Green." *South Atlantic Quarterly* 46 (1947): 109–18.

Ausubel, Herman, et al. *Some Modern Historians of Britain*. New York: Dryden Press, 1951.

Baker, J.N.L. *Jesus College, Oxford, 1571–1971*. Oxford: Oxonian Press, 1971.

Bann, Stephen. *The Clothing of Clio. A Study of the Representation of History in Nineteenth Century Britain and France*. Cambridge: Cambridge University Press, 1984.

Bevington, Merle Mowbray. *The Saturday Review, 1855–1868; Representative Educated Opinion in Victorian England*. New York: Columbia University Press, 1941.

Bill, E.G.W. *University Reform in Nineteenth Century Oxford: A Study of Henry Halford Vaughan, 1811–85*. Oxford: Oxford University Press, 1973.

Blaas, P.B.M. *Continuity and Anachronism: Parliamentary and Constitutional Development in Whig Historiography and in the Anti–Whig Reaction between 1890 and 1930*. The Hague: Nijhoff, 1978.

Brentano, Robert. "The Sound of Stubbs." *Journal of British Studies* 6 (May 1967): 1–14.

Briggs, Asa. "Saxons, Normans, and Victorians." In *The collected essays of Asa Briggs*, 2: 215–35. Urbana: University of Illinois Press, 1985.

Brundage, Anthony. "John Richard Green and the Church: The Making of a Social Historian." *The Historian* 35 (November 1972): 32–42.

————. "Radicalism and the Emerging Historical Profession in Victorian England: The Case of John Richard Green," *Nineteenth Century Prose*, special edition on "Politicians and Prose." 19 (1992): 46–59.

Buckley, Jerome Hamilton. *The Triumph of Time: A Study of the Victorian Concepts of Time, History, Progress and Decadence.* Cambridge, Mass.: Harvard University Press, 1967.

Burrow, J.W. *A Liberal Descent: Victorian Historians and the English Past.* New York: Cambridge University Press, 1981.

————. "The Sense of the Past." In *The Victorians,* 120–38. Edited by Lawrence Lerner. New York: Holmes and Meier, 1978.

————. "Victorian Historians and the Royal Historical Society." *Transactions of the Royal Historical Society* 39 (1989): 125–40.

————. "'The Village Community' and the Uses of History in Late Nineteenth-Century England." In *Historical Perspectives: Studies in English Thought and Society in Honour of J. H. Plumb,* 255–85. Edited by Neil McKendrick. London: Europa, 1974.

Butterfield, Herbert. *Man on His Past: A Study of the History of Historical Scholarship.* Boston: Beacon, 1966.

————. *The Whig Interpretation of History.* Harmondsworth: Penguin, 1973. First published in 1931.

Cam, Helen. "Stubbs Seventy Years After." *Cambridge Historical Journal* 9 (1948): 129–47.

Campbell, William. *Stubbs and the English State.* Reading: University of Reading Press, 1989.

Challen, W. H. "John Richard Green, His Mother and Others." *Notes and Queries,* n. s. 12 (1965): 4–9, 56–59, 105–108, 150–54, 185–88, 231–35, 254–58, 294–98, 345–48, 382–83, 425–29, 456–63.

Chandler, Alice. *A Dream of Order: The Medieval Ideal in Nineteenth-Century English Literature.* Lincoln: University of Nebraska Press, 1970.

Chapman, Raymond. *The Sense of the Past in Victorian Literature.* London: Croom Helm, 1986.

Cronne, H.A. "Edward Augustus Freeman, 1823–92." *History* 28 (1943): 78–92.

Crowther, M.A. *Church Embattled: Religious Controversy in Mid-Victorian England.* Hamden, Conn.: Archon, 1970.

Culler, Dwight A. *The Victorian Mirror of History.* New Haven: Yale University Press, 1985.

Dale, Peter. *The Victorian Critic and the Idea of History.* Cambridge, Mass.: Harvard University Press, 1977.

Doherty, Herbert J., Jr. "John Richard Green: Historian of the Middle Class." *London Quarterly and Holborn Review* 178 (1953): 69–73.

Eldridge, C.C. *England's Mission: The Imperial Idea in the Age of Gladstone and Disraeli, 1868–1880*. London: Macmillan, 1973.

Engel, Arthur. "The Emerging Concept of the Academic Profession at Oxford 1800–1854." In *The University in Society*, 1: 305–52. Edited by Lawrence Stone. Princeton: Princeton University Press, 1974.

Fisher, H.A.L. *James Bryce,* 2 vols. New York: Macmillan, 1927.

Forbes, Duncan. *The Liberal Anglican Idea of History*. Cambridge: Cambridge University Press, 1952.

Goldstein, Doris. "History at Oxford and Cambridge: Professionalization and the Influence of Ranke." In *Leopold von Ranke and the Shaping of the Historical Discipline*, 141–53. Edited by G. Iggers and James M. Powell. Syracuse: Syracuse University Press, 1990.

_____. "The Organizational Development of the British Historical Profession, 1884–1921." *Bulletin of the Institute of Historical Research* 55 (1982): 180–93.

Gooch, G.P. *History and Historians in the Nineteenth Century*. London: Longmans, 1913.

Grafton, Anthony. "Mark Pattison." *American Scholar* 52 (1983): 229–36.

Greene, Dana. "John Richard Green and His *Short History of the English People.*" Ph.D. dissertation, Emory University, 1971.

Hamer, D.A. *John Morley: Liberal Intellectual in Politics*. Oxford: Clarendon Press, 1968.

Heyck, T.W. *The Tranformation of Intellectual Life in Victorian Britain*. London: Croom Helm, 1982.

Higham, John. *History: Professional Scholarship in America*. Baltimore: Johns Hopkins Univerity Press, 1983. First published in 1965.

Himmelfarb, Gertrude. *Lord Acton: A Study in Conscience and Politics*. Chicago: University of Chicago Press, 1952.

_____. *The New History and the Old. Critical Essays and Reappraisals*. Cambridge, Mass: Belknap Press of Harvard University Press, 1987.

Jann, Rosemary. *The Art and Science of Victorian History*. Columbus: Ohio University Press, 1985.

_____. "From Amateur to Professional: The Case of the Oxbridge Historians." *Journal of British Studies* 22 (1983): 122–47.

Joyce, Patrick. *Visions of the People: Industrial England and the Question of Class 1848–1914*. Cambridge: Cambridge University Press, 1991.

Kenyon, J.P. *The History Men: The Historical Profession in England since the Renaissance.* Pittsburgh: University of Pittsburgh Press, 1984.

Kitson Clark, George. *Churchmen and the Condition of England 1832–1885.* London: Methuen, 1973.

Levine, Philippa. *The Amateur and the Professional: Antiquarians, Historians, and Archaeologists in Victorian England, 1838–1886.* Cambridge: Cambridge University Press, 1986.

Mandelbaum, Maurice. *History, Man, and Reason: A Study in Nineteenth Century Thought.* Baltimore: Johns Hopkins University Press, 1971.

Marriot, J.A.R. "A Historian of England. J. R. Green: The Writer and the Man." *The Times* (London), 10 Dec. 1937, 17–18.

McDowell, R.B. *Alice Stopford Green, a Passionate Historian.* Dublin: Allen Figgis, 1967.

Morgan, Charles. *The House of Macmillan, 1843–1943.* London: Macmillan, 1944.

Morton, Patricia M. "Life After Butterfield? John Burrow's *A Liberal Descent* and the Recent Historiography of Victorian Historians." *Historical Reflections* 10 (1983): 229–44.

Parker, Christopher. *The English Historical Tradition Since 1850.* Edinburgh: John Donald, 1990.

Roach, J.P.C. "Liberalism and the Victorian Intelligentsia." *Cambridge Historical Journal* 13 (1957): 58–81.

Rothblatt, Sheldon. *The Revolution of the Dons.* London: Faber, 1968.

Saab, Ann Pottinger. *Reluctant Icon: Gladstone, Bulgaria, and the Working Classes.* Cambridge, Mass.: Harvard University Press, 1991.

Schuyler, Robert Livingstone. "John Richard Green and His Short History." *Political Science Quarterly* 64 (1949): 321–54.

Shannon, R.T. *Gladstone and the Bulgarian Agitation in 1876.* 2nd edn. Hassocks, Sussex: Harvester Press, 1975.

Slee, Peter R.H. *Learning and Liberal Education. The Study of Modern History in the Universities of Oxford, Cambridge, and Manchester, 1800–1914.* Manchester: Manchester University Press, 1986.

Stedman Jones, Gareth. "The Pathology of English History." *New Left Review* 46 (Nov./Dec. 1967): 29–43.

Sutherland, John. *Mrs. Humphry Ward. Eminent Victorian, Pre-eminent Edwardian.* Oxford: Clarendon Press, 1990.

Templeman, G. "Edward I and the Historians." *Cambridge Historical Journal* 10 (1950): 6–35.

Van Eerde, Katherine. "The Uses of History: Cromwell and the Victorians." *Victorians Institute Journal* 15 (1987): 81–102.

Vogeler, Martha S. *Frederic Harrison: The Vocations of a Positivist.* Oxford: Clarendon Press, 1984.

Von Arx, Jeffrey. *Progress and Pessimism: Religion, Politics, and History in Late Nineteenth Century Britain.* Cambridge, Mass.: Harvard University Press, 1985.

Watson, Charles A. *The Writing of History in Britain: A Bibliography of Post-1945 Writings about British Historians and Biographers.* New York and London: Garland, 1982.

Williams, N.J. "Stubbs' Appointment as Regius Professor, 1866." *Bulletin of the Institute of Historical Research* 33 (1960): 121–25.

Woodward, Llewellyn. "The Rise of the Professorial Historian in England." In *Studies in International History*, 16–34. Edited by K. Bourne and D.C. Watt. Hamden, Conn.: Archon Books, 1967.

Index

About the Author

ANTHONY BRUNDAGE is Professor of History at California State Polytechnic University, Pomona. His earlier books include *England's "Prussian Minister": Edwin Chadwick and the Politics of Government Growth, 1832-54* (1988) and *The Making of the New Poor Law: The Politics of Inquiry, Enactment, and Implementation, 1832-1839* (1978).